DETOUR DE FRANCE

Michael **SIMKINS**

EBURY
PRESS

First published in 2009 by Ebury Press, an imprint of Ebury Publishing

A Random House Group company

The Random House Group Limited Reg. No. 954009

Addresses for companies within the Random House Group can be found at www.randomhouse.co.uk

A CIP catalogue record for this book is available from the British Library

The Random House Group Limited supports The Forest Stewardship Council (FSC), the leading international forest certification organisation. All our titles that are printed on Greenpeace approved FSC certified paper carry the FSC logo. Our paper procurement policy can be found at www.rbooks.co.uk/environment

Mixed Sources
Product group from well-managed forests and other controlled sources
www.fsc.org Cert no. TT-COC-2139
© 1996 Forest Stewardship Council

Printed in Great Britain by Clays Ltd, St Ives plc

ISBN 9780091927523

To buy books by your favourite authors and register for offers visit www.rbooks.co.uk

Contents

Acknowledgements

My thanks to everyone who has helped me, by accident or design, in the writing of this book. My special thanks to Andrew Goodfellow for his continuing encouragement and support: also to James Gill, Mari Roberts, Caroline Newbury and Ali Nightingale. A very special thank you to Ian Nunn, Lesley Retallack, Aude Criqui, Amelle Mouhaddib and Amanda Munroe, without whose time and patience the writing of this book would have far less fun. Certain names and locations have been changed to protect Anglo-French relations …

For Julia

Detour de France

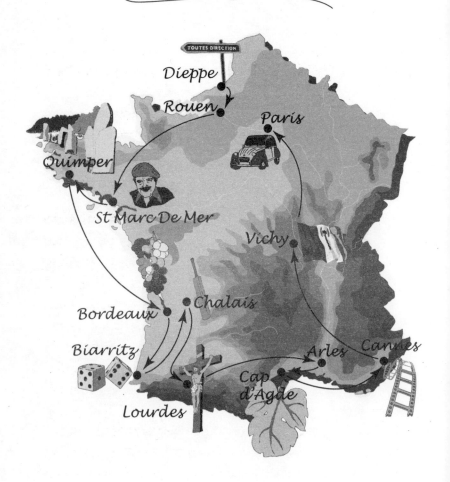

Son et Lumière

MY RELATIONSHIP WITH France began when I was inter-
fered with at the cinema.

It occurred at my local fleapit in Brighton during the summer
holidays. I can't have been more than nine or ten at the time. I
can't even recall the main feature, but the second film in the
programme was a curious French movie with English subtitles I
hadn't bargained for: *Monsieur Hulot's Holiday*.

Set in a fictional seaside resort on France's Atlantic coast, this
strange and beguiling comedy depicted the gently anarchic
adventures of French comedian Jacques Tati's alter ego during
one summer in the 1950s.

The real star of the film was the location itself: a small, sleepy
resort, complete with sun, sea, sand, donkeys, laughing children
and evening strolls along the prom. It could almost have been
Brighton, if it weren't for the fact that it was hot, elegant, exotic,
timeless, languid, and everyone in it spoke as if they'd bitten on
a glue trap.

Midway through the picture, the cinema's only other occupant, a man in his forties with greasy hair who'd been sitting a
few rows in front, squeezed between the seats, plonked himself
down next to me and moved his right hand onto my left knee.

By the time he'd manoeuvred it onto the zip of my shorts (just as Hulot commenced his famous game of ping-pong in the hotel lobby), I knew something was wrong. Yet, despite all my parents' dire warnings, so entranced had I become by the strange sunlit world that I couldn't bring myself to leave. I merely moved my seat and crossed my legs.

That had been my relationship with *la belle France* ever since. Fascination mixed with mild anxiety. Even now I can never talk to a Frenchman without feeling I'm being molested.

Déjà View

EVER SINCE KING Harold sent his army careering after William the Conqueror with the proviso, 'Mind where you shoot those arrows, you could have somebody's eye out,' England's relationship with that of our nearest neighbour has been all downhill.

You'd have thought that losing a kingdom but gaining a conqueror would have settled the issue: we'd take their foie gras, they'd take our fried bread, and we'd be one big happy family. But bad blood lingers and ever since 1066 we've been at each other's throats. From the Hundred Years War to Waterloo, from the European Union to the Eurovision Song Contest, we've remained the best of enemies.

The French see themselves as nature's aristocrat. In cuisine, manners, the arts, fine wines, philosophy and, as if all that wasn't galling enough, now even in football, they've appropriated the mantle of true class, while England is fighting relegation, both sporting and cultural, in the Beazer Homes League Division II. The French ideal is represented by a piquant blend of Juliette Binoche, Coco Chanel and Arsène Wenger. Fighting for all that we hold dear in the English corner would be Ann Widdecombe, John McCririck and Mister Blobby.

The problem is how we choose to see each other. While we may have beaten them in the run-off to host the 2012 Olympics,

Boris Johnson's flag-waving at the closing ceremony in Beijing confirmed everything for which the Brits are known on the boulevards of Paris – knock-kneed, pasty, overweight and sartorially about as well turned out as the Mayor of London's splayed feet.

We, on the other hand, see them as proud, stuck-up, rude, impatient, humourless and bombastic.

They see themselves the same way, of course, but to them these are the things that make life worth living.

MY OWN VIEW of the French, I have to confess, was still stuck in the back row of that cinema and weighed down with years of caricature. I grew up knowing little more than that we'd helped them out in two world wars. Whenever France was mentioned in our house, my dad would stare darkly into his tea cup and murmur grimly, 'Nobody ever forgives you for doing them favours.' My elder brother Pete during his college years was briefly part of something called the 'Reconquer France for Britain' Society, although that turned out to be an excuse to go on day trips to Dieppe and get bladdered. Yet the prevailing antipathy chez Simkins towards all things French was at odds with my own flickering, Hulot-kissed memories.

Sadly, I never had a chance to decide for myself. I didn't have a French pen friend, I never went on a student exchange or skiing holiday, and I failed utterly to learn the language. Not that I didn't have the chance. Au contraire: I spent four years studying French at secondary school, but there were just too many other things to do in the back row of the classroom – sticking compasses into 'Lumper' Lawrence's right thigh or perfecting my Johnny Mathis impression to mention just two.

When I was allowed to give it up aged sixteen I had little more knowledge than the opening lines of '*Frère Jacques*', and that's the way it stayed. I went straight from secondary school to drama school and to my first paid acting work, and the smell of garlic was no match for greasepaint. My wanderlust years slipped by without my noticing. Even into my twenties, my idea of a fabulous trip to foreign climes was playing Wishee Washee in *Aladdin*.

So the gap between the France of my imagination – dreamy, poetic and liltingly beautiful – and the image commonly depicted in English culture – aloof, snobbish, with a yard brush up their communal derrière – remained as wide as the Channel. I could whistle the theme tune from *Maigret*, but that apart, the strange, sunlit world I'd glimpsed all those years ago in the darkness of a provincial cinema remained a distant fantasy. Yet somewhere inside me I still dreamt occasionally about one day finding the France of Hulot.

And then I met Julia.

JULIA KNEW ABOUT France. Julia had been on student exchange visit to the French Alps as a teenager, and Julia had worked as a nanny on a yacht moored in Cannes harbour, spending her time having her toes sucked by Algerian cabin staff to Charles Trenet records and learning about fashion, style and romance.

She also learnt the language, becoming so fluent that on returning to England she'd financed her own way through drama school by working as an international telephonist in Holborn. Her French supervisors were apparently all vicious old dykes in tweed suits and monocles who required you to put your hand up to go to the toilet just so they could answer 'Wait!' while they stood about in corners gossiping with their compatriots about 'les anglaises'. But nonetheless, by the time she'd finished paying her way, Julia was as cosmopolitan as I was boiled beef and carrots.

We finally met in the less than cosmopolitan surroundings of

Harrogate Repertory Theatre. Part of the endless fascination of falling in love is discovering and sharing the other person's interests and obsessions, and I was only too glad to enlighten her at great length about mine: brass bands, county cricket, Gilbert and Sullivan memorabilia. Yet each time I tried to draw her on her early years in France, a country whose sights and sounds she seemed to know well and which I was desperate to sample, she remained enigmatically guarded.

France may be a great country, she explained, but she had no need to go back. Once upon a time she'd been dazzled by the chic and the coffee and the Gitanes, but working with the French back in London, away from the sights and sounds of their alluring environment, the more she'd steadily realised they were rude, arrogant, had no sense of humour and had to take a week off work or a suppository every time they so much as stood in a draught.

And there the matter might have rested. For the next twenty years or so we rarely spoke about the place or its inhabitants. Julia showed no inclination to return, and I certainly wasn't going there without her. In any case, there was always another play, another TV part, another job interview. What changed things for ever was my decision to celebrate Julia's fiftieth birthday by taking her to one of Paris's most historic restaurants.

La Coupole is world-famous for its food (*fricassée de poulet, glacé aux fruits rouge*), its clientele (Hemingway, Picasso) and the legendary hauteur and savoir faire of its waiters. The trip was a surprise and thus something of a gamble: but at La Coupole, I reckoned, we'd share good food and drink in elegant, formal surroundings, sophisticated, suave and expensive. If all went well it would silence once and for all these accumulated prejudices of hers, and reignite her original passion for the country, and, by implication, for me as well.

Upon being frogmarched onto Eurostar at 6 a.m. on her one day off, Julia, still knackered from an eight-show week, burst into tears. She said she'd now have to spend her one day off communicating with sneering restaurant staff, a prospect she didn't much relish on her fiftieth and that she was damned if she was going to give poncey Parisian waiters the pleasure of answering her French in disdainful English. I maintained she was being paranoid and xenophobic, and that ordering the meal was the least she could do considering I'd spent nearly two hundred quid getting her there.

And so it was a few hours later that she summoned across the waiter. In all our years together, I'd never heard Julia speak French, and I was looking forward to it.

Julia: *Excusez-moi, je pense que nous sommes prêts pour la commande maintenant. Je voudrais commencer par un croustillant de jambon, suivi d'une fricassée de poulet. Mon mari prendra la même chose. Pour boire, nous prendrons une bouteille de rouge maison mais nous voudrions aussi une bouteille d'eau minerale, et ce serait bien si nous pouvions avoir du pain et du beurre en attendant d'etre servis…*

Waiter: *Certainly, madam. Sparkling or still?*

It's funny how stress can cause you to do the silliest things. I suppose the thunderous look on Julia's face made me panic. All I know is the next moment I was telling the waiter it was my wife's birthday and could he guess how old she was?

Waiter: *I have no idea… Sixty? Sixty-two?*

WE GOT THROUGH it. Just. But one thing was obvious. If I was to separate French fact from French fiction, I was going to have to do it alone.

In truth, there was another reason for my eventual decision to take a trip there. Julia was at least correct about one thing: I was becoming stuck in a rut. Middle-aged, middle class and middle England, I was approaching that time of life when you find yourself dwelling on the things you haven't done rather than those you have. Even my obsession with acting wasn't lighting my fire as it once had. Playing detectives and unsuspecting husbands in other people's TV series had its charms – God knows it's better than working for a living – but if I was going to fulfil some of my long-cherished ambitions before arthritis and memory loss set in, time was running out. Only recently a woman had given up her seat for me on the tube: that can do a lot of harm to a man's dignity.

For many of my dreams it was already too late. I'd never be a Hollywood star, I'd never duet with Dolly Parton and I'd never open the batting for England. But discovering France was still within my compass. Not for ever, but maybe for two or three long summer months, just enough to give me a semblance of a continental education and sharpen up my sartorial act. In any case, actors of a certain vintage are never short of 'down time' in which to enjoy such an adventure: with luck, my agent might not even notice I'd gone.

Curiously, Julia was in favour of my idea. For twenty years she'd been complaining of my Little England outlook, and had quietly longed for me to develop an appreciation of the finer things in life: i.e., her. Nothing radical, just a few simple changes would have made all the difference in her eyes – perhaps to take command of a menu and know which wine to order, to wear clothes beyond M&S weekend casuals, and to make love to her without it seeming like I was trying to fix the starter motor on an Austin Allegro. Perhaps to throw off some of that familiarity and dullness that starts to grow over us all at a certain point in life, threatening to choke what we once were or might have been. Perhaps just my wanting to go offered up a certain unexpected, continental, reckless, free-thinking aspect that Julia warmed to.

And now I warmed to it too.

With the purchase of some maps and guides and the application of a soupçon of internet research, the trip slowly took shape. I began to see myself as the modern-day equivalent of those English gentlemen in centuries past who set out on the Grand Tour of the continent in search of cultural and spiritual self-improvement. What was good enough for the likes of Boswell, Byron, Wordsworth and Smollett could surely be of benefit to a middle-aged Simkins too.

I had decided to depart in classic fashion by boat (in my case, the Newhaven–Dieppe ferry), and once on the other side, to travel round as my nose took me: with nobody to answer to, no preconceptions and, crucially, no vocabulary. With an appropriate flourish, I promised to complete my odyssey by rendezvousing with Ju back at La Coupole. And this time, I'd order the meal myself: a prospect even she described as 'unmissable'.

On the eve of the trip Julia and I shared an early bird special at our local Strada and toasted my departure. Less than twenty-four hours from now I'd be sailing and there'd be no going back. But by now Julia's warmth had been frozen with dread. A rite of passage was all very well, she explained, but I was armed with virtually no contacts, no itinerary and only four words of French, and she was terrified of the scrapes I might get into. It wasn't too late to pull out. I had nothing to prove, and could stay at home and watch TV without feeling any sense of shame. She'd even let me watch the cricket on Sky if I wanted. Finally she confessed she was going to miss me.

But by now I'd got the bit between my teeth. I was looking

forward to pitting my wits against whatever *le continent* could throw at me. If all went well our next meal at La Coupole in a few months' time would taste sweet indeed.

'Well, for Christ's sake, take care,' she concluded. 'You're so parochial. One moment some bloke will be offering you a lift into the next town, and the next thing you know he'll be taking you up the Languedoc.'

Wrack and Rouen

THERE WERE HUNDREDS of ways the trip might have been cancelled at the last minute.

I might have lost the tickets, or been offered a job, or discovered my ten-year passport was out of date. There might be a wildcat strike on the Trans-Manche ferries, or at the very least my taxi to Victoria station might not have turned up – a hundred ways in which my own personal marathon might have ended by the starter gun of fate misfiring and shooting me in the thigh. But I'd thought of everything. It was the morning of my departure and all that remained was to fetch my suitcase from the top of the wardrobe and pack in time for my taxi at noon. And then Julia leaned into the lining and picked something out of the interior.

'What's this?' she said.

It was a particular voice she only uses when I'm in deep shit, the clear, crisp tone of a primary school teacher who has discovered a scurrilous message being written by the naughtiest boy in the class and is bent on reading it out in a cadence of withering contempt.

She was holding a cardboard label. The incriminating tag was off an exotic brand of brassiere, or possibly a pair of panties. 'Decadence,' she read out. 'Luxury lingerie for the discerning lover.' She looked from the label to me. 'Why is this in your suitcase?'

'Um…'

'For whom have you been buying ladies' silk underwear?'

'Er…'

'Where is the garment now?'

Her voice made it plain there were only two possible answers. Either I must refer her to the buttocks of a woman with whom I'd been sharing secret trysts in a Travelodge at Scratchwood services, or I could lift the floorboards and show her the extensive catalogue of feminine garments for my secret life as Pauline.

I hadn't the faintest idea how the label had got there, yet in the space of ten seconds, both the trip and my manhood were hanging by a thread.

For the next twenty minutes I blathered, stumbled and pontificated, while she increasingly resembled Inspector Morse interviewing a habitual criminal. By the time I replied, 'I've never seen it before, you've got to believe me,' I was even beginning to sound like one.

Eventually she lapsed into a tearful acquiescence, while I stared bleakly at my packing. She insisted I must go. I insisted I couldn't. She insisted I should have thought of that before I started buying pants for some huge-arsed tart in Potters Bar. As precious minutes ticked by, I found myself conjuring up increasingly improbable scenarios to explain the discovery. Perhaps I'd gathered the label up off someone else's present at Christmas? Perhaps it was off a costume in the wardrobe department during a recent filming gig. Perhaps –

A ring on the doorbell heralded the arrival of Zephyr Cars. Our goodbyes were short and brittle. I stared bleakly at her taut figure on the pavement from the back of the minicab as it pulled away.

Seamus, my driver for the journey, wanted to know if I was off on holiday and where I was going to. On hearing France, he waxed lyrical about a holiday he'd recently had there with his grandchildren, and assured me if the rest of the country was like EuroDisney I was in for a grand time. Yet I scarcely listened. All I could think of was my farewell to Julia. Trevor Howard must have felt like this while he waited for his train in *Brief Encounter*, but at least his reputation was still intact.

Thirty minutes later and just as we were pulling into the station, my mobile rang. 'It's me,' she said simply. 'I've remembered where it came from.'

'You what?'

'You're off the hook. I remembered where it came from. I borrowed the suitcase at Easter for Jenny's hen party...'

A faint recollection of her going on a boozy hen weekend to Birmingham with an old schoolfriend of hers swam into my mind.

'I think I bought her something with those labels on from Ann Summers. I've no idea if the firm was called Decadence but for now you're no longer a dead man.'

'So you're happy for me to go?'

'Give me a call when you arrive in Dieppe. Don't drink too much, lay off the crisps, don't talk to strange women, and remember your solemn promise not to smoke. Bye.'

Seamus was peering at me in his driving mirror. 'Good news, is it?' he asked.

'The best.'

'Ah that's grand,' he smiled, displaying a row of chipped teeth. 'Never depart on a quarrel is what my mam used to tell me. Will you be celebratin' now?'

'I will,' I replied, reaching into my jacket pocket. 'I'm going to have a small cigar...'

WHEN I WAS a kid there were few more boring prospects on earth than an afternoon's shopping with Mum and Dad in Lewes. Yet now, as my train rumbled through the Sussex weald towards Newhaven and the ferry terminal, it resembled Nirvana.

At the station, streams of trippers were struggling up the main stairs on their way to an evening's opera at nearby Glyndebourne. Chinless wonders lugged crates of champagne and punnets of M&S strawberries towards waiting taxis while their wives made twittering phone calls to their children explaining how to work the microwave and promising they'd be home by midnight.

Midnight? Obviously Wagner was having the night off. A poster confirmed tonight was the opening performance of *La Bohème*. In an hour's time they would be sitting on crisp manicured lawns drinking Pimm's as they waited for an overweight soprano with a stupendous waistline and wobbling cleavage to succumb to malnutrition and consumption in a Parisian garret.

My fate might be not dissimilar, but I was going to have to endure God knows what before I got there. The fact was, in the last couple of hours all my pent-up wanderlust had disappeared down the plughole, to be replaced by more familiar feelings: doubt, unease and a sense of profound foreboding as to what I'd find and how I'd cope.

I had a rough plan, but it wouldn't take me further than the weekend. Once over the Channel I'd set off across country via the ancient city of Rouen for the tiny village of St Marc sur Mer on France's Atlantic coast: the very town featured in *Mr Hulot's Holiday*. Beyond that I had only the sketchiest itinerary. I bought myself a Raspberry McFlurry for the onward journey and it seemed to comfort me.

In some ways Newhaven represents in miniature our obsession with our nearest neighbours. It has always had both eyes trained warily on the Channel, one for any sign of invasion and the other for the chance to have a punt ourselves. The town's main attraction (aside from the all-night cigarette machine in the high street) is the crumbling Victorian fort up on the cliff, built in the 1880s to repel the Frenchies in the event of attack.

If you discount Lord Lucan, whose car was found in a side street shortly before his disappearance in 1974, the town's only famous resident turns out to be one of the most legendary figures in Anglo-French history. Charles Wells broke the bank at Monte Carlo, correctly calling twenty-seven out of thirty rolls of the roulette wheel in a single session.

He, surely, should be my template now: no anxieties about speaking the lingo or ordering the correct wine with his food for him. He merely packed his small town ways in his suitcase, hopped on the first boat across the Channel and announced that the French banks should ensure they had plenty of cash in the vaults as they were going to need it.

Yet as I sat in a deserted waiting room in the Trans-Manche ferry terminal, I was filled with nebulous anxieties, although it didn't help that the cup of tea I'd been offered by the booking clerk was one of the worst examples I've ever had. Even as my lips felt their way through the grimy scum on the surface to the dishwater beneath I was gripped by a sense of despair.

Perhaps the whole thing was a fool's errand. A continental education was all very well, but what with British gastro-pubs serving up Michelin-starred food, a pound equalling a euro, global warming turning places like Mablethorpe into palm-fringed resorts and the EU having governance over everything from smoking in public to the admissible curvature of bananas, was there really so much difference between France and England any more, in this increasingly homogenised world? Particularly as we no longer seemed able to make a decent cup of tea. If Prince Philip and Jacques Chirac could mark the centenary of the Entente Cordiale by gripping one another by the hands rather than the throat, what differences were left to be discovered?

We were as one now, surely; our quirks and specificities eroding as reliably as those white cliffs up there on the headland.

And then I saw it. The front-page headline in a copy of the *Sun*, being read by a man in a bicycle helmet whose only item of luggage seemed to be a box of paintball pellets.

OI SARKY – WE'RE NARKY
OVER THIS EU WARSHIP MULLARKEY!

'Lord Nelson must be ready to jump off his column', it began, going on to berate France's 'pint-sized President' over his call for the EU to have its own navy, and finishing its critique by describing him as 'a Napoleon wanabee'. The photo on the front had a Hitler moustache on the face of the French supremo thoughtfully added by the design department.

I downed my tea, picked up my bag and strode across to the check-in desk with a renewed spring in my step. Perhaps I'd give it twenty-four hours after all.

THE CROSSING ON the *Marie Celeste* was uneventful. If anything, there seemed to be fewer people on the ferry than there'd been in the departure lounge. I'd imagined that an early evening ferry crossing in high summer would have been full of happy trippers all having knees-ups round the pianos in the bar and eating baguettes out on deck in the sunshine, but there can't have been more than fifty passengers on the entire craft.

I sat in a desolate lounge among half-eaten meals and bulkhead doors swinging listlessly on their hinges, watching a European Cup football match on a widescreen TV. The only indication of progress was that the further we got from land, the more the picture kept freezing. By the time we'd been at sea for an hour it was stuck for minutes on end, the same image of players caught mid-kick. It was like watching a game depicted in Fuzzy Felt.

I wandered aimlessly round the decks, passing groups of French lorry drivers playing cards or chatting up the bar staff. The on-board cafeteria was serving an extensive array of dodgy-looking meat dishes served with flaccid pasta spirals, and I looked in vain for something I vaguely recognised from Julia's more personal range of cuisine at home. It was impossible to ascertain the contents, encased as they were in yards of glistening clingfilm, but each looked as if it had been spawned in a top-secret research laboratory. Eventually I saw something I recognised. Thank God. It may have been advertised as *galette au boeuf et jambon avec des cornichons*, but I knew veal and ham pie and a wally when I saw one.

By the time I'd returned to the upper deck, the coastline of France was twinkling ahead in the dark. It was past ten o'clock and already Europe looked worryingly shut. As I trudged out of the terminal towards a bleak ring road, the sound of one of the ferry workers up on deck whistling 'If you like a lot of chocolate on your biscuit, join our club' drifted out of the hold. Funny how the smallest things make you homesick.

I blundered through revving lorries and cars full of jolly families surrounded by camping equipment towards the distant lights of the town. I briefly considered trying to hitch, but who was I kidding? A middle-aged man in a panama hat and sandals standing in the dark by the side of an unlit bypass was hardly likely to prove an appetising prospect, particularly in this notoriously formal and conservative country. I was going to have to walk.

'Allo, monsieur?'

I looked round. An elderly woman in a Renault Twingo had pulled up by the side of the road and was leaning over to talk to me through the passenger window. She launched into a stream of meaningless jumble, but the expression of gentle concern on her face was easy enough to decipher. She was offering me a lift without my even asking for one.

'Dieppe?'

'Ah oui – Dieppe,' I replied, pointing towards the distant lights.

'Bon. Montez!' she said, opening the passenger door.

Within minutes she'd dropped me at the door of the Hotel du Quesnay in the main square. Although it was closed, a key was nestling beneath the doormat as the proprietor had promised me when I'd booked the room. Moments later I was in bed, and tucking into a complimentary packet of Bourbon biscuits left on the bedside table. I was even able to make a decent cuppa.

I WOKE NEXT morning to a peal of bells from a nearby clock tower – the kind normally reserved for people suffering hangovers in bad comedies. In truth I'd spent a fitful night. I'd woken at about 4 a.m. and foolishly turned on the TV to watch *BBC News 24*, but instead of a sober-suited Nicholas Owen talking about yesterday in Parliament I'd found myself staring at a hardcore porn channel thoughtfully provided by the hotel management for people who still knew the best way to make use of such luxuries.

It had been a doleful interlude. A woman of uncertain years was in full spate with a couple of undernourished Moroccan gentlemen who were doing their best to service her in each and every available orifice. My experience of porn, particularly in hotel rooms, has made me something of an expert on the genre, and the general rule of thumb, if you'll excuse the expression, is that the more you stick on your room bill the more intimate the concomitant camerawork.

But here was something different. The angles were restrained enough, but it was evident even to my fuddled brain that in this case the skilful editing was merely an attempt to conceal the fact that neither man was able to gain tumescence.

The poor woman was dutifully moaning and grinding in the best X-rated traditions, but it was obvious that her colleagues were suffering their own particular form of stage fright. They lay on a bedspread of doubtful vintage looking down at her frantic efforts, with a mixture of profound embarrassment at their plight mixed with sheepish glances off to the side to check the director wasn't tearing up their contract.

One of the men was at least making a fist of it: or rather, he wasn't making a fist of it, whereas that was the only option open to his poor companion. Such was his stage fright that he had even kept his pants on. Eventually the two men achieved a botched climax after which all three flopped against the headboard. Now that her duties were over the woman looked thoroughly fed up at her partners' ineptitude: an expression I recognised only too well.

I CHECKED OUT after breakfast. Dieppe was raining. Knots of bedraggled tourists mingled with residents hurrying back and forth carrying bread sticks and yappy dogs. I dodged the drizzle and set off to find the *office de tourisme* on the seafront. But a notice on the main door announced that it was *fermé* till 11.15 due to *circonstances exceptionnelles*. I took refuge in a nearby café and ordered some more coffee.

There are always moments early on in any trip when you can either press on or return home. Dieppe was a pretty enough town, but the only attraction on a day such as this was to visit the beaches used for the D-Day landings. Clambering over gun emplacements in light drizzle, even if they were aimed at the Trans-Manche booking office twenty-three miles away, was hardly how I'd envisaged things.

Just then the office flared into life. A woman in a smart suit appeared from behind the counter and began switching on computer terminals and banks of fluorescent lights. I rattled the front doors hopefully, and eventually she strode over with barely concealed annoyance.

A brief exchange with lots of gesticulating soon laid out my options. The good news was that the main railway station was only a few hundred yards away. The bad news was that I'd just missed the train out of here and the next one wasn't for four hours. The return ferry to Newhaven, on the other hand, left in only fifty-five minutes. If I wanted, I could be at home with Ju watching *The Dog Whisperer* by early evening.

There was nothing for it. I set off towards the main road out of town to try my luck at hitching a lift. At least if I got picked up I'd be able to make some gags about taking the road to Rouen.

A FRIEND OF mine had given me some useful tips to increase my chances of getting a lift in a strange country. 'Make your luggage seem as small as possible,' he'd advised me. 'Smile at any passing motorist and remember to make eye contact. Ensure you're presentable, and for God's sake check that your flies are done up.'

I composed my face into an all-purpose grin, wrote ROUEN SVP in black marker pen on a piece of cardboard and positioned myself against a handy road sign. For nearly an hour I stood smiling at passing cars. Occasionally a driver would shrug his shoulders or indicate he was turning off at the next junction, but mostly they stared glassily ahead and revved away up the hill towards the motorway.

Eventually a fitter from an exhaust replacement company on the other side of the road took pity and wandered over to tell me I was leaning against a sign that said – in French – 'No Stopping'. Within seconds of repositioning myself nearer the roundabout, my luck changed. A small courier van with a sealed-off rear compartment protected by blacked-out windows screeched to a halt and the driver leaned across to swing open the passenger door. By the time I'd lumbered up to him he was already clearing a space for me in the front passenger seat.

'Rouen?' I asked.

'*Oui*! Rouen!' he answered. I clambered in.

With my cardboard sign forming a rudimentary barrier just in case he put his hand on my knee and asked if I'd ever been to a sauna, we sped off up the hill towards *la route périphérique*.

Emile's job was to drive urgent supplies of insulin to various hospitals around northern France. Despite his complete lack of English he was anxious to impress on me that Nicolas Sarkozy was a slimy pig's head and his favourite team was Manchester United. I smiled dutifully and nodded every thirty seconds or so as he kept up an unending stream of conversation, throwing in the occasional 'Mon dieu' and 'Exactement'. Emile seemed delighted by my grasp of the language.

In truth I was only able to hang on to the gist of his conversation because his favourite subject was football. Every few minutes I recognised Barthez, Vieira and Zidane. Inevitably, Eric Cantona eventually made an appearance.

'Ah oui, Cantona!' I clutched greedily at the name like a drowning man spotting a lifebelt. 'C'est magnifique, c'est vrai le philosopher!' He nodded and we sat grinning happily for some minutes as his speed increased and I tried to think of the French for sardines always following the trawler.

All was going swimmingly when he suddenly removed both hands from the steering wheel and clutched wildly at his chest, sending the car lurching towards the hard shoulder. In fact, Emile wasn't suffering a cardiac arrest; rather he was attempting to demonstrate his everyman credentials and his love of the universal brotherhood of humanity.

'Je suis un citoyen du monde,' he explained, gesticulating wildly. 'J'aime liberté, l'égalité et la fraternité!' He clutched his chest again and the car veered towards the central reservation.

It transpired Emile was full of woe for the state of affairs that this parvenu Sarkozy was taking the country towards, and that if he could get him in this van he'd throttle him until not a breath of life remained in that sleazy trickster's body.

Not that I translated any of this, but such were his powers of mime that I was left in no doubt as to his intentions. I racked my brains for the name of his former opponent for the presidency so I could take over the conversation and leave him free to concentrate on other things, like driving, for instance. But what was her name? The speedometer was now well over ninety.

Sago-something. Got it! 'Ségolène Royal!' I shouted the name so loudly he jumped.

'Ah oui, Ségolène Royal!' he said.

'Elle est très sexy!' I described a woman's hourglass figure with my hands and smiled knowingly. 'Elle est mon political champignon.'

My declaration seemed to trouble Emile. He looked puzzled and went quiet.

We'd driven barely another kilometre when he mentioned Madeleine McCann and simultaneously lurched off the motorway and down a minor road. He clutched at his T-shirt again. 'Mystérieux,' he said, shaking his head woefully. 'C'est mystérieux.'

'Oui,' I replied, feeling for the passenger door. 'Très mystérieux.'

He launched into another indeterminate sentence. I took a punt he was asking what I thought might have happened to her. By coincidence I'd recently met a documentary film director specialising in true crime who had spoken with some knowledge about the intricacies of the case. But could I translate his thoughts into Emilespeak?

'Um ... mon ami dans Angleterre qui est l'expert international de ... er ...' I couldn't think of the word for 'crime' so offered the nearest to hand, the French for 'thief', then went on to expound, 'Well, il a dit Madeleine McCann est vivante!'

Emile looked puzzled. I couldn't be sure that I'd used the correct word for thief – *voleur*. I now suspected I might have said *velo*, which meant bicycle – my friend who is an international expert in bicycles – although I might equally have said *velour*, suggesting that my friend back home claimed inside knowledge of one of the most baffling crimes in recent history thanks to his expertise in the maintenance of easy-care garments for the over-fifties.

It didn't matter. The fact was we were no longer on the main road, and without a word of explanation. The important thing was to suggest to my captor that somebody, somewhere had the ear of the highest authorities in Interpol and that even now a fleet of helicopters was being scrambled to look for me.

We turned off the road altogether and swung into a small industrial estate. He screeched to a halt, turned off the ignition and smiled. 'Une minute,' he said, and disappeared round to the back of the van before setting off in the direction of one of the warehouses.

Julia had warned me about hitchhiking. Now her dire predic- tions rang in my ears. The minutes passed. Then I saw him return, clutching what looked to be a piece of chamois leather. This was it. I was going to be chloroformed and then wake up to find myself suspended in chains and Emile in a facemask.

He got in and offered me a piece of cloth drenched in refreshing *eau de cologne*. I wiped my neck with it and muttered sheepish thanks. Then he switched on the ignition and pointed ahead. 'Rouen!' he yelled happily.

If there's one town on earth you don't want to be driven to by a man whose main method of communication is to clutch his chest, then the resting place of Richard the Lionheart must be it. As we approached the outskirts, Emile pointed to the distant spire of the cathedral and started doing his coronary impression again, this time with accompanying jungle sound effects. As we trundled through heavy suburban traffic he pointed out other points of interest: the small block of flats where he lived with his wife, his brother's house, the park where he played as a child. We drove on, Emile utilising a hitherto unseen medley of hand gestures as he pointed out *la gare*, *l'arrêt du bus* and *le prison* (removing both hands from the wheel again to perform an extensive mime of somebody in shackles).

It transpired Emile was not only taking me well past his stop, but right up to the very door of the tourist office. He parked the van, marched me up to the front desk and organised a hotel room for me less than two minutes from the main square.

'Au revoir, Michel. Vous êtes un citoyen du monde aussi.' He clutched me to his breast, gave me a kiss on each cheek, and with a final *au revoir* and an exhortation to the startled official behind the desk to take extra special care of me during my stay, he was out of the doors and gone.

Emile was my first French cliché, and, I suspect, my first French lesson. His ancestors had no doubt enjoyed introducing their local *ducs* and *duchesses* to Dr Guillotin, and in his own way he was still living the dream – liberté, égalité, fraternité. Or to recap the full phrase used during the height of the Revolutionary Terror, 'Liberté, égalité, fraternité ou la mort', sentiments that sat only too well with his driving.

He was just the sort of Frenchman I'd heard about: earnest, opinionated, and happy enough to cause a rumpus by using burning hay bales to blockade the autoroute or a rusting trawler to close down the port. Such actions wouldn't worry him if he thought the cause was just. But to Emile, this credo also meant that if you see a stranger in a strange land in need of a lift, you pick him up and make sure he gets to his destination with a flourish Louis Quatorze himself would have found hard to improve on.

I'd only stuck out my thumb in the first place through necessity, yet rather than encountering serial killers and paedophiles, I'd blundered upon real kindness, real hospitality and model humanity.

Vive la France! Vive le monde!

Vive Emile!

Monet Monet Monet

I BET THE Hôtel des Artistes in Rouen has a unique claim to fame among all the hotels of northern France. I bet it's the only one whose reception area is festooned with framed photographs of winners of the Finnish Junior Dance Championships from the 1970s.

Emile's remonstrations had got me an attic room at the very top of the building, a few minutes' walk from the cathedral. The only item of furniture apart from a double bed was a bidet. That night I sat recovering from my ordeal by happily cooling my undercarriage in its odorous waters and staring happily out at the apartments on the other side of the street.

A middle-aged woman opposite was watering her flowers, giving me a spectacular display of her varicose veins, while from the street below the chatter of happy pedestrians mingled with the occasional peal of bells from the cathedral and a distant hum of a street accordionist. Now I was away from Dieppe, a sense of anticipation and excitement was beginning to replace my former terror. I went to bed refreshed and expectant.

I was woken at 3 a.m. by shouting from the next room. A female, by the sound of it a teenage girl, was screaming the name of *The Times* cricket correspondent and author of acclaimed biographies on both David Gower and David 'Bumble' Lloyd.

'Alan Lee… Alan Lee…' she moaned.

What a hoot! I'd stumbled across probably the only other person in northern France with cricket on their mind at 3 a.m. There'd be no shortage of conversation over the coffee and croissants in the morning. Whoever she was, we could exchange views on the controversial meeting of the ICC planned for the next week in Dubai.

'Alan Lee! Alan Lee!' she wailed ever more loudly.

But the urgency of her cries and sound of creaking bedsprings soon confirmed the reality. The phrase was palpably 'Allons-y!' 'Go there!'

The orgasm approached for maybe another minute and a half. Whatever the other person was doing, he was certainly *allons*-ing her *lui* with some success. After a final yell of ecstasy she let out an endless sigh, after which everything went silent.

I was awoken again an hour later by a repeat performance, and again just before 6 a.m. As I stumbled downstairs for breakfast I halted briefly outside the room and put my ear to the door. Nothing. All passion spent. Perhaps they were already in the dining room.

But in fact I was the only diner. I sat in cacophonous silence, surrounded by the photos of the Finnish Majorettes and trying not to make too much noise chomping my Sugar Puffs. But as I passed the doorway on my way back, it opened and a willowy youth in his late teens popped his head out. I smiled knowingly and offered up the faintest trace of a wink, just something to indicate don't worry, old son, no names no pack drill, I only wish I had your stamina, who's the lucky girl then?

As I was doing so a second face popped up behind him. It was an identical twin brother. They retreated inside hurriedly and slammed the door shut. It was the last I ever saw of them. This was indeed a strange land.

IT WAS THE headline in the only British newspaper on sale that pointed my way for the day ahead. Claude Monet's famous painting of some water lilies (*Le Bassin aux Nymphéas*) had fetched the small matter of £41 million at an auction at Christie's the previous day, and the picture dominated the front pages. It was also due to be projected onto the front wall of Rouen Cathedral between six and eight that evening.

It's one of the average Frenchman's beliefs that his country leads the world in art and culture. The French sculptor Rodin said, 'To the artist there is never anything ugly', which only shows he's never been to Birmingham city centre on a Saturday night.

French art reached its grandest expression with Impressionism, a particularly Gallic innovation in which artists ripped up the rulebook and started again. Until they appeared, a house had to look like a house. By the end of the nineteenth century, all this had been shown the door, even if it no longer resembled one.

The leading exponent was Monet. He is to Impressionism what – well, what Rory Bremner is to impressionism. Anglophiles might argue that our own favourites Turner and Sisley taught Monet all he knew, but what is undeniable is that art, particularly French art, was never the same once Monet had got hold of it. As well as introducing subversive notions such as painting in the open air and at different times of the day, he also introduced – damned impertinence – the concept of tackling the same subject more than once. Or, as in the case of the water lilies, 260 times.

The resulting free-for-all provided the catalyst for everything that followed: post-Impressionism, Cubism, Surrealism,

Dadaism, Abstract Impressionism and so on down to the two yobbos in my street last month who assured me that spray-painting their initials three thousand times on my garden wall was post-Banksyism.

I have my own favourite artists, of course, notably Terence Cuneo and his legendary studies of British steam trains, especially that famous one of the *Flying Scotsman* at full throttle, but apart from him, anything more sophisticated than kittens playing with balls of wool has always left me somewhat bemused. And while I wouldn't go so far as to echo Adolf Hitler's opinion that anyone who paints a sky green or a tree blue needs sterilising, I'm definitely of the 'What's it meant to be?' school of criticism.

But Giverny, Monet's resting place and home of the famous lily pond, was barely an hour from my hotel room. Hearing of the staggering sum paid for his greatest work, I sensed it would be well worth making a half-day detour to see where it was painted. And Monet would hopefully be within my artistic compass: realistic enough to be recognisable, yet slapdash enough to be open to interpretation. I booked in a second night with the Majorettes and set off for the railway station.

MY ARRIVAL AT the nearby station of Vernon soon after midday confirmed a niggling hunch growing within me ever since I'd disembarked the previous evening: nothing in France is written in English.

You'd think such a tourist hotspot as this might offer up a gesture to the international brotherhood of travellers, but instead the idea seems to be to make it as difficult as possible for tourists to navigate their way round. I suppose it's a trick they had to employ every few years just to confuse the invading Germans. Now Americans, Russians and gaggles of bemused Japanese all wandered hopelessly up and down in search of anything resembling an exit sign or 'Le Shuttle pour les Water Lilies'. Nothing.

The only assistance on offer was a station master in white shorts, white socks and one of those yachting caps with a plastic crown, who bellowed at everyone through a loud-hailer so fast it was impossible to pick up a single word.

Outside the scene more resembled a Feydeau farce. Although the shuttle bus to Giverny was parked in a side street barely fifty yards away, there was nothing to indicate its presence or assist frenzied trippers. I made it on board just before the vehicle, only half full and with more families streaming towards its doors, lurched off in a cloud of exhaust fumes.

As we crawled towards the main road, I reflected on this famed off-handedness. I suppose the truth is the French are still at war. Not with tanks and bombs, but with language and culture. When Julia began her training as an international telephonist, the accepted international language was – could only be – French. But now, merely thirty years later, with Anglo-American culture rampant, French resistance is doomed. In the age of *Le Big Mac* and *Les Simpsons*, it's having to fight hand-to-hand, or word-to-word, in the streets. The surly bus driver, for instance, or the man with the loud-hailer yelling instructions: in some ways they're brave irregular soldiers dying for the cause. Or perhaps they're just miserable sods.

GIVERNY MAY HAVE been advertised as Monet's resting place, but he'd struggle to get any shut-eye around here nowadays. Having been dropped in an overspill car park, I followed the tide of tourists past the Monet florists, the Monet *salon de thé* and the Monet antiques shop towards the Monet centre-of-the-village and the Monet ice-cream van.

I was just choosing which flavour to have when my phone rang. It was the *Daily Telegraph* in London. I'd filed an article for the notebook section just before leaving for the ferry, a piece composed of several wry observations on current affairs, finishing off with a brief digest of my plans for the trip ahead and my reasons for going. Now a girl called Sally was ringing to explain that someone in the office had inadvertently deleted my last paragraph.

She wanted to know if I could resend it in the next twenty minutes. Just the last para would suffice. I mimed an apology at the ice-cream vendor for holding him up, but he unfurled an indulgent smile and gestured for me to take my time: it seemed that mobile-phone calls taken by frazzled customers were an occupational hazard.

'Look, if you can remember what you wrote I'll take it down in shorthand,' suggested Sally helpfully. 'But you'll have to speak up, I can hardly hear you.'

'Well, it's a bit difficult,' I explained, as a charabanc full of Italian tourists thundered past in second gear.

'What was that?'

'Never mind, here goes. Open para: *I'm going to France later this week and am looking forward to a bit of entente discordiale.*'

'*Internet* what? I missed the last bit, the line is terrible.'

'ENTENTE DISCORDIALE!' I bawled into the phone. I mimed 'sorry' to the proprietor and pointed to a tub of glistening ice cream in his display case. He set to work delicately scooping a thick curl of *caramel au beurre salé* while I attempted to reduce my voice to a mere yell.

'Um, *until now my preconceptions of the French have been in line with those of the fictional secret agent, Johnny English–*'

'Hang on,' said the voice on the phone, 'I'm trying to write with one hand and hold the pad still with the other … *Johnny English* … yes, go on.'

'*Namely, the only thing that France is adept at hosting is an invasion.*' The proprietor was now lovingly wrapping his creation in a square of greaseproof paper.

'Sorry, you cut out, is what?' said the voice.

'Look, can I ring you back, Sally? This is a bit awkward.'

'Hang on, let me write that down. *Look can I* what?'

'No, no, that was me. Never mind… *France is adept at hosting is an invasion…*' I grinned sheepishly across the counter and offered up a silent prayer that the proprietor didn't speak English, but it seems I needn't worry: he grimaced back in a gesture of mute solidarity for every man who's ever had a marital row on a mobile phone.

'Come again?'

'… *FRANCE IS ADEPT AT HOSTING IS AN INVASION!*' I noticed that the proprietor was giving me an extra dollop, presumably as a gesture of support. Here was I, condemning an uncomprehending Frenchman and his compatriots from the same mouth that would soon be hoovering up his ice cream and some of his profit. Luckily my contact on the phone seemed happy and I was able to pay up and hurry off. But it had been an uneasy interlude. Thank God I hadn't mentioned cheese-eating surrender monkeys.

MONET CERTAINLY KNEW how to live. His house, a large mansion-cum-villa with an extensive garden, had been joined in recent years by a more modern annexe to accommodate the crush of sightseers. The gift shop in particular was doing a brisk trade. I wandered among Monet calendars, books, T-shirts, postcards, paperweights, umbrellas, teddy bears, candles, micro-puzzles, jigsaws, scented notelets, pencils, bonbons, cigarette lighters, fridge magnets and tattoos. There was even a stand dedicated to Monet ties, garish affairs with insistent floral patterns in mauves and yellows that looked as if they'd been fashioned by students of Slade. The band, that is, not the art school.

By the time I'd checked out the goods it had started to rain, and I joined a crocodile of damp tourists tramping through the rooms that formed the backdrop to the great man's life. An American next to me was explaining to his wife why the grim attendant in the master bedroom had wrested her camera from her when she attempted to take a picture of the garden below. 'Well, you see, hon, people take shots of the locks on the room, the window fastenings, all that jazz, next thing you know they've got a break-in on their hands.'

With its faded sofas and threadbare furnishings, it would be slim pickings for any cat burglar today. Monet lived here for the last forty-one years of his life, and the place suggested corpulent middle age rather than the firebrand rebel popularly depicted in operas like *La Bohème*. Indeed, from the photographs displayed of Monet's second wife, Alice, it seemed the only consumption she ever succumbed to was a delivery van full of meat pies.

But the gardens were beautiful, and given added visual exoticism by a Japanese wedding party celebrating among the flowerbeds. An exquisite young girl, dressed in a demure bridal gown with a single flower in her hair, tippytoed her way among the paths, pursued by giggling bridesmaids and young men in sharp suits with brilliantined hair.

To reach the lily pond, I had to descend a concrete underpass beneath the main road. But the pond itself, silent and eerie, didn't disappoint. Suddenly you could see why he'd lived here, even if he had been forced to created the pond artificially with the aid of an army of workmen. Money well spent, I'd say.

I bought a postcard of lily paintings to send home to Julia and sat down to write it on a bench outside the shop. Here I found myself talking to Ron and Beryl from Cambridge. Ron had been here on a long weekend in the mid-1960s. Beryl hadn't been to France before and, I suspect from her sour expression, was expecting somebody to steal her handbag at any moment, or at the very least breathe garlic all over her.

'Anything you'd suggest I visit while I'm in Rouen?' I asked them for want of a better opening gambit.

'Well, the ceramics museum is very good,' replied Ron.

'If you like ceramics,' added Beryl.

'Anything else?'

'There's the medieval clock of course,' said Ron.

'If you like clocks,' added Beryl, with a knowing stare.

'And the cathedral, of course. That's something a bit different.'

'If you like cathedrals, of course,' I suggested.

Beryl nodded darkly.

By now it was nearly 6 p.m. and time to get back to the station. I joined the hordes returning to the shuttle stop, each weighed down with furled posters and bags of commemorative knick-knacks. As in all great tourist attractions, the very qualities that had given rise to Giverny's fame in the first place were now threatened by sheer weight of numbers of visitors. Yet I'd enjoyed my brief trip, and on this cool showery afternoon there had been some ravishing images to be found in among all the crush and merchandising.

I wonder what Monet would have made of the thousands of tourists blundering through his little piece of heaven? Of one thing I was sure: he might never have captured the *Flying Scotsman* at full spate, but the guy sure could paint water lilies.

THE NEXT MORNING I woke to encouraging news. Today was La Fête de la Musique, a national day of musical celebration during which every town and village in France comes together al fresco for a spontaneous national outpouring of live music and song.

Far from being a timeworn carnival from the middle ages, the event only dates from 1982, when a government official with the fetching job description of 'director of music and dance' read a survey suggesting one in five Frenchmen played a musical instrument. He decided to conduct a harebrained experiment to see if he could get them all playing at once, and this was the result.

It's now one of the biggest jollies of the year. For one day only, traditionally on the longest day of the year, every town becomes its own open-air concert venue. The only regulation is the rather pleasing caveat that the music be absolutely free. So popular has the event proved that it has spawned similar versions in more than a hundred countries, including Australia, the USA, and even Iraq Kurdistan – in fact, just about everywhere except Great Britain.

The party wasn't due to kick off until early evening, so there was time for a little sightseeing. Rouen was certainly the ideal starting point for any Rosbif trying to get his bearings in France as it has been conquered and reconquered by the two nations on an almost daily basis since medieval times.

The heart of Richard I ended up here (although his brains lie in Poitou and rest of him in Anjou) – and Henry V liked the place so much that he starved the residents to submission in 1419. His successors went even better, proclaiming the city to be part of Great Britain and barbecuing Joan of Arc at the stake while they were about it.

Nowadays there's only one way to see any new city. An electric tourist bus got up to resemble a tiny steam locomotive with a clanking bell was just revving up underneath some beech trees. I climbed in and settled down for the fifty-minute trip round the Rouen tourist trail. 'Bonjour, and welcome to the grandest little train in the world,' trilled a happy transatlantic voice emanating from some speakers secreted in the canopy. 'Just sit back and relax while we take you on a tour of some of the famous sights of this wunnerful city of Rouen.' We set off at a steady six miles an hour, slow enough for a Romanian busker in a striped T-shirt and a beret to hurry beside us for the first couple of minutes with an outstretched hat.

First we cruised round the perimeter of the cathedral. Then we viewed the Archbishop's Palace where Joan of Arc was tried. Then we visited a medieval clock with only one hand, and thence onto the house in which Gustav Flaubert, author of *Madame Bovary*, had lived, and finally round another huge church that could have done as the cathedral if the real one had ever wanted the weekend off.

The only disquieting feature was the bilingual commentary. I noticed that the French exposition wasn't always followed by an equivalent translation, but instead by a knowing yet inexplicable silence.

What had just been said that didn't require translating? And was it my imagination, or were the French couple sharing my carriage smirking every time one of these non-translatable paragraphs finished? It was easy to let my paranoia run riot.

'OK, my fellow Frenchmen, while we're going through a boring bit, why not turn round and have a look at all the English? They

won't understand this because of course none of them can under-
stand a bloody word. In any case, all they want to know is where
they can get a pint of Carlsberg and a chip bap. Well, let them enjoy
it while they can, because once they've funded the 2012 Olympics
they won't be going anywhere...'

Nonetheless, the toy train was great value. Rouen was a genuinely attractive city, full of half-timbered houses and wriggling alleyways, while the dominant presence, the cathedral, was genuinely awe-inspiring in its size and grandeur. Not that I had any desire to step inside – I'd spent too many sunny days in my youth wandering around cathedrals, and had long ago realised they're all variations on a theme: dark, cold and oddly enervating. It was time to kick the habit.

In any case, I was on my way to an attraction that had caught my eye during the train ride. The Joan of Arc Living Wax Museum occupied small tumbledown premises next to the Big Ben English pub and tearooms. From the outside it had the look of a place that counted its annual visitor numbers on the fingers of one hand, but I'm always drawn to stiff, glassy eyed figures in unlikely costume – God knows I've acted with a few in my time.

Joan of Arc is perhaps the most controversial figure of Anglo-French misunderstanding in what would in any case be a crowded field of runners and riders. Born in 1412, she became convinced of her destiny after hearing voices telling her she'd been selected by God to save her country from disgrace. I've often had the same experience myself but only after a free bar at an after-show party.

Having convinced the King that she should be given her own army to lead into battle, she gained a series of stunning victories before being betrayed to the invading English, who promptly burnt her alive only yards from the ticket booth.

The spectacle offered dioramas and effigies tracing the young heroine's life, from her birth in the village of Domrémy up to her martyrdom in 1431. I bought a ticket and entered a gloomy vestibule to find myself looking at a young waxen female wearing a smock and kneeling in a field of greengrocer's display grass.

'Visitors, listen to the story of Joan of Arc,' crackled a female voice in a French accent so thick I could hardly make out the words. I glanced back past the entranceway, through which I could just glimpse jolly tourists sitting at café tables in the sunshine. It was going to be a long afternoon.

I wandered into the next chamber. The tableau here supposedly depicted her transformation from peasant maiden into girl-warrior by having her flowing tresses cut off to the length of her signature bob cut. But the arm of the barber had slipped during its long vigil so that now he seemed to be trying to sever her elbow with a pair of gardening shears. In the next vignette, Joan, now with an arrow in her shoulder, but still with her lower arm, knelt again, this time in front of a knot of noblemen wearing improbable hats.

The scenes depicted were predictably elegiac and romantic, but they seemed sadly selective. For instance, what about the famous incident in which the French nobility assured themselves of her unblemished character by checking her virginity? Not a trace of it. No wonder this place had so few visitors.

Inevitably the exhibition mounted an inexorable progress towards her martyrdom at the hands of the English. Her dying moments, being burnt alive in a giant funeral pyre, were feebly depicted by an old Magicoal flame-effect electric fire secreted among a pile of dusty logs. The whole thing had a depressing, dog-eared quality to it, and after a solitary half-hour wandering these dank corridors I had a desperate urge to suck on a slice of fresh pineapple and wash my hair.

Yet, I had to admit, the fact it even existed was something

remarkable. It was difficult to imagine a parallel attraction in Britain being allowed to occupy such a prime piece of real estate without being bought up by Starbucks. Yet in France such oddities were not only tolerated, but were the source of civic pride.

As I was leaving, a tatty visitors' book caught my eye. Presumably there would be some entries from Brits in its musty pages, especially since we'd torched her in the first place. Perhaps here I'd find some evidence of the new spirit of forgiveness and understanding between our two great nations. I signed my own name and flicked through to see what my countrymen had made of the attraction.

The early entries would have had the architects of the EU purring with pleasure. 'Lovely', somebody from the Channel Islands had commented, while a couple from County Down had written what a wonderful spirit she must have had to pursue the cause in which she believed. The opening entry from Wendy of Chichester was rather more cautious: 'Now we know all about Joan of Arc.'

Subsequent comments included 'I woz here' by Hannah of Cheadle Hume, 'Borr-innggg' from Brett in Hackney, 'Go England' from Russell in Lutterworth, while Sue from Portsmouth had been so moved by Joan's epic struggle that she felt moved to wish her sister Claudine a fab birthday.

The final comment was reserved for Liam from Ealing: 'We Woz Robbed.' As a testimony to the 'Fog in Channel, Europe Cut Off' school of Anglo-French history, it was as eloquent as any official document.

A COUPLE OF hours later I was woken from a doze in my room by a noise suggesting Iron Maiden were performing a gig in my wardrobe.

I stumbled out onto my balcony and looked down. Where only two hours before I'd virtually had the pavement to myself, it was now barely visible. The entire population of Normandy seemed to have arrived while I'd been asleep, and they'd all brought a contribution: some were banging drums, others struggling up the street with electric guitars and amplifiers, while on the far corner of the street a woman bashing a tambourine was singing, 'I Will Survive'.

I hurried down. Bands were suddenly on every street corner and in every doorway, mostly spotty teenagers with lank hair thundering out ragged versions of twelve-bar blues to crowds of adoring onlookers. Groups with names like the Zouk Zombies and Denim Laboratory blasted out tuneless rock anthems.

I'm sure that somewhere in the city there were symphony orchestras playing selections from Offenbach or Poulenc, and had I known where to look I could no doubt have found some Django Reinhardt or even choral plainsong. This stuff, however, was indescribable, the sort of noise that wouldn't have been tolerated in the lowliest youth club back in Britain. I searched in vain for some more authentic sounds, perhaps somebody singing a ballad or some Jacques Brel, but everything here seemed to have got stuck somewhere between the Rolling Stones and Johnny Rotten: an endless landscape of thirteen-year-olds wearing waistcoats and trilbies, not being able to get no satisfaction.

It was easy to see why France has never produced a single decent rock musician. For a nation so steeped in chic, their efforts are always deeply flawed: cheesy and cringeworthy. They just don't get it. On the other hand, there's something else they don't get either. Vomit.

Not only vomit, but broken glass, and feral youths in nylon shirts singing football chants. Whereas back home the streets would already have been knee-deep in discarded food cartons and crumpled beer cans, the atmosphere here was utterly amiable, with couples pushing babies mingling happily with teenagers and elderly ladies.

For nearly two hours I allowed myself to be borne along by the crowd like a twig in a stream, sometimes washing up for minutes on end outside some pavement café before being coaxed gently down a side street towards some new attraction. Overhead people leaned out of windows with glasses of wine or bowls of olives, and the odd car driver foolish enough to be caught up in the mayhem sat happily drumming their fingers on the steering wheel in time to the music. I'd only been in France a couple of days yet I was already sensing the Channel was a lot wider than the mere twenty-three miles advertised in the Trans-Manche ferry schedule.

Eventually I found a berth on the steps of the city courthouse where a band of eccentrics was performing. The Orphean Pistons were a jiggling semi-circle of musicians ranging from seven to seventy all dressed like refugees from *Tiswas*. They specialised in souped-up novelty items, a sort of cross between Steeleye Span and Spike Jones, each tune played with enthusiasm, face-pulling and not much else.

An elderly woman on the step next to me started gabbling animatedly in broken English about the merits of her beloved Pistons. Having ascertained I was English she ranged far and wide over French tradition: the delights of their cuisine and climate, and the detrimental effect that the internet and imported American culture were having on the cultural homogeneity of the youth of her beloved nation.

At least, I think that's what she said. To tell you the truth, I couldn't hear a bloody word.

Our Man at St Marc

FRANCE HAS ALWAYS prided itself on its film industry. Rightly so, I suppose, since the Lumière brothers invented the medium in the first place. The Francophone market may not rival Hollywood, but so proud are the French of their home-produced films that they account for one in three trips to the cinema. Yet apart from my beloved *Hulot*, French films had largely passed me by.

I've seen *Jean de Florette*, of course. And *Piaf*. And I once had to take my nephew to see one of those awful *Asterix* things. Mostly I've simply stumbled upon them, usually while channel-surfing late-night television, but they always looked so dismal it was never long before I moved on to *Jackass* or *America's Next Top Model*.

The problem, as far as I can see, is that French movies are unspeakably dull. Sorry, but there it is: the same unsmiling couples sitting in parked cars having tortured debates about their relationship. I can get that experience several times a week at home without having to go to my local arthouse cinema for it.

So why was I now feeling the need to hurtle halfway down northern France to see where *Hulot* was made? I sat pondering this question as I stood among the Finnish Majorettes waiting for my room bill to be processed.

In fact, I knew why. I needed to check if it was for real. That small piece of dreamy Atlantic coastline formed the template for my imagined France. Even those opening frames, a mood-establishing shot of gentle waves breaking on the beach, has always seemed to me the essence of summer. Whenever relationships or work or traffic jams on the M25 got too much to bear, I'd found comfort in imagining myself bathing in that sea, on that beach, in front of that same homely Hôtel de la Plage. And now – with luck – I'd be there in less than three hours.

The movie itself was something of a torturous affair. The filming, which began almost to the day back in June 1952, was supposed to end in August but what with typical funding crises, plus unseasonably chilly weather and a stiff wind that drove salt and sand into every orifice, both human and mechanical, shooting lasted nearly into October.

None of this comes across on screen, of course. The film's other-worldliness always seems part of just a perfect day, and I'd like to spend it with Hulot. The virtual absence of dialogue also compounds its ethereal quality. Apart from the odd muttered exchange, the only sounds are sound effects, on which Jacques Tati worked for months after filming finished: the whoosh of the sea breaking on the shore, the children's laughter echoing between the buildings, the murmur of chit-chat mixed with clattering cutlery, and, best of all, that trademark *ba-doingg* of the dining-room door as waiters pass back and forth.

And there's Hulot himself. His bungling awkwardness is encapsulated in the final shot, where he sits with the children on the beach, resigned to his inability to exert any control over a world destined to remain a baffling mystery. I've often felt the same about my own life.

Visiting places made famous by movies can be a dangerous business. It's a bit like going backstage to see the glamorous blonde you've fallen in love with under the spotlights – and God knows I've done that enough times. The end of the performance often reveals a reality not apparent from the stalls. Nothing is more illuminating than a single 40-watt light bulb in a tatty dressing room.

I recall some friends of mine once travelled to the hotel featured in *Some Like It Hot*, only to find it was actually situated at the end of a military runway used by the Mexican air force. They spent their time bellowing at each other from adjacent sun loungers while being strafed by jet aircraft. And have you ever visited Brighton's West Pier, which was featured in *Oh! What A Lovely War*? Well, you can't any more: it's fallen into the sea.

As I climbed aboard the train from Rouen to Nantes, I was under no illusions as to what I might find at the end of my own flickering rainbow. If the way Britain protected such sites was anything to go by, chances were either the whole of St Marc sur Mer had been bulldozed to make way for an arterial road, or, worse, it would now be some Disneyfied Mr Hulot experience. If some out-of-work actor in a felt hat and sand shoes tried to press a tennis racquet into my hand on the promenade, I'd already resolved to deck him.

Yet, what if?

What if the French did things differently to us Brits, and had left intact my sleepy high street and my rickety promenade? What if the beach still had keep-fit classes and overweight businessmen running across the sand to answer important transatlantic telegrams? What if the walls really did resound with echoing children's laughter?

As I was rummaging for my tickets on board the train, I discovered nestling in the middle of my carefully folded T-shirts a small, gift-wrapped rectangle. It was a present from Julia. This was just the sort of understated romantic gesture I'd expect from her. Never ones for overt declarations of affection, we were always slipping little billets-doux into each other's luggage when one of us went away: notes, miniature photographs, tubes of Love Hearts. Inscribed on the wrapping of this one was a simple message: 'Please open in case of emergency.'

What could it be? A spare travel wallet perhaps; a photograph; or even a first edition of some famous travel book by Colin Thubron or Eric Newby?

It was a tiny manual. *Instructions for British Servicemen in France 1944,* published by the Foreign Office towards the end of the war. An olive-green hardback about the size of a postcard, it was issued to every soldier in the army, including, presumably, my own dad, in his vital wartime role as principal tenor saxophonist in the Guards Armoured Division Dance Band. I broke open some crisps and settled down to read.

The aim of the publication was evidently to apprise British troops, many of whom would have been unfamiliar with continental ways, of what to expect and how best to relate to the inhabitants. After some useful opening facts such as its size (five times that of the UK), its population (60 million) and its religion (mostly Catholic), it attempted to summarise relations between them and us from the Battle of Hastings right up to D-Day. 'It is fair to say that at times we have parted on the bitterest terms,' the author concluded with admirable understatement.

Having then emphasised the new comradeship between the two nations, the book offered some handy tips 'against which to measure contemporary cross-Channel relations'. If the FO were to be believed, the average Frenchman's concerns were the family, the land and national identity, in that order.

It certainly seemed so now. The country we were speeding through was populated by rolls of golden hay and huge toffee-coloured cows, interspersed with villages, many of which had the French *tricolore* fluttering from the town hall or local war memorial.

Just as I was popping the book back in my bag, I saw an inscription from Ju on the inside cover: *Please memorise pages 46–47.* Headed 'Useful Phrases in Case of Emergencies', among the sentences she'd marked in yellow highlighter were 'Fetch a doctor', 'Come and help quickly', 'I have been wounded', 'Bring boiling water', 'Can you lend me some tools?' and 'Where is the police station?' It seemed that in Julia's eyes I was not so much Eric Newby as Eric Sykes.

MY FINAL APPROACH to St Marc itself was via a ten-mile taxi ride to the coast. As we got nearer I found myself becoming absurdly nervous, as if I were about to meet a long-lost love after many years of separation. Would I recognise her? What if she were now some powdered hag, or an old boiler in a shell suit? Whatever she looked like, I was committed to spending the night with her, even if I had to creep out first thing tomorrow morning while she was still sleep.

It was nearly midnight when we rounded the curve in the road and I saw him. Mr Hulot, leaning like a drunken stork by the railing of the promenade, his hands clamped on the back of his waist as if suffering an attack of lumbago, staring out at the ocean.

It wasn't him, of course, but a life-size bronze statue, erected in 1999, and so perfectly sculpted and so beautifully positioned as to delight fans of the film yet not give any unknowing visitor an inferiority complex.

Despite the lateness of the hour, I asked the taxi driver to drop me alongside. Hulot's bronze likeness was the only presence on the promenade. I stood with my arm round him for some minutes, looking out at an ocean lapping gently under a huge yellow moon.

As a piece of commemorative sculpture it was pitch-perfect, so much so that I found myself recalling with a shudder similar examples back home. The RAF fighter pilot on Cleethorpes seafront, for instance, who looks like one of the Homepride flour graders; or the replica of Southampton footballer Ted Bates that had to be removed after being dubbed the third Krankie. Even the statue of Brunel at Paddington station looked like one of Ken Dodd's Diddymen. Why couldn't we come up with something as perfectly proportioned and evocative as this? I turned for the hotel, resolving to write a letter to *The Times* first thing after breakfast.

EARLY THE NEXT morning I was woken up by a familiar noise. It was the sound of echoing children's laughter. I opened the curtains and found myself on a film set.

Everything in front of me was exactly as Tati had captured it fifty years before. Dead ahead across the sand was the tiny concrete spit jutting out into the ocean, along which the elderly couple in the film endlessly strolled each evening after dinner, she always two yards in front. To my right was the same quaint promenade, now with the addition of the statue, and behind it in the distance the rocky cliff on top of which Hulot set off the shed full of fireworks in one of the film's most memorable scenes.

Some children barrelled down the steps from the prom in

swimming costumes and cardigans and ran towards the sea, chased by a frenetic collie dog. On the foreshore a lone jogger plodded through the sand. There was even a set of old-fashioned wooden beach huts and a solitary volleyball net.

I stood for some minutes on the balcony with a cup of tea, taking in my new home and gently humming the theme from the movie, when a voice called out to me. I looked up to find a middle-aged Frenchman wearing only a crumpled T-shirt standing in the window above and glaring down. 'Please – if you must sing at this time in the morning, lower your voice,' he said sternly.

I mumbled an apology and he disappeared back behind the net curtains. His comments would have carried more gravitas if he hadn't been entirely naked below the midriff. Appearing at hotel windows like that might be all very well in northern France, but if he tried it on Brighton seafront he might get more than he bargained for.

I spent the morning ambling about the tiny promenade with a sense of wonder. The town seemed to have been left virtually untouched. The only disappointment was the inside of the hotel itself, which had been kitted out in the antiseptic hues of an American corporate chain. Perhaps I shouldn't have been surprised – I'd read somewhere that most of the interiors had been shot in a Paris film studio – but it was disappointing not to be able to sit in that chaotic lounge where Tati had played cards or enjoy a bowl of soup in that dining room with the clunking door and the harassed waiters.

I tracked down the manager to ask him about the relationship between hotel and movie, but our meeting proved one of the dampest squibs since Michael Parkinson interviewed Meg Ryan.

'Do you get many people visiting the hotel because of the film?'

'It's difficult to say.'

'Were any of the actual bedrooms used in the movie or were they, too, filmed in a studio?'

'I do not know.'

'Have you ever seen the film?'

'I have yet to watch it.'

By the time I'd finished exploring it was lunchtime. Even the weather was similar to that which had so hobbled Tati's filming schedule almost sixty years before: a blustery wind was sweeping in from the west and ominous storm clouds lurked on the horizon. For forty years I'd been looking forward to a dip in the sea here, yet even as I strode purposefully towards the shoreline, my resolve faltered.

I knew this would happen. This is how I always spent my summer holidays: sitting on a beach staring forlornly at the waves, trying to get up the confidence to go in, while Julia cajoled, exhorted and ultimately threatened me with divorce if I didn't at least take off my pully.

But today the stakes were far higher. My entire trip had been predicated on this one moment. Yet now I was here, my inherent Englishness welled up once again. Of course, it would: you don't get rid of genetic traits just by having a black coffee and a baguette.

Now all the old prejudices that had bound my wanderlust in mental hoops of steel gripped me again. It's too cold, the wind's too stiff, I might get a stitch, I've just washed my hair, I mustn't get sunburnt, there may be jellyfish, I may step on a sea urchin and have to be flown to Luton by air ambulance: all the usual bollocks that have kept me swathed in towels on every hotel balcony I've ever sat on.

I had to go in. No matter I was the only bather. No matter it was starting to rain. I had to pluck up courage and wade in. If not now, when? Break my 'I can't find my little willy' karma and who knows what fabulous experiences might yield up their mysteries in the coming weeks. But revert to type, and I might as well go home now.

If only it didn't look quite so bloody cold…

And then I noticed him: about fifty yards off, and the only other occupant of the beach. A small stout man, probably in his late thirties, with a mop of curly black hair, sitting all alone on a tartan rug. He wore a cream and orange sports shirt underneath a beige jacket and matching slacks, with his feet encased in old-fashioned rope-soled shoes. Apart from the absence of a duffel bag, he was perfectly equipped for a day's trainspotting at Clapham Junction. A transistor radio was pressed to one ear, his fingers fiddling intently with the dial.

I recognised him instantly. He was a mirror image of myself. But what was he doing here, sitting by himself on a windswept beach-front? Obviously not a businessman on a lunch break, as beside him lay all the assembled paraphernalia I associated with my own summer holidays: sandwiches, a thermos of tea and biscuits.

It's easy to become overly romantic abroad: to imagine chance encounters were designated by fate, and that footling coincidences are pregnant with hidden meaning. Yet somehow this odd, solitary figure, sitting barely yards away without apparent purpose, seemed to offer a reflection of the old me I'd come here to escape.

How many holidays had I sat on beaches, in my own version of jacket and slacks, telling Julia I'd take my T-shirt off 'in a minute', as the best hours of the holiday and of my youth ticked silently away?

This seemed to be his misfortune too. Instead of feeling the sand between his toes or the clear cool sensation of salt water lapping around his bare calves, he seemed intent only on fumbling with the dial of his transistor in search of a familiar world represented by favourite radio programmes. Julia will tell you, there are always three of us when we go on holiday: her, me and Edward Stourton.

A watery sun broke through the clouds and shone faintly off the surface. Forward or back? Which was it to be? Dive off the board or retie my swimming trunks? Seize the day or my winky?

I stripped off, pulled on a pair of navy blue bathers specifically purchased for this moment and laboured down to the shoreline. The water seemed icy to the touch. I turned to check my lone compatriot wasn't already rummaging in my bag for my credit cards. But he was exactly where I had left him. And he was watching me.

I turned, counted to three in French and ran in at full pace, shrieking like a big girl's blouse at the first numbing shock of Atlantic water on my midriff. With a last desperate surge I plunged beneath the surface.

When I came spluttering up for air a few strokes later, my doppelgänger had already gathered up his things and was trudging back up the sand towards the promenade. I ran back out, retrieved my camera and took a photo of his departing figure, just to prove to myself he hadn't been some self-indulgent hallucination. Within seconds he'd disappeared from view and I'd headed back for the sea and another surge of endorphins.

YOU'VE GOT TO hand it to them. The French don't worry about being one huge collective cliché. My afternoon walk along the cliffs provided as many stereotypical images of *la belle France* as you'd expect in an entire series of *'Allo 'Allo*.

As I rounded the first bend on my way up out of the resort, I noticed on the rocks below a man in a white suit playing arpeggios on an alto saxophone. A little further along I came across a group of Girl Guides, each sporting blue uniforms with toggles and beret, attempting to catch butterflies with nets on bamboo poles.

No sooner had I left them than along the path came a group of children dressed as cowboys and Indians, all singing 'Sur Le Pont d'Avignon' and carrying a large wooden crate in which sat another child, dressed as Big Chief Sitting Bull.

It got better. As I retraced my path later in the afternoon, the sound of clopping hooves hurried me back to the Hulot seafront. A wedding party was approaching down the main street, the bride and groom sitting in the back of a flower-covered donkey cart, led by a man in moleskin trousers. Behind them stretched a procession of upwards of a hundred guests, each holding glasses of champagne.

Bertrand and Yvonne had just tied the knot after a whirlwind courtship, and the extended family of both celebrants were in St Marc to share their big day. Bertrand was obviously in the army, and, like him, virtually every male well-wisher under the age of thirty was a square-jawed Max Headroom hero, kitted out in fabulous sky blue uniforms and draped in enough lanyards to knit a sweater.

The wedding photographer was barking frenzied orders down to the party below us on the sand. I'd read somewhere that although the French *se mettent sur leur trente-et-un* (dress up to the nines), the occasions themselves are often relatively simple affairs. It certainly seemed so here. The emphasis was on discreet elegance, and framed against the pale sand and the grey sea the celebrants looked the epitome of romance.

The restaurant directly underneath the prom had been booked for their wedding breakfast, and despite my feeble protestations, a glass of champagne was pressed into my hand along with exhortations to join in the *vin d'honneur*, the traditional part of any French wedding between ceremony and banquet when guests toast the happy couple with a cocktail or two.

As I stood there, relatives of the bride and groom introduced themselves and attempted to make small talk. I replied to each incomprehensible enquiry with a shrug of the shoulders designed to suggest, 'Oh well, that's the thing about young love, isn't it?' a gesture that not only kept me out of trouble but actually seemed to delight them. I made a mental note to try it out at future TV drama castings when the writer asks what I think of his efforts.

Eventually the function moved into the restaurant for the feast, and with the smell of sizzling garlic floating in the breeze I decided this was the appropriate moment to become acquainted with real French cooking.

Up till now I'd lived on baguettes, croque-monsieurs and croissants; all very well in their way, but it was time to strike out. During my odyssey I intended to try all the signature masterworks, the pig's trotters, the frog's legs, the snails; but tonight I'd wade in gently with something Gallic yet familiar. Having once more given my *félicitations* to Bertrand and Yvonne, I set off up the steps towards the main street and my own banquet.

It was the phrase *plat du jour* that decided me in favour of the tiny Restaurant La Gavotte across the road from the hotel. Julia had advised me about this. Much the best away to eat in France, she said, the *plat du jour* offered the best food at the cheapest price. In any case, she continued, 'It's almost impossible to find a bad meal.'

I took a table by the window and studied the menu. Some of the words I didn't recognise. Garbure? Grenade? Never mind, the main dish had the word *saucisson* next to it, and that was enough for me. A sausage would be just the job tonight. How different can a sausage be in any case?

'Le plat du jour, saucisson andouillette avec frites et aussi une petite bière, s'il vous plait.' The waitress smiled and headed off to the kitchen. I sat looking out onto the very street up which Hulot's eccentric little *un-cheval* had first puttered its way into my consciousness.

The meal arrived. A big fat fulsome sausage on a modish wooden board, with a few legumes and some French fries pleasingly arranged round its base in a neat crescent. Until now I'd still felt like a fraud, a Little Englander creeping around in the shadows of this complex culture, but I was gaining in confidence. Far now from all things English, I'd had my first swim and had ordered my first proper meal in the vernacular. The country and its strange ways were opening up to me at last, and so was this sausage. I took up my knife and began cutting.

The knife pierced the thick, yellowish skin and plunged into the interior. A curl of steam billowed up and wrapped itself round my nostrils. The waitress stood at a beaded curtain, nodding appreciatively. I lifted my head and took in deep olfactory draught of my first taste of proper provincial restaurant cooking.

I may not be Gordon Ramsay, but I know drains when I smell them.

My instinct was to turn away, but the girl was still watching and in any case there were other diners at the next table. Instead I inched my way inside, now using my knife and fork as if performing some delicate brain surgery. The meat inside had an unfamiliar terraced texture to it, slabs of pink meat interlocked as if in some fleshy jigsaw. I fumbled desperately for my hand-kerchief and opened it just in time to cough discreetly without upsetting my fellow diners.

As I did so, *Instructions for British Servicemen in France* fell out of my pocket and onto the floor. What on earth had I summoned up here? I picked it up and flittered through the booklet until I came to the section at the back: 'ordering meals'. What was the word next to *saucisson* I'd so blithely disregarded?

Here we are. '*Andouillette.* Pig's intestine.'

Bon appétit.

Allez. Oops.

ACCORDING TO JULIA, the two unfunniest things in the world are the French, and circus clowns. What she makes of French circus clowns is unprintable in a book aimed at a general readership.

It's not that the French don't have a sense of humour, or so she maintains. They do. It's just that their sense of humour is crap. Give them *The Office* or *Dad's Army* and they regard you as if you've just put your finger up your nose and then deposited the findings in their *bavette à l'échalotte*. But offer up someone gurning in a spangly leotard while spinning plates and just watch as tears of uncontrollable laughter course down their cheeks. It's as if Ken Dodd has walked on stage.

Except, of course, he hasn't. If Ken Dodd thinks the second house at the Glasgow Empire is a tough call, he should try an audience of Frenchmen. Take one of Doddy's best. 'I've always wanted to meet the man who invented cat's eyes. Just as well he didn't pick the other end or he'd have invented the pencil sharpener.' Try that over here, says Julia, and the only sound you'll hear is that of the mistral blowing through the auditorium. But bring on a man in a stilt-walker and a multi-coloured boiler suit, and they'll blow the roof off the theatre.

As for her second pet hate, circus clowns, we have to be

56

tolerant of her views, as when she was a child in Lincolnshire a schoolfriend was eaten by a visiting circus lion and the episode has rather tainted her view of the genre. But I'm with her every step of the way. If I wanted a laugh I'd sooner watch a documentary on contagious diseases than a load of men in baggy trousers and red noses falling out of a collapsing car filled with shaving foam.

Thankfully, there aren't any clowns in Britain now. They've all been flushed down our heritage plughole as a by-product of the animal-rights campaigns that have done for circuses in general. Billy Smart's, Bertram Mills, they've all gone to the wall or had to change their shows to incorporate juggling with chainsaws and naked trapeze acts. Jolly good thing too.

But across the Channel they're everywhere. You can't walk down a main street without seeing prancing horses and men with grease-paint smiles grinning at you from billboards. There are estimated to be over two hundred separate outfits trundling round France during the summer months, as well as countless smaller outfits consisting of barely trained teenagers performing feeble stunts in precincts and converted church halls. At least we've maintained that tradition. It's just we've renamed them the Edinburgh Fringe.

I'd noticed the big top on the other side of the bypass as the taxi had driven me into St Marc sur Mer the previous evening, a huge canvas tent picked out in light bulbs and surrounded by a laager of trailers on a piece of scrubby waste ground.

And they were after me. I was queuing for some *Arret* at the local pharmacy the morning after my meal at La Gavotte, when a minivan festooned with speakers rumbled up the main street.

The circus was in town. To be precise, Circus Joseph Bouglione. They were advertising their latest show, the spectacular Etoile Piste (literally: Star Ramp). The fevered tones of the announcer suggested he was in no doubt that this was the greatest show on earth, and just in case we were in any doubt, the sides of the van were plastered in colourful posters showing troupes of jugglers and flying acrobats.

In any other circumstances I wouldn't have contemplated it, but St Marc was deathly quiet once night fell, and with another hearty dinner firmly out for the immediate future I was struggling to fill my final evening. It was either the circus or *A Touch of Frost* dubbed into French in my hotel room.

MY TAXI DUMPED me by the entrance to the field just before curtain up at 6 p.m. It was a balmy evening and the air was thick with the smell of trodden grass and smoke from an assortment of whirring generators. A flock of angry geese surged back and forth across the grass in pursuit of some imagined enemy.

Although I'd arrived deliberately early in order to bag a seat, a queue of expectant punters was already gathered patiently at the entrance. A young man, looking like Aled Jones's gayer brother and dressed in a dusty bellhop's outfit, stood at the tent flap tearing tickets.

It may have been the midges, or the grass, or the exhaust fumes, or just the fact I was in France rather than West Hampstead, but there was a grubby allure about it all. The scene was like something out of *La Strada*. Swarthy stagehands stood in groups smoking roll-ups, while between the trailers I caught glimpses of skeletal women in grubby leotards holding ballet shoes and ice packs.

An elderly woman in the ticket trailer with bleached hair and tired eyes smiled wearily at the news 'Je parle un petit peu français' and pointed to a dog-eared plan of the auditorium propped against the glass. I decided to eschew the deluxe loge ringside seats and plump instead for the more competitive *gradins* from where I would have a panoramic view of the backs of the performers' heads.

Aled tore my ticket and ushered me over to a deserted corner where wooden benches teetered uncertainly on wonky rostra. Above me, three giant swags of material in the colours of the *tricolore* hung listlessly above the ring.

À la recherche du temps perdu. Was it Proust who wrote about the memories of things past? Old sawdust and dusty lamps, the air pungent with the smell of dung mixed with stale sweat, greasy chairs separated by pieces of plywood draped in rotting curtains? Was I recalling some long-forgotten visit to the circus as a toddler, or merely my bedroom as a sixteen-year-old? A teasing shiver of ill-defined nostalgia rippled through me.

Six o'clock came and went with no sign of anyone resembling a ringmaster. A sad, sweet-faced young man in a crimson leotard, with huge biceps and cheekbones you could open letters with, wandered disconsolately up and down with an old-fashioned ice-cream tray containing coloured fibre optic fronds. A family in one of the deluxe ringside loges bought one for their three-year-old, who immediately burst into tears when told she couldn't eat it.

By 6.15 we were still waiting. But just as I was thinking of bumming a lift back into town, the lights dimmed and two figures emerged from behind a blue drape decorated with cardboard stallions and marched confidently into the centre of the ring.

It was Aled, now with rouge on his cheeks and having forsaken his bellhop combo for a powder-blue overcoat and a large sweeping brush which he carried jauntily over one shoulder. He was joined by a girl I'd seen serving ices from a fridge on the opposite side of the tent, a slim teenager with dark Slavic features and smouldering eyes. She was dressed as a French maid, complete with feather duster, black stockings and teetering heels.

I'd been hoping for a man in a top hat and red tailcoat proclaiming 'Laydeees and gentlemennnn', but instead the two performers conduced a laborious mime in which the French maid persuades Aled to sweep the perimeter of the ring. Every time his back is turned she picks up more flecks of sawdust from her feet and deposits them where he's just finished. It was hardly the Mighty Boosh, but the audience seemed to love it and applauded loudly when the act eventually petered out.

Things soon pepped up when a huge shambling camel emerged from behind the curtain to a thumping disco version of 'La Vie en Rose'. It was followed once more by Aled, now in a lime-green blouson and juggling bowling pins.

My zoological knowledge may be founded entirely on *Animal Magic*, but if there's one thing Johnny Morris taught me about camels (apart from the fact they all speak like art critic Brian Sewell), it's that they're capricious. Fabulous for crossing the Gobi desert, but you wouldn't want to rely on one for your synchronised animal gymnastics act on *Britain's Got Talent*.

Yet the creature on display tonight seemed remarkably adept, loping gamely around for several circuits, walking backwards to order, and even rolling on its back on request, a manoeuvre that threw up further clouds of dust into an already gamey atmosphere.

No sooner had it lumbered to its feet and sped off than five white horses with plumed heads skittered through the curtain and began careering round the ring in frantic circles. They were followed by a man in a paisley shirt, custard-coloured corduroys and riding boots, carrying a whip and with a smouldering cigar clenched between his teeth. Try to imagine former BBC controller Alan Yentob having decided to attend a fancy dress party as Erich von Stroheim.

With the merest flick of cigar ash he sent the animals in the opposite direction. Round and round they went, barging blindly into one another and sending gobbets of froth spraying into the loges. A team of muscular stagehands swarmed above them, unfixing the drapes and lowering them onto hooks fastened to the saddles of the excited steeds.

The horses now began an intricate figure-of-eight routine, kicking and blundering into each other as they went, weaving their strands of cloth together in a gigantic maypole dance. Yentob stood in the midst of them with a look of sublime contentment, as if he'd just seen the latest viewing figures for *Omnibus*.

If this had been offered up on ITV, Piers Morgan would have buzzed them before they'd even got halfway on stage, but the crowd here seemed entranced, and I realised that I too had been staring with my mouth open. A young boy in front of me at ringside level sat bewitched, his face only inches from their rumps, vanilla ice cream mixed with horse gob dribbling untended down the sleeve of his pullover.

The next act was even more surprising. It was a troupe of performing cows. A line of toffee-coloured heifers gambolled the ring, complete with clanging bells strung from their necks. Yentob had now been replaced by a bovine dominatrix: a buxom woman with acid blonde hair scraped back into a bun encased in a decorative lace hairnet, and dressed in the type of dirndl-skirted and frilly-white-bloused combo so favoured by employees of Spanish riding schools, all nicely finished off with stiletto-heeled leather boots.

The heifers made the camel look positively sophisticated by comparison, lumbering round clockwise and then anticlockwise until they shuddered to a halt and gingerly put their front hooves up on some wooden rostra. Yet it was strangely impressive, though I imagine the rehearsals must have been monotonous.

It became clear long before the end of the first half that multi-tasking was an important prerequisite of life with Circus Bouglione. The ability to scoop an ice cream, play the drums or flog off your nightly quota of optic fronds to hungry children was obviously as important as walking the high wire or fire-eating. Contrary to the cast of thousands depicted on the posters, Circus Bouglione consisted of a cast of about five.

Aled demonstrated audacious balancing skills on a flimsy tower fashioned from wooden rollers and whisky glasses, then the dominatrix juggled flaming torches, and then Aled and the Slav girl did some synchronised tumbling over the backs of cantering Thelwell-type ponies; even Yentob had a turn on the drum kit.

The only member of the troupe who seemed excused ring duties was the sad-faced, chiselled youth with the paperknife cheekbones I'd spotted before the show. In this multi-tasking environment surely he wasn't pulling his weight. Perhaps he drove the vans?

Then, with the end of the first half fast approaching, he appeared from nowhere in the very centre of the ring. His features had that classic look of resigned suffering that only the Russians seem to be able to manage. Having surveyed the audience with a look of infinite apology, he began scaling a specially constructed platform stretching high up into the air.

The spotlight followed him up into the darkness. Now seemingly weightless, he hauled himself carefully on top of a tall pole some fifty feet into the air. With extreme care, as if trying to make safe an unexploded bomb by touch alone, he began performing a set of extraordinary physical contortions, using only one arm to support himself.

By now Yentob's energetic drumming had given way to something more intimate, a strange, unnerving Islamic descant full of longing and mystery. There was something strange and unnerving too about this muscular youth, suspended midair in a pool of light, delicately positioning and repositioning himself into extreme angles with only the prospect of falling head first onto compressed earth and camel hair to look forward to if he failed. In fact, it struck me that–

'You are journalist!'

The old woman who'd sold me my ticket out in the field had sidled up in the darkness. She was now clutching my arm.

'Er–'

'You are journalist!' she repeated in a whispered rasp. 'I see you writing.' She gave an accusatory nod of her head in the direction of my notebook. Word must have got round that the middle-aged man sitting by himself in the cheap seats was making surreptitious notes. To a troupe of travelling showmen I must seem suspiciously like a council official out to cause trouble, or worse, an animal-rights activist travelling incognito.

'Je ne suis pas journalist,' I stammered. But she had me by my sleeve.

'You are writing,' she instead. 'You work for paper?'

'Non, je suis un –' I could see Yentob's dark curranty eyes squinting at me through a gap in the curtain.

'Je suis un author,' I blurted. Or rather, 'Je suis un author-rrrrrr.' Why did I always suppose that by inflecting any English word like the compère of *Eurotrash* I would immediately make myself understood? But she was shaking her head, either in incomprehension or disbelief I couldn't tell. Then she fixed me again with a gimlet stare as her grasp tightened.

'Il y aura entracte dans cinq minutes,' she rasped, poking me in the chest with a bony finger. 'You explain with my daughter, she speak English.' With that she scurried back around the perimeter of the ring, and was soon lost from view behind one of the stanchions.

By now the gymnast was reaching the climax of his act with a gravity-defying manoeuvre, propelling his entire body weight round and round on top of the pole by one arm only, the spotlight bouncing off his sequinned leotard and throwing shards of light in all directions like he was a giant glitter ball. In other circumstances it would have been a magical climax, but the elderly woman's confrontation had concentrated my mind on other things.

Any minute now I was going to be frogmarched to a back room for what would certainly be a searching enquiry from a woman dressed as a dominatrix wielding a riding crop. I'd read enough Famous Five stories as a child to know about circus folk. Enid Blyton barely wrote a story which didn't involve them crashing through the narrative at some point, and hers was a picture of a closed, mistrustful, suspicious and largely tribal society, hard-working, courteous, but wary of interlopers and constantly on the lookout for troublemakers. All I could hope was that they wouldn't be able to understand my hurried notes. Something told me they would be settling this particular matter out of court, probably with a handful of fibre-optic fronds.

Even as the house lights were rising, a huge grubby hand landed heavily on my shoulder. A burly roustabout straight out of the *Ladybird Book of Neolithic Man* was scowling at me.

'We go,' he said simply.

I got up and followed him round the perimeter. Aled was already back in his bellhop's outfit and now selling plastic bags of candyfloss, and I attempted a look of mute appeal for assistance, the type I imagine people in car hijacks attempt in slow-moving traffic. Nothing.

At the refreshment stall on the far side the dominatrix was already serving a crowd of children with popcorn and crisps. Beside her a chubby child with bristly hair was restocking a whirring fridge with cans of Coca-Cola.

I decided to speak first. 'Pardonez-moi, je parle un petit peu français–'

'No worries,' she replied in a creamy transatlantic drawl. 'I speak English. Would you like a Coke?'

Her name was Dandrine. She'd noticed me out of the corner of her eye while juggling the blazing torches and had sent her mother over to find out what I was doing. 'I kinda figured that if you were sitting by yourself without a child then you were probably a journalist. I told my mom-in-law to invite you over so we could give you any help we can, but her English isn't so good. Hope she made herself understood.'

Leaving her mother to take over the stall, she joined me on a couple of upturned crates by the side of the ring. Over a packet of complimentary fromage 'n' onion Lays and a can of Fanta she told me in an educated New England accent about her life in the circus.

It may have been the relief of not ending up with a broken nose, or the sugar rush from the Fanta, or perhaps – and this I think the likeliest explanation – that she was called Dandrine, quite the most absurdly wonderful name ever conceived for a female performer in the circus, but within thirty seconds I was entranced.

The Bouglione family was one of Europe's oldest troupes; in addition to this touring company they also had a permanent mooring in parkland just outside Paris. Dandrine had spent the last twenty years of her life travelling round with them after falling in love with Yentob, and in between performances had even managed to spawn four healthy children. Together her family now formed the nucleus of the show this evening.

'This is my eldest.' She leaned across the counter towards the chubby juvenile and patted his bristly black hair. He grinned back. The kid can't have been more than ten, yet in contrast to most other kids of his age, who on a Friday night would be hanging about gusty precincts on bikes boasting about their latest ASBO, he spent his life here in a world of performing heifers and mystical acrobats.

I complimented her on the quality of her dancing cows and gyrating camels. 'The audiences have to have animals,' she explained. 'It's the only thing the parents want to know when they ring up to book seats: "Will we be getting animals?"'

So why no ringmaster? She grinned knowingly. 'We tried them once but every time they came on we lost the audience. The children would start fidgeting, running about or wanting to go to the washroom. It was like this...' She traced a wavy line in the air to demonstrate the fluctuating interest whenever a man in a top hat and shiny boots walked on.

I could have sat at her feet for ever hearing about life in the circus, but already the audience was returning to their seats for the second half. 'I gotta go,' she said, reaching across and retrieving her riding crop. 'I have to be ringside for the next act, just in case my husband gets into trouble...'

'Trouble?'

I turned to look. While we'd been talking the ring had been enclosed on all sides by steel bars. Inside the makeshift cage were huge upturned tubs decorated with painted stars, each connected to its neighbour by wooden planks.

Unless there was going to be display of forcible milking, Circus Bouglione was about to up the ante.

THERE WERE FIVE of them. Tigers that is. Huge great things with slavering jaws, resplendent whiskers and, crucially, a full set of gnashers. And they were terrifying. No sooner had the lights dimmed than they slunk in through a hastily erected mesh tunnel leading from backstage.

The first to arrive, obviously the leader of the pack and possessing the largest pair of testicles I'd ever seen outside the pages of *Viz*, made a presidential circuit of the ring before lifting his tail and squirting a disdainful arc of musk with pinpoint accuracy through the bars and onto the boy in the picnic chair, a task it celebrated in suitable style by turning its head and luxuriously licking its balls.

They were followed by Yentob, now carrying an upturned chair. He strolled into the cage and bolted the gate behind him. By now the beasts had settled themselves on their tubs and were snarling at him with suppressed fury as if they'd like to have him with a little *beurre et confiture d'abricots*. Dandrine and Aled stood outside with a look of concern that only comes from witnessing genuine danger.

In truth the tigers proved barely more skilled than the heifers. There was a bit of leaping from rostrum to rostrum, some synchronised rolling over and finally a little surly paw offering as if at some nightmare version of Crufts. What was completely gripping was the psychological negotiation going on within the cage. I can't imagine what Yentob's life insurance premiums must be like, but I wouldn't offer him a quotation.

Even with an upturned chair it was demonstrably five against one. These animals didn't seem sedated, and their teeth looked horrifyingly their own, so a momentary lack of concentration and Yentob was toast. The tigers knew it, he knew it; even the little boy with the candyfloss knew it. The result was mesmerising.

But he wasn't toast. After a lot of eyeballing and some ill-tempered stand-offs, the tigers completed their tasks and, with a final look of fury, four of them slunk back out through the tunnel.

That left Big Daddy. Without breaking eye contact for a single moment, Yentob reached out through the bars and accepted a gas hob lighter handed to him by his wife, before holding it to a large metal hoop on a stand, which burst into flames. Big Daddy sat surveying the conflagration with an air of world-weary resignation for several seconds, and then, as if saying, 'Oh for Christ's sake let's get this over with,' set off along the duckboards and with stupendous dexterity leapt through the flaming hoop, landed on a nearby platform and was gone. Within minutes the cage had been dismantled and we were back with Aled and the French maid having more fun with the sweeping brush.

By 7.45 it was all over. To a final rousing fanfare the entire company, all five of them – six if you include Dandrine's bristle-haired child – paraded round the ring with the camels and the heifers, waving goodbye and wishing us all *bonne soirée*. I stood and clapped and waved a frond, wondering why I felt like crying.

You'd have thought they'd need to put their feet up after all that, but instead they invited the children in the audience to enjoy free donkey rides round the ring. The sight of huge razor-scarred roustabouts delicately leading lines of ecstatic infants round the arena summed up the whole captivating blend of informality mixed with derring-do.

Afterwards I hung around like a love-struck stage-door Johnny until Dandrine, tiny troll-like children now hanging from every available limb, spotted me and invited me over to meet the company, and I found myself solemnly processing along the line and shaking each artiste by the hand. Expecting a non-event I'd left my camera at the hotel, but now, in response to my entreaties, they promised to send me photographs of them all in action.

We shared a beer from the fridge and Yentob offered me one of his cigars. 'It is a shame you weren't here at the weekend,' he said as fumbled for his lighter. 'When the place is full, it's really something.' I assured him it was already really something. I'd been taken aback by the show's power to enthral a generation used to Gameboys and CGI. But what was it about circuses that they could still captivate a twenty-first-century audience?

'It's because they are... how you say?' He drew on his cheroot while he thought. 'Primeval,' he said at last. 'Is that the word? They are primeval. They affect you still, right here...' He pressed his hand tenderly to his heart.

He was right. I'd gone along tonight anticipating some tatty, fifth-rate farrago, a clapped-out hokum provided by the remaining rump of an entertainment long past its sell-by date. But instead I'd experienced something alive and visceral. It may not have had the shimmering expertise of Cirque du Soleil, with state-of-the-art equipment and three-month sojourns at the Albert Hall, yet this tiny group of performers, faced with a Friday matinee to about a hundred people, had performed as if their lives depended on it – which in some senses it had.

There had been no safety nets, no cables attached to their

midriffs to protect them as they teetered yards above the ground on platforms of old planks and glass tumblers, and no security guards with loaded rifles in case their nightly game of Russian roulette with a cage full of wild animals went wrong.

And, most wonderful of all, no health and safety officials clustered round the ring with clipboards droning on about risk assessment and the deleterious effects of young children consuming foodstuffs sprinkled with old wood shavings and tiger pee. The whole evening had had a startling, earthy quality to it – just a crowd, a drum roll and unadorned skill illuminated by spotlights.

It was time to go. The troupe had to do it all again, after which Dandrine and her husband had to feed the animals, cook the supper and get their four children safely to bed. She gave me a kiss on both cheeks and offered up the youngest of her adoring trolls for me to blow an affectionate raspberry to.

Yentob was the last to say goodbye. He shook my hand and finished with a rib-busting bear hug. Then he stepped back and scrutinised me like a tailor measuring a customer for a bespoke suit. 'You are the perfect shape to be a ringmaster,' he said proudly. 'You know Norman Barrett?'

Norman Barrett. For a minute I thought he was the bloke who used to present BBC's *Nationwide*. But from somewhere in a long-neglected memory bank, I recalled his name. Once as familiar to me as Coco or Charlie Cairoli, he'd been the ringmaster on the Blackpool Tower Circus when the BBC used to screen it live on Boxing Day. It was years since I'd heard him spoken of, although, now I came to think of it, I had recently seen him, or someone like him, on afternoon TV, rheumy-eyed and with a stoop, advertising denture fixative.

'You should train with us,' said Yentob affectionately. 'You are strong, handsome and have a loud voice. You would be perfect. Michael Simkins, the next great ringmaster!' They all applauded.

'And now we take you back to your hotel.' Dandrine clapped her hands, and as if on cue, the minivan I'd seen earlier that day in town drew up outside the tent flap and a young man with glasses waved through the driver's window. 'Guillaume here will give you a lift,' she explained. 'We'll have you home in fifteen minutes.'

Guillaume and I passed the journey back vigorously debating art and entertainment, and its place within the wider framework of society and culture. He maintained passionately that the secret of great art was in the soul and in its intention. 'We do not perform the shows for ourselves,' he said, with the clutch at the heart that was by now so familiar, 'we perform it for our audience, and through them we validate our own happiness.'

It was a stirring sentiment, although Guillaume's admission a few minutes later that his role in the outfit was merely driving the minivan and putting up posters left me puzzled as to his own emotional epiphany. When I asked how long he might stay in his current occupation, he merely shrugged his shoulders.

I found myself recalling the gag where a bystander accosts an old man shovelling shit at the rear of a circus parade and asks why he doesn't give up the job and go and do something more well paid and dignified instead. The old bloke replies, 'What, and give up show business?'

Guillaume was still a young man, but if he was to live the life espoused by circus tradition he'd better start learning to juggle some flaming bowling pins pretty soon. The fact was, he was almost certainly star-struck. Like me, he'd wandered into the big top one evening but had simply never left. Still dazzled, and probably in love in some innocent way with Dandrine.

And now so was I. My clothes smelt of the sawdust and tarpaulin, and I wanted more than anything to put on a leotard and balance on whisky glasses, or tame wild tigers with an upturned chair, or even tear tickets and sell fibre-optic fronds to tiny children.

If Al Gore is indeed correct and we're heading for a global catastrophe, there will come a day when everything stops: *Britain's Got Talent*, *Les Misérables*, even *Cirque du Soleil* will simply run out of juice, and have to pack their bags and walk home. And when that day occurs, Dandrine and her troupe of acrobats and tigers will still be here, in this tent, offering something timeless and mysterious. Something primeval.

As night fell I stood on the promenade, my arm wrapped round the bronze Hulot, staring out to sea. My two days in St Marc sur Mer had proved even better in reality than on film.

And even more wondrous, there'd not been a clown in sight.

Quimper and Contrast

BACK IN THE 1970s I'd briefly dated a girl from Roedean School whose parents owned a holiday home near Brest in Brittany, and during our few chaste months together she regaled me with tales of rocky coastlines, dark country lanes, ancient stone circles and a haunting form of country dance known as *fest-noz*: part French, part Celtic; wholly mysterious.

Regarded by Parisians as being as backward as it is rough-hewn, this secluded peninsula abutting the English Channel and the Bay of Biscay is in some ways the soul of old pre-homogenised France. Less than a hundred years ago, nearly 50 per cent of the population of the region still spoke the ancient tongue of *Brezhoneg* as their first language, and even today it still has its own flag, its own dialect and its own version of the notorious Cornish piskies in the shape of Breton elves, scatter-brained mischief-makers that make life unbearable for the unwary traveller.

Yet ethnic fervour burns far more brightly than scraps of folk-lore reprinted on tea towels. Such is Brittany's sense of separateness that until recently they were getting up to the same sort of antics as the Sons of Glendower and ETA: blowing up holiday homes, torching foreign cars and daubing local statues with graffiti.

Odd when you think of it. Only a few miles across the Atlantic the spirit of Cornwall burnt just as fiercely, yet they undermined their conquerors by coming up with the Flambards Experience and Ginsters pasties.

Regional pride in these parts is distilled each summer into nine days of untrammelled cultural tub-thumping in the shape of the Festival de Cornouaille, one of the largest folk-dancing festivals in Europe, and it was here I hoped to sample *fest-noz*. Normally I tended towards Sir Thomas Beecham's dictum of trying everything in life once except incest and folk dancing, but in the interests of personal development I was willing to make an exception. Just as long as I wasn't required to wave a hankie.

I ARRIVED IN Quimper (pronounced 'kam-*perrrrrrr*') just after 7 p.m. on Saturday. This ancient medieval town is the capital of Brittany and the beating heart of the region, a place where, according to the guidebooks, the old dialects can still be heard if you know where to go. By the time I'd settled into my attic room on the top floor of the Hotel TGV opposite the station, it was a beautiful evening, and I headed off towards the town centre and the spire of the cathedral with a spring in my step. Apparently the town has 3,000 performers and 250 separate acts crammed within its walls during this brief annual festival, and I was looking forward to running into some of them, particularly if they came with plenty of *fest-nozzing*.

Fest-noz literally means 'night dances', and enthusiasts claim it's what a rave would have been like in the time of the Domesday Book. The routines themselves are remnants of traditional floor-stamping rituals by which peasants smoothed down God's good earth with their size nines so as to have a solid floor for farm work. But these ancient farmyard hoe-downs also performed another, far more crucial function in the continuation of life, love and the pursuit of happiness than merely providing a firm base for your milking stool.

As any teenager will tell you, there are as many ways to trample a floor as there are to wear school uniform, and at one stage the Catholic Church even banned the particular *fest-noz* dance variant known as *kof-a-kof* (stomach to stomach) because of its potentially corrosive effect on youthful sensibilities.

Nowadays guitars and amplifiers have augmented knackers and crumhorns, yet the event allegedly remains as potent as in medieval times, and devotees of *fest-noz* often talk of reaching a state of trance-like contentment during the dancing. If I were to hear for myself the far-off voices of ancient France, then it would surely be here.

But Quimper was empty. I walked down the main street past empty cafés and bars without seeing a soul. A lone diner in a grubby Vietnamese restaurant glared at me as he hoovered up an enormous platter of prawn crackers, while from a nearby balcony a solitary canary in a cage twittered in despair. Apart from that, nothing: no pedestrians, hardly any cars, not even the sound of a television set playing in a distant room. Merely shuttered windows, desolate streets and an air of overpowering stillness and fustiness about the place. I'd worried that a mere weekend may not be enough to see Quimper in full spate, but after a brief walk along the main boulevard it appeared I'd disastrously overestimated. This was advertised as the epicentre of *fest-noz*, for God's sake.

Then I rounded a corner and my question was answered. The entire population of the town, estimated by guidebooks at 60,000, was in a large tent. And they were dancing.

THE MARQUEE WAS so large it was impossible to determine if it was permanent or temporary. In the distance was a vast stage on which a group of musicians were pumping out an amplified and adrenaline-fuelled melody on an assortment of instruments ranging from the time of William the Conqueror to about last Thursday. The principal performer, dressed in tie-dye T-shirt and jeans and sporting a Mohican haircut sharp enough to put your eye out, was playing what looked like a baby oboe and sounded like one of Rolf Harris's stylophones. He was supported on identical instruments by a couple of prop-forwards wearing hiking boots and kilts, while behind them stood two electronic accordionists and three saxophonists, with robust support by a flailing drummer and several don't-muck-me-about electric guitars. It was as if the Chieftains had decided to link up with the Grateful Dead. Perhaps I shouldn't have been surprised: standing in this tent here tonight I was probably nearer Dublin than Dollis Hill.

And in front of them, crabbing sideways across the dance floor, were thousands of people dancing: pensioners, businessmen, teenagers, hoodies, entire families snaking round the hall as if attempting to edge their way along an imaginary window ledge. Each participant was linked to their partner only by their little fingers, which were discreetly intertwined as if about to serve afternoon tea.

I grabbed a festival programme from a stack on one of the seats and turned to the section marked *Samedi Soir*. The group providing the music rejoiced in the name Hiks, and the instrument looking like an oboe and sounding like a deflating balloon was the Breton bombard, cornerstone of traditional Breton music-making and described in an unwieldy English translation as a 'rustic hautboys'. The aim of Hiks, it continued, was 'to make war with composition indelibly, enriching many savages with bassist grooves, thus perfectly de-haunching you'.

I'd never seen an entire marquee de-haunched en masse, but whatever it involved, it was going down a storm, particularly with the older participants. I sat at the far end and watched in wide-eyed wonder as a sea of bobbing heads straggled this way and that, all of them fixed with expressions of utmost solemnity. One old dear who must have been in her late seventies didn't leave the dance floor for the entire time, merely standing gravely in the centre between numbers with her hands clasped behind her back as if waiting to testify in court.

It went on like this for three or four items, until the melody changed without warning to something more sprightly, an act that caused the entire population to celebrate with a sort of sideways bunny jump, their hands simultaneously winding down imaginary car windows as they did so.

In some ways the spectacle resembled a traditional Celtic ceilidh, yet there was none of its flagrant exuberance: here, the dancing was conducted with all the sobriety of a state opening of Parliament, the dancers apparently only too aware of the powerful symbolism inherent in each step. To look at the grim expressions on their faces as they slewed past me, you'd have thought the penalty for bunny jumping when you should be de-haunching was being taken out and shot with a high-velocity rifle.

Nonetheless these endlessly bobbing processions were curiously hypnotic, like a human art installation. It was difficult to think of any comparable activity back home: Morris dancing perhaps, but there weren't enough hankies in M&S to furnish the sort of numbers I was looking at here. Line dancing? I'd once stumbled on a display in a shopping precinct in Doncaster, but for all its obvious allure, it was only an imitation of something imported lock, stock and barrel from Memphis – men in NHS specs with Stetsons and bejewelled cowboy boots striding back and forth past the entrance of Holland and Barrett.

What was on offer here was no crude facsimile: it felt nothing less than an affirmation of identity. Nobody needed instruction in the various steps by grinning leaders with radio mikes, it was ingrained in all but the very youngest of them, and even they were catching on before my very eyes.

Dancing has never been my strong suit. My description in the actors' directory, *Spotlight*, mentions that I'm good with move-ment, which is a showbiz euphemism for 'give him three weeks one-to-one remedial tuition with the choreographer and he may just make the back row of the chorus'. But as regards summoning up an impromptu physical expression of my inner spirit, I'd never recovered from my first date with Julia at a discotheque in Harrogate, when she'd observed I danced like an insurance salesman.

But she wasn't here. And I'd come to *fest-noz*. With luck I might even get a chance to practise my stomach-to-stomach technique, and God knows I was ideally qualified. Like most red-blooded Englishmen, there was only one thing I needed before I took the plunge. It was time to head for the bar.

Outside the marquee on the grass a long wooden counter was dispensing pints of draught Guinness under a starlit sky. In Britain it would have taken hours to get served on a night like this, yet tonight the bar was virtually empty, and even those that were drinking had one eye back on the marquee lest they miss the chance to do some window-winding. Men preferring to dance rather than drink draught Guinness? This was a strange country indeed. I gulped down a pint and it did the business. Bunny-hopping? Window-winding? You want some de-haunching? Bring it on.

I returned in belligerent mood and found a convenient pillar behind which to practise my hand movements. It must have looked to a casual observer like a particularly exotic line in self-abuse, but better that than I disgrace myself on the dance floor. At last I felt comfortable with the upper body action. The rest would have to take care of itself.

Up on the stage Hiks was screeching to another grandstand finish with their fusion-meets-folk-meets 'dustbin-full-of-spanners-being-thrown-down–a-cement-staircase'. The dancing stopped, hands instantly unclasped and everyone applauded. Any moment now a new melody would be striking up and they'd be linking hands again. This was my opportunity. Time to catch the wave.

But even as I blundered onto the dance floor the next number was commencing, and I was overtaken by a fresh tide of revellers. Everyone was so gagging for a chance to crab sideways while winding down windows that it was impossible to get a finger hold. Before I'd got my bearings the amorphous mass had grouped into fresh spirals and closed ranks. I felt like a submariner whose vessel submerges while he's out swabbing the deck.

I capered along hopefully on the perimeter, desperate for an opening. 'Pardonez-moi, excusez-moi,' I blurted hopefully to the back of people's heads, but I was now drowning in a sea of dancers. I blundered through weaving chains, treading on people's corns and bringing girls' slippers off at the heel, until at last I reached the edge and flopped down in the front row of the seats, spent and exhausted.

Fest-noz was trickier than I'd thought. But if at first you don't succeed… During the next break in the music I tried again. This time I managed to persuade a small stout woman to offer up her finger, but an old bloke on my other side in a zip-up cardigan seemed to react to my taking his little finger in mine as if I was making a proposal of marriage. He threw it off roughly, and a second later my place had been taken by a young girl whom I hope for both their sakes was his daughter. I blundered back to the edge again and sat down to regroup.

After another fortifying pint at the bar I returned for a third attempt. Now I would time it perfectly. The dance was already in train, but directly in front of me a mother had identified some friends entering the marquee and broke off from her chain to greet them. Quick as a flash I was in. One finger enfolded mine on one side. Another grabbed me delicately by the thumb. I was on board.

But no. The music abruptly finished, and within seconds the intricate patterns had evaporated like morning mist. I was alone on the dance floor with my arms still out, as if attempting a Larry Grayson impression.

It seemed we'd hit an interval, and while a new band began assembling on stage, a man in a moleskin waistcoat approached the mike and launched into a long speech about forthcoming events. I smiled hopefully at people on nearby seats in the hope of igniting conversation and being offered a leg-up, but the fact was the *fest-noz* felt a family affair, and my faltering presence here stuck out like a dog's balls. After a final desultory attempt I gave up and trudged back to the hotel with the sound of renewed de-haunching mocking me on the breeze.

Perhaps I was trying too hard. Perhaps if I just throttled back and let Brittany come to me, tomorrow might bring richer results. After all, tonight's event was only the curtain-raiser. The festival programme itself ran to over sixty pages, and the listings for *Dimanche* alone ran to three: young Enya-types in trailing velvet smocks playing Celtic harps, solitary guitarists, groups of accordionists, choral societies, female dance troupes: there'd be plenty more opportunities after a good night's sleep.

And then, just as I was about to put out the light, I read something that made my blood run cold.

Tomorrow was dedicated as a mass bagpipe festival.

ALFRED HITCHCOCK ONCE suggested that the inventor of bagpipes must have been inspired when he saw a man carrying an indignant, asthmatic pig under his arm. I must say I'm with him all the way. Like most things, they're fine in their place – at the Edinburgh Tattoo, for instance, I've heard they go down quite well, and I've found them to be very toothsome on the odd Christmas pop song when accompanied by footage of bleak Celtic landscapes or with the pipers themselves surrounded by lashings of dry ice – but little and seldom is my motto.

Not in Quimper. The Bagadou is a nightmare musical invention in which bagpipes, bombards and snare drums are all brought together into one fiendish coalition. According to the brochure, nearly every town in Brittany has one such band, and in some cases two or three. It transpired that all of them were due to converge on Quimper between noon and 2 p.m.

As it was the first band woke me soon after 7 a.m. With more of them arriving by train every few minutes and using the station car park as a rehearsal room, sleep was soon impossible. By 11 a.m. you couldn't move for the things.

I wandered down the side of the main canal looking in vain for some more traditional dancing, but bagpipes were suddenly the only show in town. They were everywhere, blowing furiously on street corners, tuning up in shop doorways, marching in straggling convoys along the river, each contingent supported by squealing bombards and flailing drums. Tourists sat stoically under the trees or at the kerbside vainly attempting to converse in sign language.

The participants came in all shapes and sizes: huge James Robertson-Justice types with flaring eyes and W.G. Grace beards, contingents of female librarians in crocheted waistcoats, and others who'd obviously modelled themselves on their distant cousins in Ulster: stern men with jutting chins, wearing menacing sunglasses and festooned in white and orange sashes.

At its height around 2 p.m. I counted nearly forty separate outfits within a hundred yards of the Cathedral Square, all of them in full spate. It was like a grotesque world record attempt. I half expected to see Norris McQuirter with a stopwatch. The odds were insuperable, so I bought a tea towel inscribed with Breton proverbs and some Nurofen, and returned to my hotel room. With my rail ticket booked for first thing Monday morning, it seemed my dream of joining the spirit of the dance had evaporated forever.

AT 6 P.M. I WOKE with a cricked neck. I'd fallen asleep to with the TV on, and it was now blaring out a Gallic equivalent of *You've Been Framed*, a show called *Video Gag* consisting of people walking into glass doors and babies throwing spaghetti about.

But at least my headache had disappeared. And there was more good news. It was only when I turned off the set that I heard it. Nothing. The sound of silence.

I dressed hurriedly and set off back for the centre. The transformation was remarkable. Where bagpipes had once held sway, now, as if by magic, were the sweet sad sounds of a fife, fiddle and two acoustic guitars. On a stage along the cathedral wall, a tuneful ceilidh band was in residence, dispensing irresistible rhythms full of the sort of twiddly bits that would have Michael Flatley busting his spandex to get in among. Beside them, underneath a massive awning, lines of trestle tables had been set out, and a team of blushing teenagers in plastic aprons were doling out portions of mouth-watering dishes to a queue of diners, each clutching a raffle ticket.

Each volunteer had a job description scrawled in Magic Marker down the front of her pinny. I passed Miss Moules, Miss Couscous and Miss Pommes Frites, and joined the end of the queue. Minutes later I was sitting in the sunshine, wolfing down a delicious bowl of Cotriade, Breton fish stew with parsley, white wine and potatoes. So intense was my relief to have my sanity back, I didn't even mind that the main ingredient seemed to be conger eel.

But best of all, the window-winders were back in town. Between the band and me was a distance of no more than thirty yards, yet if I'd had to run across to the fife player to tell him his instrument was booby-trapped I couldn't have managed it for worlds. Long chains of dancers were once again crabbing back and forth, including many I recognised from the previous evening. Round the perimeter stood thousands more, watching and waiting for their chance to join in.

An heni na avantur netra, nà koll nà gounid ne ra, runs a proverb on my tea towel. 'The one who does not risk anything does not gain or lose.' I resolved to try my hand one last time, but I wouldn't repeat the mistakes of the previous night and go blundering in. Instead I'd find a vantage point at the top of the cathedral steps and prepare for a lengthy stakeout.

As the sun dipped behind the spire I surveyed events over several glasses of local *cidre*. A pattern began to emerge. After a while I began to identify the ones who weren't interested in accepting interlopers from the ones who might prove more receptive to an Englishman in a panama hat. I just needed to find the weak link in the chain, the one as useless and confused as me.

And then I spotted him. The runt of the litter, the one who could be picked off before he could run for safety. He was a lumbering tourist, like myself, with an unwieldy haversack on his back, great fleshy sunburnt feet encased in dusty sandals, and his features stretched in the telltale look of bewildered happiness that Americans often have in Europe, The face that says, 'Shucks, just wait till I tell the folks back home the things I've done.' He'd already joined one of the chains and was lurching around desperately trying to keep up, oblivious to the mayhem his flailing haversack was wreaking.

If I could just get near him…

A gap opened up. With a single bound I was down the steps and grasping for his spare hand. New recruits were already streaming onto the courtyard to join the procession, and for a ghastly second I thought I'd missed my chance, but then his huge flapping fingers closed gratefully round mine and we were away; he even found a moment to flash me a huge sweaty smile of greeting. Never was a man so relieved to have someone equally hapless at his side.

We set off, clumping our way across the flagstones towards the queue of diners and back again. I'd made it. I was part of the festival.

It was about to get a whole lot better. Someone else had grabbed my trailing hand and was holding it at regulation midriff height, as prescribed by Breton tradition. When I glanced behind I found I was linked to an attractive older woman in her mid-fifties, the sort you always hoped to meet as a teenager, warm, unthreatening and experienced, a person who would guide you across the sexual Rubicon with a steady hand mixed with delicacy and understanding. Think Susan Sarandon mixed with Meryl Streep.

She, too, was obviously a stranger to Breton ways. But better still, she had the largest pair of ripe, bountiful, fifty-something breasts that had ever had to endure a country dance. They were now bouncing up and down and landing on my hand with a satisfying slap each time we hopped, which without looking at my wristwatch I reckoned to be about every three seconds.

I momentarily considered withdrawing my fingers from hers as a gesture of supreme gallantry: but what would that achieve? It would only break the chain, and in any case she was so rapt in the sheer delight of the dancing and the cathedral and the slanting sunlight and the smell of conger eel and her efforts to get the steps right that it would achieve nothing by disturbing her.

The *fest-noz* had proved every bit as mysterious and powerful as I'd imagined. Here now, in the shadows cast by the symbol of the very Catholic Church that had once viewed this ancient cere- mony with such alarm, I could appreciate the complex blending of Christianity and ancient pagan traditions that influenced so much French culture hereabouts.

As to the dance's sexual efficacy: all I knew was that in the glow of a July evening, in France's greatest ethnic music fest, I danced as I've never danced before, with a pair of 38DDs slap- ping the top of my right hand.

Appellation Spring

AN ACTOR ACQUAINTANCE once told me of a gig he'd got filming a movie in rural France. During the lunch break on the first day, he was horrified to find himself being offered wine with his meal on the location catering bus.

'Please don't,' he pleaded with the puzzled cook. 'If you do, I'll drink too much and won't be able to work.' My friend wasn't a drunk, or an alcoholic: the point was, he was English. This simple story sums up the difference in attitude between the two nations on the subject of wine.

Think of wine, and you think of France. Never mind those New World parvenus, France is the gold standard by which everyone else is judged, and wine drinking is part of the warp and weft of French life.

From the time they've barely worked out how to use a cup, French kids are encouraged to acquire an appreciation and respect for the stuff: always with food, always in moderation and always in company. The average Frenchman consumes ten times more than the average American, who, let's face it, doesn't normally have his arse whupped in any tests involving the consumption of foodstuffs. Just as well, as France annually produces between 7 and 8 billion bottles.

But it's about much more than that. Some observers have

even suggested that drinking wine is a cultural bonding ritual. A bit like dogs sniffing each other's bottoms, the French drink wine in order to strengthen national and tribal ties, reinforcing pack identity against the increasingly invasive culture of the outside world.

My own palate is somewhat rudimentary. It's not that I can't manage the techniques vital to the appreciation of a good vintage – slurping it up through my teeth, sloshing it around my tongue like mouthwash and then making a noise with my cheeks as if trying to produce sound effects for an adult movie – it's just that I tend to use them when eating soup.

My knowledge was forged by witnessing my dad's attempts to make his own wine back in the 1970s. He fiercely guarded his artistry, but I knew the secret, which was to strain each consignment through an old pair of my mum's pantyhose before bottling, a process that he claimed not only reduced the sediment but gave the wine darker, richer tones. He also routinely added a slug of vodka before corking: 'Just to assist the fermentation process.'

On my sixteenth birthday he allowed me to share some with him, and I still blame the two glasses I choked down for the fact that my palate is shot to pieces. Forty years on, I still have a single bottle under the stairs, and one day, when I've lost control of my physical and mental faculties, I intend to drink it in a single sitting, thereby saving Julia the heartache of having to book me into a clinic in Switzerland. In the meantime, I still crave sweet sugary things, and my idea of a perfect accompaniment to a little lightly grilled lemon sole is a large tumbler of Vimto.

Now I had the chance to put it right. The Dordogne is where many of the household names in viniculture hail from: St-Emilion, Merlot, Graves, Haut-Médoc, and the one that tastes like cream soda, Sauternes. Hopefully a day or two here would unlock the mysteries of one of France's national obsessions. My destination was Bordeaux – gateway to the vineyards.

Although I'd chosen Bordeaux much as I might choose my wine, namely by shutting my eyes and pointing at a map, it turned out I couldn't have chosen a better place. Bordeaux means 'along the waters', in this case the Gironde estuary and the rivers Garonne and Dordogne, the sun-kissed banks of which are key to the success of wine-making in these parts.

Better still, the region's antecedence is decidedly English. The marriage of Henry Plantagenet with Eleanor of Aquitaine in 1152 made this province English territory, and the export of Bordeaux wines to the tables of London began at once in earnest. We even gave the region's trademark brew our own name – claret. From the twelfth century to the nineteenth, claret was the Blue Nun or Carling Black Label of the English dinner table, and while it was still part of the empire, we fiercely defended Bordeaux and its alcoholic bounty against French assaults in order to ensure supply.

Yet despite this, French wine remains a minefield for the novice. That's why so many of us prefer the New World stuff, which has made choosing a decent bottle of plonk about as risky as purchasing a bag of sugar. The French, however, prefer things to be a bit less straightforward, continuing to cloak the appreciation of a good wine in snobbery and moribund protocol.

Why classify wine according to the type of grape, as everyone else does? That would be far too easy. Instead, they insist on a complex and impenetrable method of codifying the producer or the vineyard and bugger all else. This is why we Brits find our sphincters tightening at the appearance of a French sommelier; they possess the only rulebook and it's not printed in a language we understand. Ordering wine is not about ordering wine, but rather proving yourself worthy of ordering wine.

Not for much longer, of course. With a soupçon more climate change and our shared geology, the Brits will soon be able to grow the stuff on the South Downs or the Hackney marshes. But in the meantime, a wine-tasting course in Bordeaux should ensure an easy passage, not least down my neck.

I'D BEEN LOOKING forward to the five hour train ride from Quimper not least to catch up on sleep and do some preparatory reading about viniculture. Anne-Sophie had other ideas.

She got on at Vannes, a salty, flag-fluttering seaside resort an hour into the journey. Her principal interest was lighthouses. If she hadn't spoken such good English I would have sworn something had become lost in translation, but to avoid any misunderstanding her overnight bag was covered in stickers of the things.

Apart from this one eccentricity she proved to be very jolly company. An immensely tiny woman, like a character from *The Hobbit*, and dressed from head to foot in a sort of baby blue jumpsuit, she pointed out various points of interest on the journey and even offered to share some of her *ficelle et Philadelphia* with me.

We talked of many things. Music was another passion. Her favourite group was Boney M, closely followed by The Clash. Best of all she liked film music. She reached into her bag and showed me her collection of CDs, together with her Disc Walkman, a machine I hadn't seen in public for some years and which now struck me as grotesquely old-fashioned and cumbersome.

In fact, there was something old-fashioned and cumbersome about Anne-Sophie. Her mobile phone was big enough to use as a weapon, and her choice of music too betrayed a woman who had got stuck in an eddy somewhere, even if it was only one of the Nelson variety. She showed me her cherished discs: *Dance avec les Loups, Petit Déjeuner chez Tiffany, La Panthère Rose*, and, most surprising of all, *Zulu*.

'Have you ever seen *Zulu*?' I asked.

She confessed she hadn't, but she liked the soundtrack very much. 'Is it a love story?' she wanted to know.

I decided to forgo the main thrust of the plot and instead concentrate on describing Ivor Emmanuel's spontaneous rendering of 'Men of Harlech'. Anne-Sophie hadn't heard of 'Men of Harlech' either but wrote down the name of the tune so she could buy it later.

At Bordeaux we hurriedly exchanged email addresses. She still had a two-hour journey ahead of her, but for me it was time to find a hotel and a wine-tasting course. At the last moment I turned back to give her a final wave. Her tiny form, almost hidden among the bustle of the platform, flapped furiously back before she was lost from view.

Wine-tasting in Bordeaux is obviously big business. So many were queuing for places that the front doors of the tourist office had to be wedged open, and I found myself jostling for attention at a special desk set up to cater for the overspill. The array of packages was vast, from week-long courses with inclusive accommodation down to vineyard bicycle tours, wine-tasting river cruises and even a chance to assist with the grape harvest.

There were two types of trips available for the aspiring sommelier on the day I visited: an escorted coach tour of a chateau, or an all-purpose *atelier de dégustation* at the local Ecole du Vin. The receptionist explained the château tour came with a discount voucher for a local restaurant at which we could try out our newly acquired skills later that evening. Five minutes later, and fifty euros lighter, I was on board.

The half-day *excursion* was to explore a relative newcomer on the block, a region called Entre-Deux-Mers, or as our guide Sylvie explained, 'Between two rivers.' Looking like Olive from *On the Buses* with huge bottle-top glasses and a curious mangled English accent that distended each and every vowel sound, she welcomed us aboard. 'I am 'appee to meet you,' she trilled. 'The region ees a mosaic of exceptionelle soils, containing all the vivacity of the Sauvignon, the plenitude of the Semillon and the fruit of the Muscadelle.'

Understanding Sylvie was a bit like discovering the intricacies of French wine itself; just possible as long as you constantly repeated the information under your breath and had some paper and a pen to hand. But I was too distracted by my fellow *dégustationnaires*. The mix was nothing if not eclectic. There was a lone Japanese male weighed down with cameras, a hefty female Canadian backpacker, the ubiquitous American college boy with acne-pocked cheeks, a party of blushing Irish spinsters, a crisp German couple with a tiny toddler in a sling and a gnarled old Aussie in a sweat-stained hat. And of course a middle-aged Englishman in a panama.

While Sylvie got things moving with a few opening facts about the Gironde, I turned to look out of the window. Bordeaux seemed to be a city of elegant squares interlaced with huge monuments and impressive fountains, many of which were playing host to the feet of sweltering residents.

I've always subscribed to the view that instant gratification is not soon enough, and I was already salivating at the thought of soaking my tonsils in something crisp and white. Yet the combination of Sylvie's mangled commentary and the rapidly climbing temperatures meant that by the time we crossed the river itself, my head was already lolling against the shoulder of the Canadian backpacker next to me. Not that she was complaining: she'd fallen asleep as well, displaying an enormous mouthful of pristine gnashers.

'–and you swirl the wine een a circular motion…' I woke with a start. Sylvie was at the front of the gangway, her impressive Gallic hooter buried deep within a glass, demonstrating the correct way to identify the bouquet. We were barely out of the city precincts and, fool that I am, I was already missing vital information.

I blinked hard and resolved to stay alert. But there was just so much to take in. The types of grapes, the strength of the alcohol, whether it was silky or rough, flat or flabby; having finished her opening remarks, Sylvie handed the microphone over and invited us to talk about our own knowledge of wines.

The responses were varied. The American boy was hoping to go into the catering trade, the blushing spinsters admitted they merely wished to return home with enough knowledge to order the correct accompaniment to a meal of meat and potatoes, the Germans professed an unassailable preference for Riesling, while the Aussie assured her as long as it was wet and alcoholic he didn't much bloody mind. I decided to omit my experiences with my mum's pantyhose in case I was turned over to the gendarmerie.

Vox-pops complete, Sylvie moved onto the important question of standards and the complex system of awarding *appellations*, the system that confirms France's status as the Lord Snooty of viniculture. 'So what do we call an appellation?'

I dug my nails into my palms as I clung on grimly to her meandering exposition. There was something about 'terroir', something else I didn't quite catch, and the last thing I recall is Sylvie talking about 'the Gallic-Roman time, an age of prestige'.

I woke with a start. It was half an hour later and our coach was trundling over a speed bump into a dust-filled courtyard. As we came to a halt, a small frazzled-looking woman in glasses was hurrying out to meet us, followed by a couple of overweight Labradors. God knows what vital information I'd missed during my nap, but it was too late now: I'd have to busk it.

The woman with the dogs turned out to be the owner of the vineyard. Madame Blanche-Gaston had obviously gone to the same language school as Sylvie, but it didn't matter much as most of her welcome was drowned out by a braying donkey in an adjacent field. Formal introductions concluded, she led us towards a complex of sheds that stood baking in the heat. At last my education was commencing in earnest.

Our *dégustation* got off to a slow start. Instead of the anticipated bottles of chilled whites I'd set my heart on, the first building merely contained several stainless-steel vats, each with a blackboard hanging over a tiny tap at shoulder height. Next to them was a wooden desk containing pots full of rubber bands, lengths of tubing and pairs of latex gloves.

'And now, a little 'eestory.' Madame Blanche positioned herself next to one of the vats and began describing her family tree. It was no doubt fascinating to genealogists, and I'm sure her ancestors were a credit to their parents and kind to animals, but ten minutes later and with her having only reached 1850 she was starting to lose her audience. 1800 came and went, then 1750, and when she finally announced that there were no reliable records before 1650, I heard the Aussie murmur, 'Thank Christ for that.'

But she wasn't finished yet. She now launched into an

exhaustive explanation of the influence of rock and water on the finished product, followed by a summary of fermentation procedures, the rules for checking the transformation of the sugars and the preferred bandwidth of temperatures to achieve the best results.

Knowledge of bandwidths was all very well but it wouldn't be much use at my local branch of Pizza Express. Instead I found myself scrutinising my fellow travellers. It's funny how different nationalities seem to behave according to type when thrown together.

The American with the acne, for instance, was making copious notes as if he intended to start a company specialising in bandwidths the following morning. Beside him the Irish women stood uncertainly, cheeks flaming, as if waiting to go into confession, while the German family nodded in mute assent at Madame Blanche's theories. Further back the Aussie dabbed at his neck with a creased handkerchief and muttered something under his breath about 'wringing that donkey's bloody neck if he doesn't shut his racket'. In the far corner of the shed the Japanese tourist was taking a series of close-ups of a jar full of latex gloves.

'White wines generally gain colour as they age...'

It was now nearly two hours since we'd left the tourist office and still Madame Blanche's commentary showed no sign of concluding. We were due back in the centre of Bordeaux by five thirty, and if we didn't start getting some plonk-on-plonk action soon we were going to have to really cane it once it eventually arrived.

I reminded myself that quality not quantity was the defining concept of the trip and that it was exactly these primitive Anglo-Saxon traits I was attempting to re-educate by coming here in the first place: but old habits die hard. Bordeaux alone produces

70 million bottles per year, surely it wasn't expecting too much for one to ship up hereabouts? I noticed the German toddler sitting astride his dad's shoulders was near enough to one of those spigots to turn them, and I found myself willing his hand to stretch that tiny bit further. His fingers found the tap, but would he have the strength to twist it?

'– and that is why everything here today is empty.' Madame Blanche shrugged her shoulders and slapped a distinctly hollow-sounding cask with a rueful smile.

Empty? Everything is empty? The German dad allowed himself a curt smile, as if this was just the sort of thing you'd expect from such a disorganised country, while the Aussie slumped onto a nearby table. Even the Irish spinsters looked at each other in panic. Only the Japanese photographer seemed unperturbed, immersed as he was in taking a series of snaps of some empty detergent bottles on the floor. It was all very frustrating. By this stage in the afternoon I'd anticipated talking about insolent little devils with their background of blackcurrant and naughty little afterglow of lemon and toffee.

A third room offered for our collective scrutiny brought only more misery, containing the sort of equipment you'd find in a catalogue from your local branch of Travis Perkins: mud-caked trolleys, things with nozzles at the end and odd cranking mechanisms on metal feet. 'We use these for racking up,' explained Madame Blanche, an announcement that sent the Japanese with the camera into overdrive, as if his entire journey had been solely in pursuit of racking-up apparatus.

By the time we reached the fourth room an air of insubordination was beginning to set in. Even the spinsters were giving way to grumbling complaint. But then Madame Blanche trotted across to a sliding partition. Behind it, grinning broadly, stood

Sylvie with a large tray of wine bottles and a corkscrew. If she'd been dressed as Marie Antoinette she couldn't have received a more enthusiastic response.

Hers was a well-rehearsed routine, and within seconds the room was echoing to the popping of corks and the murmuring of appreciative punters. I edged my way in, trying to balance the conflicting interests of not being left out and not looking desperate. But what to do once I'd got some? All around me people were studying the liquid with microscopic scrutiny, holding it up to the light and tapping the rim of the glass, while the young American swirled it round the sides. When I tried to follow suit half of my sample sloshed out over the side and ran down my arm.

Thankfully the Aussie was still awaiting his sample, and I studied him carefully. Sylvie had placed a number of spittoons on the table, but I noticed he downed his glass in one and even stuck his hand out for a refill. I followed suit and stood smacking my lips, waiting for something to emerge. Vanilla, *n'est-ce pas*? With a faint afterglow of apple? Whatever it was, it was excellent. Perhaps I should have another helping just to make sure.

The next glass tasted even better than the first. Just as I was about to ask for yet another to confirm my suspicions, Sylvie reappeared through the sliding door with trays of food. Bowls of tasty aperitifs were placed along the length of the room: delicate squares of creamy cheese, anchovy-flavoured spreads, morsels of baguette and slivers of sausage speared on cocktail sticks.

More bottles were uncorked. We were invited to try another white with a citrus flavour and an aftertaste of yellow flowers and Tizer; and then another white, and before I knew it my beaker was being filled with a bulbous red. I sat down at the far end of the room, savouring each new sample and blowing raspberries at the gleeful toddler.

I was beginning to enjoy myself enormously. And there was no doubt about it: the first two had definitely been whites, and this one was most certainly a red. Beyond that I wouldn't yet want to commit myself, but it was a start. Perhaps another sample might help me to differentiate further.

Thankfully Madame Blanche was already approaching with a Merlot. I held the glass of russet pink liquid up to the light and then held it under my nose.

I was still inspecting it when the Aussie wandered over and asked if he could join me. His name was Stan, he'd been a stoker in the Merchant Navy before retiring to the suburb of Hornsby in New South Wales, and was on a pan-European trip with his wife, who, most wonderfully, was called Sheila. He'd only come on the wine tasting to avoid having to go round the art galleries in Bordeaux with his wife. 'I didn't really fancy either, to tell you the truth, but at least coming here I'd get some down my neck,' he confessed, before moving on to the thorny questions of whether Flintoff had a drink problem and if London is going to make a right shite-house out of staging the Olympics.

I liked Stan. He was just the sort of no-nonsense bloke who was typical of his country. I toasted the Aussies, then he toasted the Poms, and then we both toasted the fact that the sonofabitch Prime Minister John Howard had been defeated at the polls and was finally out of power after ten calamitous years. As we drank Stan talked about the plight of the Abbos, who, he explained, were becoming hopelessly reliant on drink due to general deprivation and lack of a decent education. I observed we'd be in the same boat if we stayed here much longer. We asked for a refill and toasted Australia's indigenous race.

Indeed, it seemed to me now that the wines of each country seemed to mirror their representatives here today. Take Stan, for instance. Straightforward, consistent, with a sunny disposition and no unexpected aftertaste. Or the Germans, currently folding Sylvie's paper napkins into quarters and stashing them for later. Weren't their indigenous wines crisp, efficient, lacking flair, and with a fatal weakness for sugary sentimentality? I sensed the finer points of my wine education seeming suddenly less important. Surely the crucial thing was to enjoy what appealed to you rather than worrying about bourgeois trends: and just now everything was appealing. Even Sylvie. Funny, I'd never noticed how attractive she was till now.

By the time Madame Blanche had explained the château's protracted efforts to gain an official appellation, an exhaustive process that she expected to take up to five years, she was struggling to make herself heard. The respectful silence of thirty minutes ago had now given way to the buzz of raucous chatter. Stan was telling Sylvie about a journey he made to visit his relatives in Saskatchewan after the war, the Canadian backpacker was delighting the young tot with an impromptu game of peek-a-boo, while the Irish women were discussing the merits of leaving a legacy in their wills to a donkey sanctuary in County Cork.

I sat happily watching my new friends while I rootled with a cocktail stick for slivers of sausage lodged between my teeth. Wonderful, when you come to think of it: this knot of international travellers, thrown together by a common desire for self-improvement through the small but crucial niceties that make life worthwhile. I decided to conduct an experiment to see if tipping the glass of white I was holding in one hand into the glass of red I was holding in the other would result in a decent rosé. The resulting brew seemed very acceptable.

It was only when I tried to get up that I realised my plight. I sat down again and the room stopped spinning, but by now most of the others had already deposited their glasses and were following Madame Blanche out into the sunshine for a look at the all-important vines. Only Stan remained, pouring the left-overs into a single glass. 'You all right, chum?' he asked. I smiled cheesily and raised my glass in a facsimile of a toast, and he followed the others out.

Eventually I managed to stand, and pursued the swimming vision of my fellow travellers. I now realised I must have put away the best part of a bottle of red plus a full bottle of white in a little under an hour, and life suddenly didn't seem quite as much fun.

Outside it was roasting. Madame Blanche was pointing out the vineyard, row after row of identical bushes stretching into the distance, and explaining the various factors to consider when purchasing. Luckily, she explained, the shop was currently open, at which we could buy some samples of the chateau's various products at competitive prices. She moved off in the direction of some outbuildings, where an assistant was already laying out some gift packs. A moment later and I was alone.

Thankfully there was a decorative well surrounded by a stone parapet a few yards beyond the coach. I laboured across and sat down heavily on the gravel with my back against the parapet. Sometime during the last five minutes I'd heard Madame Blanche talking about a procedure called 'laying down'. Perhaps I'd just try it myself.

The next thing I remember is being woken up by Sylvie. It was forty minutes later. The coach had just been pulling out of the car park when one of the spinsters had looked out of the window and noticed my feet sticking out from behind the wall.

THAT EVENING I visited the restaurant with my voucher. It had taken till 10 p.m. for my hangover to abate, and from the look of the crumpled napkins strewn across the tables, the majority of my companions had already eaten and departed for home.

The only diners I recognised were the pockmarked American sitting at a nearby table with the Canadian backpacker. As I entered they withdrew their hands from where they'd been entwined across the table. I smiled politely but it was evident from the frosty response that at some point during the return journey on the coach I'd crossed the line. Perhaps it was when I treated them, if memory serves me right, to my Tommy Cooper impressions.

While I was still trying to focus on the menu the restaurateur strolled over to the couple and presented the wine list with a flourish. Had they enjoyed their trip to explore Entre-Deux-Mers? he enquired. *Peut-être* they felt a little more confident as a result?

'Let's find out, shall we?' replied the American. He stared confidently across at his new companion. 'You happy for me to have a go?'

She nodded enthusiastically.

'Well now.' He retrieved his notebook from a rucksack beneath the table. 'Let's see what we've got here. I'd suggest we go for something pretty light; we don't want to smother the taste, do we? They have some very nice Bordeaux Supérieurs, or we have a Terres Douces down here. Or if you wanted something lighter they've got a Lamotte Joube, which will just blow you.'

She giggled and they let the words hang in the air between them.

Eventually he selected a Château Grand Barrail Larose, a choice which seemed to meet with approbation from the restaurateur, who nodded sagely before returning with a dusty bottle from which he dispensed a tiny amount with a flourish.

The American smelt it appreciatively and curled some expertly round in the glass. After a long lazy sniff he slurped a small amount gently through his lips and let it roll about on the front of his tongue. The restaurateur flushed with delight.

'Boy, that's good. C'est parfait.'

The restaurateur bowed deeply, filled their glasses and wished them bon appétit. Then he wandered over to my table. 'Have you found your trip useful, monsieur?' he asked.

'Well, let's find out, shall we?' I stared queasily at the wine list. Today may not have taught me much about fine wines, but I'd learnt a bitter lesson in the field of social anthropology. All afternoon I'd been quietly mocking my fellow travellers for behaving exactly like their national stereotypes, yet I'd ended up the worst culprit, perfectly representing my countrymen by going berserk at the first sight of free booze, drinking far more than I could handle and then having to be helped back into the coach by strangers.

I closed the menu and looked up.

'I don't suppose you could do me a cup of tea?'

High Rollers

THE NOTION OF even sitting at a gaming table, let alone playing roulette, is so beyond my psychological compass as to be unimaginable. Apart from my annual trip to the bookmakers on Grand National day with a crumpled fiver, I've always ascribed to the notion that the best way to double your money is to fold it in half and put it back in your pocket.

France, however, is synonymous with such sport. The perception of Gallic temperament is of sudden impulse, grace under fire, trusting to one's intuition and the readiness to stake all on the turn of a wheel, content in the knowledge that win or lose, life and love will go on.

This attitude finds perfect expression in roulette. The game itself is inherently French, originating in Paris in the nineteenth century as a by-product of an attempt to invent a perpetual-motion machine. In 1842 the first proper casino opened in Monte Carlo, where, according to legend, the devil shared with the owners his secret of how to beat the odds. To this day the game's customary traits of nerve, flair and systematic analysis come with a heavy dose of superstition.

For an inert, rather-not-cause-too-much-fuss Little Englander, these are frightening notions. When it comes to risk assessment, I've always preferred a GPO savings account to Icelandic hedge funds. Few things trigger such a feeling of profound comfort and security in me than the sound of that nice little lady down at the post office clunking a mechanical date stamp down on my pass book. And as for gambling, if I wanted to waste my hard-earned money simply handing it over to a load of anonymous crooks, I could simply fill in my tax returns.

Yet it hadn't been lost on me that the most famous of all gamblers, Charles Wells, 'the man who broke the bank at Monte Carlo', once resided in Newhaven. I suppose anyone who hailed from such an unprepossessing place would tend to have a certain carefree philosophy about life, but nonetheless his story is remarkable.

In 1891 he arrived in Monte Carlo with £4,000 – albeit money defrauded from investors with claims of various fake inventions – whereupon he promptly broke the casino bank no less than twelve times in a single eleven-hour session.

He returned later that year and broke it again, this time to the tune of one million francs over three days, including one extraordinary sequence in which he placed five consecutive bets on the number 5. Despite hiring ten private detectives to watch his every movement at the table, the casino could find no evidence of chicanery. In the meantime, millionaires, beautiful women and the cream of society courted him assiduously, hoping to discover his secret.

'The average gambler lacks courage,' he once said. 'He will not risk sufficiently large stakes and he is afraid of his losses.' Just to prove it, he returned to break the casino on six more occasions.

What's certain is that a roulette table is not the place for faint hearts. It's a place where your philosophy and your bank account are defined by your actions: a spiralling theatre of dreams in which you can act out your own fantasy future without a script.

It is your deeds that define who you are, or so the great existentialist thinker Jean-Paul Sartre claimed, and, more frightening still, responsibility for those deeds rests with you and you alone. Each day you may mint your destiny afresh. But only if you have the nerve, *mon ami*.

Would a night on the roulette table bring me liberation from those frigid twins Prudence and Probity, set free the existential hero within and make me a new man – a Camus, a Hemingway or even a Bond?

Rien ne va plus.

MY DESTINATION WAS Biarritz, jewel of France's Atlantic coastline and playground of the rich and famous. Famous for its flashy opulence and world-class surfing, it's also home of the biggest and grandest casino in the region.

The fortunes of this tiny coastal resort changed irrevocably after Empress Eugenie, wife of Napoleon III, Emperor of France, visited on holiday in 1854 and liked it so much she persuaded her husband to build a palace there. The swarms of European royalty who flocked to fill the guestrooms soon transformed the town from the French equivalent of, well, Newhaven, come to think of it, into a place synonymous with carefree, sophisticated living, and in the space of a few years, feasts, balls, bathing parties, receptions, diplomatic intrigue and, above all, gambling became part of the fabric of daily life.

The brand new casino Municipal, built at the turn of the twentieth century, confirmed the resort's status, and even fifty years later everyone from Bing Crosby to the Duke and Duchess of Windsor were still flocking here to play the tables.

And now it would be my turn.

The train down to the Atlantic coast was crowded with holidaymakers, so much so that I was squashed hard against the sort of unappetising young French couple who give their country a bad name. He a guitarist by the shape of his luggage, she a singer, probably with one of those hopeless breathy voices as evidenced by the French president's current wife, they oozed body odour, garlic and recent sexual congress in equal parts. He wore a goatee beard, a trilby hat and carefully contrived NHS-type specs with designer sellotape holding together one of the arms. Her contribution was a mini skirt made of antelope hide with endless sweat stains radiating out in concentric circles. I found myself crushed up against her hairy armpit as we clenched a handrail. Just when I thought it couldn't get any worse, they broke into an impromptu rendering of one of their songs.

The station turned out to be some way from the centre of the resort. Because of a computer fault afflicting all the ATMs in southern France, I hadn't been able to replenish my wallet before leaving, and thus found myself virtually broke some kilometres outside a town famous for its intolerance of poverty. A superstitious man would already have read the runes and caught the first train out of here, but the story of Charles Wells has emboldened me.

I stood for some minutes attempting to thumb a lift as convoys of open-top convertibles sped past full of open-top convertible people. Just as I was about to filter my own urine through my T-shirt in order to provide a nourishing and life-saving drink, a bus appeared around the corner and pulled up alongside. 'Combien pour le billet à centre de Biarritz? Les distributeurs est kaput!' I croaked. I had no idea if 'kaput' was a word recognised in these parts, but just to make my plight crystal clear I went into a desperate mime, slitting my throat, turning out the lining of my trouser pockets and making farting noise with my tongue.

When the driver picked over my shrapnel and grudgingly dispensed a ticket, I would have kissed her on the mouth had her demeanour not suggested she wouldn't be interested in such things. Half an hour later I was deposited in the town centre and, minutes after that, solvent once more. Crisis over.

I recognised Biarritz. It was Scarborough with money. The seafront had that same appearance of nature tamed by humanity for fun and frivolity, but whereas Billy Butlin had crafted Scarborough, Biarritz owes its grandeur to Napoleon III. Need I say more?

And it was very rich. I sat with a Coca-Cola Lite at a bustling café on the promenade watching hundreds of bronzed angels surfing out in the bay. Thousands more lazed on the sands or pottered past me on the esplanade. There were no shortage of English people, and they all seemed to be arguing. Snatches of overheard conversation were variants on an identical theme: 'All I'm saying is...' – 'For Christ's sake, Angela...' – 'Well, if you're going to behave like this, we might as well go home tomorrow...'

Nonetheless, on a flawless July afternoon it was a treat to be here. From far off, huge Atlantic rollers were thundering towards hundreds of expectant body boarders. In fact, a swim was just what I needed to restore my spirits and give myself courage for the stiffer tests ahead.

But I'd come without a beach towel. I wandered up and down the shops on the Esplanade in search of a suitable item, but with the prices for everything here up to a fifth more than anywhere else in France, even the baldest bit of old terry towel was going for forty euros a pop. Eventually I found a small outlet selling them at half price and hurried in before they changed their mind.

It was only when I unfurled my purchase on the sands a few minutes later that I realised the reason for the special reduction. My first purchase in Biarritz had the words FUCK OFF emblazoned in huge white letters on black across its entire length. I swallowed hard and assured myself it wasn't God's way of telling me to stay away from the gaming tables.

I TRIED TO ignore the casino for a day or two, but you simply couldn't ignore such an imposing edifice. Its art deco frontage seemed to leer at me wherever I was in the town. How would Charles Wells have reacted? He wouldn't be cowed like this, sidling about the prom having endless cups of tea. It was time to redefine myself by action, purpose and decisiveness.

I got about three words into my introduction.

'Passport please, monsieur,' the receptionist said, barely looking up from her desk.

'Well, actually I have it with me, but the point is–'

'Driving licence?'

'No no, you don't understand.' I allowed myself a chuckle. 'The fact is, I don't want to play tonight, I just wanted to know if someone could show me the ropes so that–'

'Henri!' A man who looked as if he meant business was already padding across the plush carpet.

'Good evening, sir, is there a problem?'

The woman rattled off several phrases I couldn't understand, but which obviously ran along the lines of the lines of 'this deadbeat refuses to show me any proof of identity and by the way have you seen the state of his shoes'. I noticed I was being filmed by no less than seven different video cameras, which was more television coverage than I'd managed in thirty years of acting.

Eventually I showed them my passport. The image on the inside suggested someone off the photo gallery in *Crimewatch*, but it seemed to satisfy, and I was able to move on to explaining my mission to play roulette and perhaps receive some basic tuition in the process. After yet more consultation and a phone call, I was assured that if I were to turn up there at 8 p.m., 'when hardly anyone is here', one of the cashiers would be deputed to show me around. The inference was obvious; get this guy in and out before he starts removing his shoes under the table and leaving sticks of Kit-Kat on the baize.

'The average gambler lacks courage,' wrote Wells. I'd better find some, and fast.

I spent the long hours leading up to my date with destiny at an internet café near my hotel. I'd assumed gaming was basically about luck and nerve, but typing in 'How to play roulette' brought forth thousands of websites and articles, each of which needed a degree in applied mathematics to appreciate. There was no shortage of systems and strategies available, each of which claimed a winning formula by which to beat the odds, and one in particular, owned by a Mr Pfeffer in America, offered guaranteed returns: in fact, his system of adherence to a series of sequential numbers made gaining a million sound as easy as slow-cooking a casserole. I broke open a jotting pad and started writing it down.

His theory sounded plausible enough until I reached his final section – vital tips – which read like something out of an MI5 handbook. Among the rules indispensable to the success of his system, Mr Pfeffer insisted on your never spending more than twenty minutes at a table at one time, avoiding playing at all between two and three in the afternoon, and not attracting attention to yourself by donning garish clothing. 'I do not know why these rules seem to apply but they just do' was his final thrust.

Of course. This is why casinos always flourish, because the world is full of madmen like Mr Pfeffer, who put all their belief in a system that has taken them twenty years to devise, but which ultimately only works if you always knot your tie clockwise or wear the same underpants.

Far from living the high life in Vegas, my erstwhile hero was probably holed up in some trailer park in Arkansas with the world's largest collection of ring pulls and his wife's head in the fridge. In the end I decided to rely on my own system. It had certainly stood me in good stead when choosing the winning number last Christmas in my local theatre's Bonus Ball contest.

WHEN I ARRIVED at eight the casino was largely empty. I was shown down a flight of illuminated glass steps into the basement, past a number of leathery-skinned sun-worshippers in golfing shorts or sarongs, already sitting diffidently at rows of fruit machines, distractedly filling them with coins while examining their sunburn.

The assistant who'd been deputed to look after me was called Isobel. A crisp woman in her late forties with the look of wry resignation reserved for divorcees whose husbands have left them for younger models, she'd been working at the casino for fourteen years. But she turned out to be a magnificent tutor. Both she and her employers had spared no efforts in their attempts to make it easier for novices such as me to hand over our savings. After a guided tour of the complex, including its three restaurants, indoor swimming pool and roof terrace overlooking the ocean, she led me to what appeared to be the gaming equivalent of a flight simulator.

The machine offered instruction on a whole array of casino games in a safe, cyber-space environment, and within minutes I'd mastered the rudiments of both blackjack and roulette. From here I moved on to some actual fruit machines with a copper beaker of half-euro pieces in one hand and Isobel in the other.

Casinos are nothing if not psychologically sophisticated. They trade on anticipation. I tried a number of different machines – Zorro, Money Tree, Them Thar Hills – and on each and every spin it seemed I was always about to win something.

What about this one for instance? Look, there's a Bonus come to rest on the winnings line, and now an Extra Winnings has lined up beside it, and here's a Triple Bells arriving nicely on the third reel–

–but at the last moment a Banana appeared from nowhere and spoilt it all. 'Oh no, you are so unlucky,' said Isobel despairingly. 'Never mind, you must 'ave anozzer go.'

I fed in another coin and pulled again. And another. One by one they disappeared, until my beaker was nearly empty. I pushed back my stool, ran my fingers through my hair and prepared to leave. All this existential stuff about being defined only by your actions sounds all well and good, but right now I was more persuaded by the philosophy offered by my beach towel. But Isobel sat me down again. 'Michel,' she said with delicious severity, 'you must 'ave... how you say?'

'Perseverance?

'Exactement. Perseverance. Good. We try again.' We moved on to one called Break the Bank and I inserted my final coin. This time it sprung into overdrive, flashing its lights and filling the hall with a synthesised bugle call. I'd won.

My prize was a ticket promising me a special mystery free gift to collect from the cashier's table at the end of the evening. What could it be? A table lighter? A set of picnic chairs? One of those devices that picks fluff balls off old sweaters? Isobel wouldn't be drawn. But of one thing she was now certain.

'Michel,' she joyously proclaimed, 'you are now a gambler.'

It was now nearly 9 p.m. and the casino was starting to fill up. 'Now you can change some money and 'av fun!' she said simply, kissing me brightly on both cheeks. 'I see you at the end of the evening. We stand on the terrace together, and you can show me your free gift. There is a fireplace display on the promenade.'

Fireplace display? Perhaps the citizens of Biarritz were easier to entertain than I'd thought.

A HUNDRED EUROS bought me so many counters that when I put them into my trouser pockets the crotch dropped to my kneecaps. I lumbered across the carpet like a deep-sea diver searching for clams and plodded up the staircase, rattling loudly. Already Isobel's careful tutelage about the rudiments of the various games was starting to blur into a morass of numbers and vulgar fractions, and I hadn't even got near roulette yet.

The blackjack table was already colonised by a group of young surfing dudes. No more than eighteen or nineteen, they exuded effortless confidence. I eyed their insouciance with envy: when I was that age I was still listening to Acker Bilk and building Airfix kits. Their garb, too, was crushingly casual. Standing beside their cut-away jeans, carefully distressed tops and dishevelled hair in my M&S suit and polished shoes, I looked a like a Scout leader at a surfing party.

A sour-faced youth sporting a baseball cap turned backwards was indicating whether to pass or play with a barely perceptible nod of his head. He was less nervous than the croupier, a young girl with auburn hair and freckles who shuffled the cards like a fumbling children's entertainer. A stern overseer with an earpiece scrutinised her efforts from the far end of the table.

At last a space became free and I shimmied into a seat. But even before I'd settled the cards were sliding towards me. An ace and a ten. What did Isobel say? I nodded at the blushing croupier, who flicked another card in my direction. A three. That made... um, hang on, eleven and ten plus three–

'Play or not play, monsieur?' the overseer with the earpiece was addressing me with barely disguised irritation. The fact was that my mental arithmetic just wasn't strong enough, yet I could hardly start counting on my fingers. One by one my stock of chips started to decrease.

It may have been the champagne, or the sympathy I felt for the beleaguered croupier, but after some minutes I started to relax, and with it my luck turned. Perhaps there was something in all this fatalist gubbins after all. As in life itself, once you released yourself from your inner angst, the game no longer held you in its suffocating thrall.

In fact, what changed things was the realisation I wasn't the most clueless person at the table. The poor dealer could hardly think straight for the basilisk glare of her superior bearing down upon her, and while I was similarly out of my depth on the other side of the baize, at least my livelihood didn't depend on it. At least, not yet.

I won back my stake in the next round: then another, and suddenly I was back where I'd started. I held my nerve: refusing to be rushed, allowing my brain time to think, and using the excuse of a sip of champagne to buy me precious seconds to evaluate the risk.

When the fumbling apprentice was eventually replaced by an

older, more experienced colleague, I took it as a sign to quit myself, and I wandered out onto the balcony with another glass of champagne to take stock. I'd already scrawled down my preferred sequence of lucky numbers for the forthcoming roulette wheel on a scrap of paper back at the café, but even were crib sheets allowed, I had no need to remind myself of them. These were seminal indices from my life, and I was going to stick by them.

It was a wonderful starlit evening. The beach, though dark, was still busy with couples lighting fires or smooching by the sea, while further out the surf was picked out every few seconds by the beam from a distant lighthouse. Anne-Sophie would have liked it here. I was already thirty quid up on the night, and yet my biggest test still awaited me. Roulette was what I'd come here for, with its tumbling balls and the eyeshades and other gamblers all looking like Steve Buscemi flicking chips over your shoulder. And it still waited to be conquered. I swigged back the dregs of the champagne, loosened my tie and strode back in to try my luck.

I ARRIVED TO find the table already doing a brisk trade. There were some sleek businessmen, a couple of spry retirees, some younger pale-faced habitués, and a beautifully dressed woman with hair the colour of strawberry gobstoppers who seemed to be on first-name terms with the croupiers.

It was some minutes before I risked my first stake. A split bet between 4 and 2: the date of my birthday. With each minute new punters were joining the game, and the croupiers were moving the counters about with all the expertise of young WRAFs plotting the latest positions of Messerschmitts over the Kent coast.

My next bet was another split between 5 and 7, the year of my birth. Then a split bet – 32 and 36 – the house numbers of the first two properties I ever owned. At first I was barely aware I was in credit. But then one of the businessmen leaned across and brusquely suggested I tidy my chips, and I realised that the chaotic mess of counters on the baize in front of me was all mine.

I spent some moments stacking them into tiny piles, an act that was more satisfying than I could ever had thought possible. Somehow I had acquired nearly a hundred and fifty quid's worth. Like the lucky golfer who keeps thwacking the ball onto the green, events seemed to be evolving without my active participation.

After a brief pause, I put bets on Julia's birthday (15), Dad's birthday (30, 3, 16), Mum's (2, 11, 18) and the number of times my name has been in lights in the West End (1). The stack of chips continued to mount. I ordered a cocktail.

How he deals with unexpected success can say more about a man than anything else. For some it spurs them on to even greater heights of derring-do, while others, suddenly realising how ludicrously high off the ground they are, freeze and fall to their doom. 'Gambling is the son of avarice and the father of despair,' someone once said. Or was it the other way round? Either way, it was only once I realised I had nearly three hundred smackers that my nerve started to fail.

I thought of all the things I could put the money towards back home if I could only quit now. A half-decent second-hand car. Six months of gas bills. A Velux window in our attic conversion. Even a week's holiday in Spain if we were prepared to go allocation-on-arrival. There'd be no shame in throwing in the towel, as long as it was only the metaphorical one. It was already way beyond my anticipated finishing time, and I wasn't sure I even had the door code to get back into my hotel.

But another voice was whispering in my ear. It was the voice of champagne, of Isobel, of a provincial Englishman travelling alone in a foreign land. Possibly of Charles Wells himself. 'You've waited fifty-one years to be here tonight, and your luck's in.'

Another cocktail. My first-ever weekly wage (47). The number of times Sussex have won the county cricket championship (3).The voices remained, but they were lower.

By 10 p.m. I reckoned I had nearly five hundred quid. The woman with the gobstopper hair was now smiling shyly at me each time our eyes met, and even the croupiers seemed to be paying me more deference, carefully coaxing my winnings over with their sticks instead of pushing them at me like their weekly laundry delivery.

A new sofa for the living room, a season ticket for the tube, a more powerful laptop – there was a knot in my stomach.

The table was now crowded with people waiting to join the fun. I had nearly a grand and one remaining lucky number in my sequence: the date of my wedding to Julia: 24.

That Sunday afternoon back in April 2001 when we'd tied the knot surrounded by all the friends and relatives who'd expended so much time and effort coping with our back and forths over a quarter of a century. Twenty-four was the date when I'd stopped fannying around as a bachelor-manqué and committed publicly my lifelong adherence to the only woman who had ever held my interest and my affections. If one were being fanciful, one could argue that that 24 was the start of the chain of cause and effect that had brought me here tonight.

'The average gambler will not risk sufficiently large stakes and he is afraid of his losses,' Wells said. In life, 24 had marked the moment when I'd finally thrown caution to the wind and committed myself to a course of action that had paid nothing but dividends ever since. If it came up trumps again tonight, I could expect to walk away with three or four big ones. And if not...?

Sartre himself talked of this tipping point in every gambler's life, what he termed as the moment of 'vertigo': a state of anguish caused not by the fear of falling over the edge of the precipice and losing all, but of consciously throwing oneself over – or, put another way, fear of the future in the moment before we become it. 'I must rediscover the fear of financial ruin or disappointing my family,' he once wrote. 'I perceive with anguish that nothing prevents me from gambling...'

I carefully pushed my counters across the baize and eased back in my chair. As the ball curled round the edge of the wheel I took a final swig of cocktail, and pulled my top lip back down off my teeth.

FIVE MINUTES LATER, I was back out on the balcony. It was a peerless evening. I lit a fresh Café Crème, inhaled deeply and stood against the balustrade, looking out to sea. What a night.

The ball hadn't come to rest on the date of my wedding anniversary after all. It had ended up somewhere else on the wheel entirely – I forget now, 3 or 5 or something. At the time I'd been too shocked and surprised to notice or care. It was only in the numbing aftermath of all my counters being scooped away into the bag that I realised my mistake. I'd staked all on the wrong number. We'd actually got married on the 22nd.

Viewed from one perspective, my lapse of memory hadn't made a jot of difference to the outcome. But viewed more philosophically, the coincidence was tantalising. I'd only come unstuck when I'd misconstrued my magic formula. Was it happenstance or hubris that had sent my tiny ball veering so spectacularly off course? God, I was even beginning to sound like Sartre. Or worse, like Mr Pfeffer.

And yet I found myself wanting to laugh. The evening had set me back in total about sixty-five quid, seventy if you include this final glass of champagne. About the same as a meal at the Ivy, or a ticket to a musical, or an afternoon at a Premier League football match: for which it had given me nearly four hours of entertainment. What did it matter that I hadn't won anything? It'd been a gas, and good for my soul. Prudence and Probity may not have been sent packing, but at least they'd been put to bed early for the night.

Just then Isobel hurried onto the balcony.

'Michel, I thought I 'ad missed you,' she said breathlessly. 'How did you manage? Are you a millionaire?'

I toyed with an enigmatic smirk, but instead settled for a genuine smile of gratitude, one she winningly returned.

'I've had great time, Isobel. I ended up not winning anything, but it doesn't matter.'

'Non, non, you 'ave forgotten,' she replied. She rummaged in her jacket. 'Your mystery prize from the fruit machine? You remember?' She presented me with a thin package wrapped in crumpled polythene.

It was a small Basque flag, in red, green and black, about the size of a large handkerchief and attached to an oversized ice-lolly stick. And it was mine.

I found myself pondering on the temperament required by the successful gambler. Towards the end of his life, Charles Wells had admitted that his system of placing bets had been nothing more sophisticated than a lucky streak. That much at least we had in common.

But unlike me, he'd gone on too long, eventually becoming

bankrupt and having to change his name to Davenport to escape his creditors. And – inevitably – he died broke in Paris: whereas the casino he'd so famously brought to its knees prospered to such an extent from the attendant publicity that it spent the next hundred years happily creaming off the life savings of the middle classes who flocked here to emulate their hero.

My biggest gamble by contrast had been on a chilly Sunday in April in north London seven years ago, and it had come up trumps. No need to be greedy: I may only have come away with a toy flag, but I still had a shirt on my back. And at least I wouldn't have to change my name to Davenport. That in itself was a blessing.

Isobel was being paged. As she left she kissed me on both cheeks and took a final photograph of me, tie loosened, cigar clamped between my teeth, an empty champagne glass in one hand and the other defiantly waving my flag.

Behind me, hundreds of exploding fireplaces filled the sky.

Hello Children Everywhere

HAVE YOU EVER watched those TV series in which families who've had enough of Britain attempt to relocate to the continental good life? It always seems to involve retired couples from the West Midlands deciding to invest their life savings in a derelict French farmhouse, with a view to converting half of it into a holiday *gîte* to fund their retirement.

He weighs about thirty stone, and she comes out in blotches whenever the temperature reaches 16°C and can only eat beans on toast. Their combined knowledge of continental ways is based solely on his thirty years as a forklift-truck driver at British Leyland.

You can imagine the rest. After a series of toe-curling cock-ups, they end up returning home due to chronic homesickness, and with their entire life savings shot to buggery.

Theirs is only an extreme example of a collective insanity that's taken hold over the past thirty years. If there's one thing France has too many of, it's the English. Since the 1970s we've relocated here in droves, subsuming most of the northern coastline and threatening to spread to all points of the compass. Hence the moniker – Rosbifs.

The term first stuck to our English boots as far back as the eighteenth century, when the French realised that it was about

the only meal that visitors from across the Channel would coun-
tenance. Our obsession for sticking anything with four legs and
a tail in a slow oven at gas mark 7 soon resulted in other Anglo-
French dishes acquiring similar titles, such as like 'rosbif de
mouton', but by 1850 the phrase had come to refer to the two-
legged variety.

Our cross-Channel spats over foot and mouth and BSE have
kept this insult alive and well, particularly since the locals, with
admirable regard for their finest traditions of cussedness, refused
to import the roast beef of old England long after the rest of the
EU had declared it fit for consumption. In fact, the International
Racial Slur Database lists hundreds of national insults based on
what people eat, including 'locust-eaters' for Afghans, 'salmon-
crunchers' for Alaskans and 'goulash-heads' for Hungarians. It's
just that the French, as in most things, have refined insubordination into an art form. But I suppose that's the Frogs for you.

The latest census estimated there to be 100,000 Brits living
here, although some figures put it as high as half a million. In
Dompierre-les-Eglises, a village of four hundred inhabitants in
central France, fifty-five British families have bought houses,
while the town of Bourbriac in Brittany witnessed vehement
anti-British demonstrations and ceremonial burning of estate
agents' details in the main street after the local populace found
their supermarché inundated with couples in replica West Ham
shirts all complaining about the lack of Branston pickle.

It's perhaps hardly surprising that expats should want to
huddle together for warmth. Cautionary tales from the many
who've tried and failed to relocate paint a picture of France as a
cultural maze and legalistic mantrap, just waiting to sever your
bank account at the knee.

Common laments include impenetrable legal procedures,

sudden preservation orders just as you've signed the title deeds to the land, workmen who take four-hour lunch breaks and hopelessly optimistic business modules that end with the wife sitting knee-deep in unpaid bills, while the husband puts his fist through the only wall they've managed to successfully plaster in the entire summer.

I'd been wondering for some days about trying to touch base with the expat community. Were they simply holidaymakers who'd been seduced by looking in too many estate agents' windows, or fundamentally a different breed? As if on cue I received a call from Ric.

I was surprised to hear from him. Squatter, tree-hugger, poll-tax rioter and, the guise in which I'd met him, keen pub-team cricketer, he'd found love late in life after meeting a woman called Lindy in the mud of Glastonbury. They'd since had a set of male triplets whom they nicknamed Larry, Curly and Mo, in a tribute to the slapstick comedians the Three Stooges, and rumour had it the tots were leaving no stone unturned in their efforts to behave in a manner befitting their filmic counterparts.

'I called your house. How do you fancy a game of cricket tomorrow?'

'Ric, I can't, I'm in France doing some travelling.'

'I know. Julia told me. Biarritz. I'm about a hundred miles east of you. Lindy and me have bought a derelict farmhouse in the Dordogne and we're over here doing it up. It turns out the local village has its own cricket team and they've roped me in to play. We're one short for a match tomorrow afternoon. Ju said if I could track you down you'd be sure to help out.'

'Um–'

'If it helps you can stay at our place. The beds are damp and we've an infestation of caterpillars in the kitchen, but you won't get much sleep anyway as you'll be woken at five by screaming toddlers. Fancy it?'

'Are they Frenchmen or expats?'

'Simmo, don't be a tosser. The French don't play cricket. You can't move for expats where we live. Remember, we live in Dordogneshire. It's no pressure, the game is only an in-house fundraiser; apparently they need a new septic tank for the pavilion. The set-up here's well worth a look. They're a funny old bunch. The club secretary wears a panama hat. He's an absolute twat.'

I removed my hat and put it under the table while I considered his invitation. On the one hand this was the sort of opportunity that might fast-track me right to the heart of Fortress Angleterre. But set against that, Ric was the least likely expat you could wish to meet: laid-back, unfussy, unmaterialistic, and with an unsentimental love for all things English. It's only people who proclaim Britain's gone to the dogs who move four hundred miles south and then try to recreate it in miniature. Ric was hardly a representative sample of the type I was looking to study.

He clearly sensed my prevarication. 'All right, what about this? The secretary's a retired stamp collector called Barrington Hancock. That clinch it?'

Barrington Hancock. If there was a better name for the sort of expat I would like scrutinise at close quarters, I couldn't think of one. I had an entrée straight to the beating heart of the Rosbif community, and Bazza had an eleventh man for their crunch game the following afternoon.

'IF THE FRENCH nobility had been capable of playing cricket with their peasants, their chateaux would never have been burnt.' So said G.M. Trevelyan, the most English of historians. We certainly share many things with France: rugby, football, a hatred of the Germans, yet cricket hasn't made it any further across than the Isle of Wight.

Perhaps there's something in the game that repels a country brought up in the spirit of liberté, égalité et fraternité. Visiting a match in the nineteenth century, a young Frenchman, Gaston Berleman, couldn't get past the fact that the match seemed to be five and half against one, 'Which to me does not sound quite fair, but they say I will understand better when the game begins, which will start as soon as it stops raining.'

He would have been surprised that less than fifty years later France would win the Olympic silver medal for the sport in the Paris games of 1900. Although it has to be said only two teams competed, the other being Great Britain, who won gold. Yet since those giddy heights the game had struggled to attract attention. Recently I'd heard the odd anecdote about various West Indian and Asian leagues still operating in the hinterlands of the capital, and this summer I'd read of a native Frenchman making it to a professional English county. But what surprised me from Ric's invitation was that today's game should be this far south. If there were Rosbifs around, a cricket team would surely attract them like bees to a honey pot.

I arrived just after 1 p.m. the following day. The station I got off at should have been renamed Dead Man's Gulch: I was the only person to alight, and as I waited for my lift I was scrutinised in total silence by a gaggle of unsmiling Frenchmen sipping coffee at a dingy café on the opposite pavement.

Thankfully the sound of crunching gears announced the arrival of Lindy. A jolly, knockabout sort of woman who still wore dungarees and her hair in bunches, she was famous for her joie de vivre, her capacity to hold stupefying amounts of booze and her infamous driving. Indeed, she'd only passed her driving test by default, after her emergency stop in Chigwell High Street had resulted in the examiner getting a pencil embedded halfway up his nose, requiring her to drive him to the nearest A&E.

The windows of her camper van were misted up but I could dimly make out a small army of toddlers. The soundtrack of what I dimly recognised as *Shrek* poured forth from the van. She swung open the door. 'Get in! We've won the toss and are batting and you're in at number four. Ric's texted me to say they've already lost a wicket, so we've no time to lose.'

Inside it was mayhem. The front seat was submerged in stale bread crusts, polystyrene cups and discarded packaging, while the upholstery was covered in what appeared to be cat litter. As I climbed in I became enmeshed in the coils of wires and plugs that trailed haphazardly from the dashboard to a video screen positioned on the rear of the driver's seat.

'OK, kids, here's the deal,' she shouted, looking behind her and addressing the children directly. 'Simmo's buggered the video so we're gonna have some singing. *Hello Children Everywhere*, please, Simmo, it's on the dashboard, can you stick it in, my darling.' She indicated a stack of greasy discs piled by the windscreen, the top one of which seemed to be doing service as an ashtray. I fumbled gingerly among them and slipped the appropriate one into the CD player.

Hello Children Everywhere ('fifty years of popular hits for kids') hit me while I was still strapping myself into the seatbelt. I'd already prepared myself for the odd frisson of British culture to surface during my day with the ex-pats, but being assailed by Terry Scott singing 'My Bruvver' only seconds after arriving was far more than I'd bargained for.

It was decades since I'd heard these songs, and now they unlocked a deluge of unbidden childhood memories of days spent sitting in the back of my own parents' car on picnics and holidays. 'The Runaway Train', 'The Big Rock Candy Mountain' and 'Nellie The Elephant' soon had my lip trembling like a lovesick teenager. Legend has it that Don Bradman was out for a duck on his final innings due his eyes being misted by emotion as he approached the wicket. Unless I pulled myself together sharpish, 'My Boomerang Won't Come Back' seemed likely to do the same for me.

As we drew into the club car park, it started raining. Out in the middle I could see Ric's lanky frame and trademark pony-tail peeking out from under a batting helmet, while another, stockier individual in a red cap was playing a sumptuous off drive that wouldn't have disgraced David Gower. It could have been a game on the outskirts of Beaconsfield.

I was curious to see the sort of welcome I might get today. Even I'd been on enough foreign holidays to know how oddly Rosbifs behave upon running into one another abroad, and Scottish author and traveller Tobias Smollett had already identified the tendency while travelling through France as far back as 1764:

'When two natives of any other country chance to meet abroad… they embrace like old friends, even though they've never heard of one another… : whereas two Englishmen in the same situation maintain a mutual reserve and diffidence – like two bodies endowed with a repulsive power.'

Sheltering by the boundary under a large golf umbrella was a huge flabby man wearing a hat, who seemed amply endowed with just the sort of repulsive power Smollett presumably had in mind. Seeing an unknown white English male approaching, he behaved perfectly to type, namely by looking the other way while reaching into his pocket and jingling change.

'Barrington?'

'Yes?' He focused grimly on the scorebook. It wasn't quite the warm expat welcome I was expecting, but I pressed on.

'Michael. Thanks for letting me join in today.'

'Oh yes, jolly good, the fact is, we're two down now and you're in next wicket down so better get padded up. You'll find some kit in the pavilion. Help yourself to whatever you can find. It's a matting wicket so spikes are out. Pad up, will you, bloody Monty has pulled a hamstring, he shouldn't even be out there.' He indicated the man in the cap who was pulling the bowler for a massive six into an adjoining field of sunflowers.

'He looks fit enough to me.'

'Yes, well, you don't know. Fact is, we need him for next week's Zonal cup match against Bordeaux. Can't have him crocking himself in a Mickey Mouse knockabout like this.'

Bordeaux? Cup match? A tantalising glimpse of a whole new world opened up before me, but it would have to wait for later.

Once inside the pavilion the parallels with suburban Britain continued. While the term 'garden shed' may have been a more accurate description than pavilion, it was warm and waterproof, and the drinking water had the familiar stagnant aftertaste that is such a comforting feature of genuine village cricket.

Once sorted, I wandered outside for a recce. It really did appear to be England in miniature. There was a sightscreen, a full-sized roller and even a working scoreboard with pleasing little tin numbers. I strolled across to introduce myself to the operator, a bloke smoking a roll-up who, by the murderous look on his face, had obviously been out first ball of the match. Long years of practice told me to leave well alone: a dodgy LBW decision looks the same whatever the other continent. Instead I wandered over to introduce myself to my teammates, who were knocking up in a net.

If Barrington's greeting had been tepid, my approach now was met with all the enthusiasm one might display to an approaching double-glazing salesman. How odd the English can be. I hadn't expected to be led into the nets on a donkey with my path strewn with palm leaves, but I'd anticipated that a new face being invited into such an enclave would at least be the subject of minimal curiosity. Yet there seemed to be a studied indifference as to who I was and what I was doing here.

By joining in with a little ritualistic pocket fumbling and change jingling, I soon persuaded them to open up. Apart from Ric and one young Sri Lankan who worked for Barclays International in Toulouse, they were all grey-haired retirees with ample paunches who had obviously relocated here to seek the good life. Graeme was a retired stockbroker, Hugh had worked as a wine merchant and now owned his own tiny vineyard, and the bloke with the roll-up and the murderous expression was an investment banker called, most wonderfully, Gordon Bennett.

With the rain increasing and we soon abandoned our practice in favour of the shelter of the pavilion. Barrington had taken refuge in it too, and as we approached he was describing to the opposition's twelfth man, a young boy of no more than thirteen, the selection policy of Kent during the inter-war years.

It was obvious that this entire set-up was his baby. He'd not only purchased the ground from the local council but performed every task from mowing the wicket to upgrading the club website: for which colossal service I suspected he and his endless stories were rewarded with stoic tolerance by his recruits.

Nonetheless his ownership exacted a heavy toll. Over the next twenty minutes he talked without drawing breath, all of it on cricket and cricketing matters. France had obviously tailored the sport to fit its infamously complex administrative system – the game over here received government subsidy, nobody was allowed to play without a medical examination and there were now some fifty clubs with 850 licensed players (I'd only ducked the medical because today was a friendly). Barrington predicted a bright future for French cricket.

When at last he was called out to do some more umpiring, the mood lifted instantly. The rain was now giving way to blue skies and sunshine, illuminating a landscape of gently undulating hills and thick forests. Like all well-brought-up guests, I expressed my envy of the circumstances and lifestyle available to my hosts. But did anyone harbour any regrets about leaving England, I wondered. My query was answered by enough snorts to satisfy the gents' toilet at the Soho House on a Saturday night.

'Are you joking?' Graeme, the elderly ex-stockbroker, spoke first. 'Traffic jams, knife crime, nowhere to park your car, and those fearful surveillance cameras. Why do you think I moved here?'

'And the constant roadworks,' added Hugh. 'And that Kerry Katona: what do people see in her?' Now lanced, the litany of complaint poured forth. Casual violence, immigration, lack of respect for authority, the rotten education system, post office delivery times, teenage pregnancies: it began to sound like an edition of *The Jeremy Kyle Show*. 'All that binge-drinking culture,' complained one, before going on with barely a pause for breath to criticise high pub prices back home.

'So you don't miss anything?' I asked.

Graeme's face clouded for a moment. 'Beer,' he said quietly. 'I miss a decent pint.' Then, after a moment's reflection: 'And support stockings.'

'Support stockings?'

'Mmm. The ones you get over here have a different weft. It

catches in my leg hairs. They look like a Remington Ladyshave's been on them.' He lifted up his right trouser leg to reveal the trademark pins of an elderly cricketer: varicose veins, mottled skin and the smell of liniment, but unnervingly as smooth as Kate Moss's.

Graeme's observations quickly segued to a wider discussion about France and the French way. A straw poll revealed that the best things about France were the food, the space, the food, the formal politeness of everyone, the food, the weather and the food. But particularly the food.

'You can't eat a bad meal in these parts,' said Hugh enthusiastically. 'It's absolutely impossible. The most bog-standard restaurant in the area is better than anything back home. It puts the English to shame.'

And the worst?

'Can't think of anything,' said Graeme, shaking his head.

We broke off to offer a smattering of applause as the player in the red cap hoisted another towering six into an adjacent field. Eventually Gordon, the one who'd earlier been smouldering by the scoreboard, returned to my enquiry.

'The bureaucracy gets on your tits, I suppose,' he said. 'It drives you up the wall. It takes ages for anything to be sorted, from getting broadband right down to your car repaired.'

After another brief pause, an elderly man wearing a sweater embossed with the logo of Cricket Thailand, who answered to the name of Ernie, spent several minutes vilifying the tax situation over here. 'You have to pay tax on what the authorities predict will be your profit,' he said. 'It's bloody ludicrous. Some years I pay more tax than I actually earn.'

The delivery of goods seemed to touch a raw nerve. 'You ring up to order something, pay in advance, then on the delivery date, after you've stayed in all day, they call up to say it's still in the workshop or some such balls, and in the end you're lucky if it turns up before Christmas. It's bad enough if you're a native, but once you start getting shirty and they hear your English accent come out you may as well go piss up the wall.'

'And you try taking something back to the shop once you've bought it,' added Hugh. 'Consumer rights over here are a joke. If you want to learn some juicy French expletives, just walk in and politely tell them their item isn't fit for purpose.'

'And they don't smile. Ever,' added Wally, a retired accountant from Poole.

'And they never admit they're wrong,' shouted Glyn, a solicitor.

'And they always think that France has nothing to learn from other countries,' added another.

'And the television programmes. Bloody awful. Nothing but game shows and reruns of rubbishy old British detective series.'

I nearly interjected, if only because at some time or another I'd appeared in most of those rubbishy old British detective series. But minute by minute the litany of disadvantages to the dewy-eyed expat life continued to seep out until it started to look like a parody of the 'What have the Romans ever done for us?' sketch.

We'd just got past the flushing mechanisms on French toilets and their infuriating insistence on protocol when a clatter of stumps signified one yahoo too many. I was in: which was a pity, because I was hoping we'd soon get to 'They're all cunts' and I'd have a title for my book.

What an unpredictable trip it was proving to be. To be playing cricket in the Dordogne to the distant soundtrack of the Chipmunks singing 'Ragtime Cowboy Joe'. Who'd have thought it?

My innings was something of a farce. Matting wickets exert a hypnotic effect on me. In England they're associated with practice nets, and anyone who has ever batted in one knows that the natural instinct is to try to hit the ball straight back to the bowler, so time isn't wasted having to retrieve it from coils of netting or distant duck ponds. So it was now, with the result that after half an hour I'd scored only three and was batting to mid-off and mid-on, long-off and long-on, and with a couple more at straight hit. Thankfully my agony was soon over and we wandered off for the interval.

Tea was one event I had been looking forward to. Here, if in nothing else, cricket in France would put the home-grown event to shame, particularly as the nearby town of Périgord was reputed to be the world capital of foie gras.

Thus I was surprised to see Barrington Hancock unwrapping a carton of jam tarts. It was the first industrially packaged food-stuff I'd seen since I arrived in France, but perhaps it was some recherché nod to the world of suburban English cricket they'd thankfully left well behind. 'See if you can track down a packet of jam tarts, Bazza, remind ourselves what the poor saps back home are having to endure.'

But the tarts proved the zenith of the experience. Instead of the plover's eggs on rustic *pain*, the *pâté de campagne* and plat-ters of gently quivering cheeses I'd anticipated, the tea at St Savieure cricket club turned out to be one of the most spectacu-larly bad cricket teas I'd ever had: supermarket bread, flaccid pizza slices, fondant fancies with dry, cracked marzipan edging and fillings like something you'd find in your handkerchief – even those dreaded pork pies injected with industrial-strength pickle. Where on earth had they sourced such awful foodstuffs?

Perhaps there was something more subtle at work here. My companions may have publicly trashed the denuded culture back in the old country, but the delight with which they attacked the Scotch eggs and corned beef suggested a culture perhaps not fully discarded.

Over tea Barrington introduced me, with almost Uriah-Heep deference, to Monty, their star player, he of the hamstrings and the red cap. I soon realised why he held the others in his thrall: a small, squat man, younger than the rest, with an almost impenetrable Nottingham dialect, he'd briefly played in the Yorkshire Leagues before spending several winters with the likes of David Boon and Mark Taylor in grade cricket over in Oz. He'd returned to Mansfield to join the fire service, but following a brush with the business end of an exploding gas canister he'd used his extensive payoff to relocate and was now in blissful semi-retirement. Unless Kevin Pietersen was taking a luxury weekend break for two in Paris, there was a fair chance that the man with whom I was sharing a cheese bap might be the greatest player currently in the country.

Whatever I'd imagined about the organisation of expat life in these parts, I'd obviously underestimated hugely. Details of a hugely sophisticated cricket set-up filtered out during the chit-chat, even down to an umpire's federation (the NUA), leagues, cups, knock-out trophies, dinner dances, conventions and under-XI competitions. Indeed, Barrington himself was going to a meeting of umpires in Paris the following weekend.

Was this normal expat life I was looking at, or something strange and bespoke? Spending your time in the middle of France travelling vast distances to go on umpiring courses when you could have done the same thing for free back in Richmond-on-Thames and had time to pop up the road for the final session at Lords afterwards? It seemed a curious compromise.

THE SECOND HALF of the game took considerably less time than the first. Once Monty brought himself on, he wrapped things up within minutes, taking five quick wickets with fizzing off-breaks and confirming my suspicion that while the set-up was Barrington's pride and joy, it was Monty's plaything.

As the shadows lengthened on a peerless summer's evening, we sat while Monty held court once more, this time with tales of facing Merv Hughes and batting with Ritchie Richardson. For the first time since I arrived, a touch of the real France was allowed in under the door when Ernie produced from the boot of his car several bottles of local red that were (and I speak now as something of a connoisseur) extremely drinkable.

Eventually the chat found its inevitable way back to the bucolic glories of the expat life.

'Well, I wouldn't move back for all the tea in China,' said Monty, uncorking another bottle. 'Me and the missus love it here. Why would I want to live in some Barrett home on a ring road near the A1 when I can sit here and look at this?' He waved his hand expansively to indicate the sun-kissed vistas stretching in every direction. He had a point.

But there was general consensus that you had to do your homework first. All agreed that the most crucial element of relocating here was to learn the language. 'I'm afraid unless you can talk fluent French it's very difficult,' concluded Graeme. 'Think how you'd feel if the boot was on the other foot. Would you want to spend hours trying to converse back home with a neighbour who could only speak French?'

I had to admit, probably not.

I wanted to know more, but with the sun dipping below the trees and the Three Stooges fading fast, it was time to go. While Ric and Lindy strapped them into the van, I retrieved my case from the pavilion and began a collective thank-you for a great day.

But even in those precious thirty seconds I'd been away, something had changed. Heads had turned, hands been thrust back into pockets and coins were copulating once more. Was it my traveller's paranoia, or was their previous air of indifference descending before my eyes like a stage curtain?

What had changed in those precious seconds, of course, was that I'd reminded them I was leaving: not only for other parts of France but ultimately back to Britain. It occurred to me that apart from Ric, not one player from either team had asked me a single question about myself all day: what I was doing here, where I was going next or what I thought of the place. My mere presence was a stark reminder of the compromises the others had made in order to be here.

Had these Rosbifs truly embraced the French lifestyle? In a recent survey of British expats, the Royal Society for Medicine found that 29 per cent of all emigrés admitted to missing the traditional British fried breakfast. I suspect the real figures might be a lot higher.

In the end I departed without ceremony. My final sight was of Barrington, silhouetted in golden evening sunshine against a field of sunflowers, his panama perched on his head like a Scoutmaster's hat, holding forth on the subject of how best to counter Muttiah Muralitharan's doosra.

Lourdes a Merci

I LIKE CHILDREN. After all, I was one myself once. But having never had any of my own, I was unprepared for the week I spent at the farmhouse with Ric and his family. He'd been exaggerating when he warned me I'd be woken at 5 a.m. each day by blows to the head; in fact, it rarely commenced much later than 4.30. I never realised anything with only three heads and twelve limbs could make such so much noise, extrude such copious amounts of waste from every orifice or cause such monumental damage.

That's not to take anything away from the parents. On the contrary, they were, and if they're still alive still are, the most wondrous parents any child could wish for. It's just that looking after three kids, each of whom has realised that if he could only destroy his rivals he'd have three times as much food, toys and attention, is an overwhelming task.

I would have taken to my bed with the strain of it all, except that here I merely became a sitting target. Sooner or later one of the tots would attempt to test the ability of the human skull to absorb directly applied kinetic energy, as applied by a pair of discarded fire irons or play bricks. When, on the third morning, Curly decided to ring the changes by surreptitiously waking me to show off his collection of slugs, I nearly cried with gratitude.

Yet St Savieure was an idyllic spot. Apart from the occasional group of disorientated ramblers or a lumbering farm tractor, the location was completely off the beaten track and wonderfully remote. I sat playing with the kids in their paddling pool for hours on end under limpid skies. With reveille soon after dawn and no TV, radio or internet to break the monotony, the days seemed impossibly long, and I became accomplished in un-familiar pastimes such as playing cards, organising nature trails, building tree houses, and, once the kids were asleep, sitting outside with my hosts in the darkness staring up at a night sky more full of stars than I would have thought it possible to cram into a single hemisphere.

On my last day we went *en famille* to a local municipal camping site-cum-beauty spot known as Les Pins. The location offered a huge lake of crystal-clear water surrounded by ravishing woods, with a small sandy beach, handily positioned sundecks and diving spots, as well as a picnic area, a café and cycle trails.

With the holiday season now in full spate the area was full to bursting with French provincial bourgeoisie by the time we arrived: yet nobody played loud music or dropped litter or went around snapping branches off the trees or shouting, 'Leave it, Kev, it's not worf it…' Everyone just got on with enjoying himself in that formal, slightly detached way that seems to be a trade-mark of French life.

The only eyesore in this otherwise idyllic spot was Barrington Hancock, dressed only in his panama and a pair of flannelette mini tennis shorts, sprawled against a tree a few yards away from our picnic rug with one of his testicles protruding from the bottom of the gusset. I had intended to try once more to engage him in conversation, but decided that having my head held underwater for minutes on end by warring toddlers might be a more life-affirming experience.

All too soon it was time to go. I could sense the dreamy bliss of provincial French life in high summer, with its drowsy hilltop villages and long leisurely lunches, sapping my will to travel. If I didn't pack up and leave now it would ensnare me.

The family dropped me back at Dead Man's Gulch the following Sunday afternoon. As I waited for the train back to Bordeaux, my final sight of the Three Stooges was of them sniffling unhappily through the rear windows at the departing sight of Uncle Simmo. This from three boys who had spent much of the previous five days trying to kill me.

Funny things, kids.

Back in Bordeaux I hit my first shit hole. The Hôtel des Lapins, located in a seedy area adjoining the station, seemed aptly titled, as that's how most people obviously behaved who stayed there.

My room had cigarette burns on the bedspread and stains on the towels. When I tried to use the loo the toilet seat slipped off onto the floor, and the sheets had an unpleasant musk of three hundred different types of men's aftershave. As I was putting out the light I noticed a small, anonymously wrapped package lying on top of the wardrobe just back from the front edge. I stood on the bed and prodded it gingerly with my *Instructions for British Servicemen*. It could have been flour, or sugar, but whatever it was, it wasn't meant for me, and I didn't fancy spending my final hours being pursued by gangsters across the French rail network. So long as the item didn't move about in the middle of the night, I was going to leave well alone.

MY DESTINATION THE next day was Lourdes, the great centre of pilgrimage and one of the most iconic, and icon-filled, locations in the entire nation.

France is sometimes known as the 'eldest daughter of Catholicism', mainly because 77 per cent of its population is estimated to be followers of the faith. Its ninety-eight different dioceses and 23,000 priests are stats that the Catholic Church in England could only dream of.

The vice-like grip it once exerted over affairs both temporal and pastoral may have been prised open in recent decades as successive governments have legislated to separate church and state, but its influence is still enormous. Indeed, some traditional groups are calling for a return to basics, contending that the nation has forgotten its 'divine mission' as a Catholic country.

As regards Lourdes itself, what was once just a rocky wild grotto has now become one of the great pilgrim destinations of the world, principally because of its apparent ability to heal the sick and cure the dying. Since the records began back in 1883, some 7,000 supplicants, of the millions who have been immersed in the famous springwater baths, claim to have benefited from celestial intervention, and although the official figure is a more modest sixty-seven, such is the reputation of Lourdes that it still attracts visitors in considerable numbers each year. The small matter of six million of them, in fact.

The last accepted 'miracle' was declared as recently as 2005, when an Italian woman with severe heart disease, Anna Santiella, was carried to the baths on a stretcher, and left walking unaided on her own two feet. In fact, she'd made her visit back in 1952, which by my reckoning means they took some fifty-three years to come to a decision on the matter of whether it was a miracle. Yet even now dozens of seriously ill people leave the grotto convinced they have been cured. Thus it has become both a place of immense hope and comfort to those requiring its particular magic, and a source of suspicion and pity to anyone who doesn't.

Not being a Catholic, I had little to go on apart from anecdotes from parents of friends, but the mere fact that this medium-sized town in the far south-west of the country had more hotels than anywhere else outside Paris spoke more eloquently than anything about its importance in French cultural life; and as it was about to celebrate its 150th anniversary, with no less a personage than Pope Benedict himself due to appear in little over a month's time, my visit there could scarcely be better timed. If six million individuals thought it worthwhile to travel all that way for a dip, it had to be worth a couple of days of my own itinerary.

The train from Bordeaux to Lourdes was delayed, and I passed much of the time waiting for it by following signs on the station forecourt to *les toilettes*, a process that entailed following the same loop up and down the same escalators for nearly twenty minutes, until a kind official pointed out that *les toilettes* were actually in entirely the other direction.

When my train finally arrived it was an hour late and the platforms were in chaos. In the end I merely made a beeline for the train that had the most nuns. I sat in a cramped compartment full of chattering families. With no room even to open a paperback, there was little to do but study my fellow passengers, and I found myself trying to work out which of them might be ill enough to contemplate a pilgrimage.

That little baby over there across the aisle, for instance, being dandled on its mother's knee. She looked healthy enough, and she certainly had a fine pair of lungs on her, but was her parents' amiable demeanour masking some darker purpose? Or that woman with dyed brunette hair in an enormous frizz, cradling three fingers wrapped in a bandage? That'll teach her to poke her fingers in electric sockets.

Or what about the man opposite me? Perhaps his peptic disposition and his gesture of offering everyone around him except me a Polo mint was borne of some deep psychological anxiety that only Lourdes could solve.

By the time we reached the city of Pau, thirty kilometres from our destination, I'd decided everyone in the carriage had a contagious disease. As if reading my thoughts, the guard entered the carriage and turfed everyone out. The authorities, needing the locomotive back in Paris, had decided to decant the entire population onto a replacement bus service for the final leg of the journey. It was almost like being back in Britain.

It was pouring with rain by this time. I managed to store my luggage in the hold of three successive motor coaches already positioned outside for our arrival, only to find that by the time I'd struggled round to the front there were no seats left. I found a berth on the final vehicle, but by then the barrier to the station car park had malfunctioned in the deluge, and we sat in a rapidly misting coach for a further half-hour. I was going to need a miracle to get to Lourdes at this rate.

It was nearly 6 p.m. before we arrived. Although the rain had stopped, a low bank of cloud had crept down from the encircling hillsides and Lourdes was dank and shrouded in a clinging mist. I needed to get out of my damp clothes and have a bath, so I wandered into the first decent hotel I came across, a large, gloomy building with ornate balconies by the main bridge into town, called, appropriately, the Splendide.

The signs were promising: a bright foyer liberally decorated with comfy sofas and cacti in plastic pots. Sitting at the front desk playing computer patience was an elderly man with one of the ten worst toupees I'd ever seen. It was as if a coconut husk had dropped on his head. I stared desperately into his eyes, and by force of will managed to keep them there while I asked if he could offer me a *chambre avec douche* for *deux nuits*?

My query seemed to strike a humorous chord with him, as he burst into laughter before replying happily that indeed he had. So hearty was his response that for a moment I wondered if I'd perhaps committed some ghastly solecism in his native tongue. But when I requested to see the room before confirming my booking he started cackling again, and was still shaking with laughter three floors later as he unlocked the door. A final hilarious rib-tickler, in this case reciting the digits on my credit card, and I was home and dry.

My new home was a huge high-ceilinged room, furnished with items of massive oaken furniture, whose walls were decorated by framed prints of scowling cardinals. But it had a double bed and a pleasing balcony looking directly down onto the main street, which I noted was itself liberally sprinkled with nuns all streaming into town. Within minutes I was lying happily on the bed among the cardinals watching the TV.

THE STORY OF how Lourdes became the pilgrim site it is today is well known, but it's worth a brief resumé. In 1858, a young maiden named Bernadette was fetching wood from this anonymous garrison town near the Spanish border when she looked up into a nearby grotto and saw, about thirty feet up, the image of a lady dressed in white and wearing a blue sash, who later told her she was the Immaculate Conception.

Over the following couple of weeks, Bernadette had seventeen more visitations from this apparition, with each visit attended by more and more locals as word spread. The apparition gave strict instructions for the young girl to eat the grass growing there, and to go to the spring where she was to take a drink and wash herself. Even by her last encounter, thousands of people were crowding in after her.

Such is the legend. What is certain is that from that moment, people started claiming miraculous cures for illness and infirmity, and the fame of Lourdes was assured. Nowadays the Catholic Church steers well clear of such claims, stressing instead the individual's connection with Christ in all things and rebranding the site as a place of affirmation and pilgrimage. To make their point, they've even removed the display of discarded crutches and callipers that until recently adorned the walls of the famous grotto.

According to one source, forty cases are presented to medical officers for consideration for miracle status every year. Is that why so many people still travelled here hopefully? I decided to begin my investigations at the Cross of Jerusalem pizza house.

In the event I went for the healthy option: chicken and salad, but it was a truly terrible meal, the sort of thing only tourist traps can come up with. However this poor animal had died, its execution had been enough to send every muscle in his body rigid with fear. Yet every cloud has a silver lining, for as I stared mournfully out into the street, I saw an intriguing sight.

It was nuns holding chips. Or at least, the paper cones in which chips normally come. At first just a trickle in ones and twos, marching purposefully past the pizza house down the rue de la Grotto towards some unknown destination, all of them clutching cones. And all determined not to be late.

I leaned across and asked the only other diner, an elderly priest who would have been a dead cert if the life story of Alastair Sim were ever filmed, what the commotion was. Father

Alphonse was from Verdun and was here with a party of pilgrims from his diocese. After wiping his lips on a napkin, he began a stuttering response. I noticed a book lying on the table in front of him, *Le Sacrement pour Les Maladies*. Obviously he'd visited the restaurant before.

'C'est une...' he began. He made little walking motions with his fingers across the tablecloth before miming an action that seemed to suggest his hand was on fire.

'La promenade d'illumination?'

'C'est ça!' he announced delightedly, and raised a glass of watery rosé in triumph. I thanked Father Alphonse, settled up and set off after the nuns.

The rue de la Grotto itself was a brightly lit, bustling sort of street that wound steeply downwards before disappearing intriguingly round a corner. Shops and businesses fringed both pavements and even at this time of night were doing a roaring trade with an astonishing medley of mementos and knick-knacks. I was already braced for Immaculate Conception key rings and scent bottles. But Bernadette's grotto glass snow-storms? Or Lourdes baseball hats? Here the devoted could buy almost anything they could fit in a suitcase. Even the suitcase. One of the most popular items was the Bernadette of Lourdes plastic jerry can, the sort of thing you buy when your local water treatment works fails. Anything was possible in the rue de la Grotto.

At the bottom it turned sharply left, whereupon it opened out onto an elegant bridge looking down on a foaming weir. Here I found myself staring at something which, if not an apparition, certainly defied logical explanation.

About 2,000 metres ahead, at the end of a long oval lawn, was the castle from Disneyland: a huge, crennellated chateau with tall towers spiralling upwards and ending in neat little cones, each with banners flying on top. From somewhere on the battlements, loudspeakers were broadcasting a tremulous male voice singing a chorus of 'Ave Maria', although had he been singing 'When You Wish Upon A Star' it wouldn't have seemed out of place.

I was looking at the Basilica of the Immaculate Conception, built on an outcrop of solid rock in the grand Gothic style and consecrated in 1876. It was both absurd and incongruous, and yet, framed by lowering hills, themselves silhouetted against an angry sky, there was something thrillingly theatrical about it. And in front, still many metres away but advancing steadily towards me along one side of the lawn, was another extraordinary visitation.

There are an estimated 45 million Catholics in France, and most of them were walking towards me at a steady two miles an hour. They came in all shapes and sizes, all of them carrying paper cones, now illuminated from inside by tiny pea bulbs.

The first ones to pass me were mostly elderly folk being pulled along in huge, old-fashioned invalid carriages with retractable rubber rain hoods by straining nurses, with yet others pushing lustily at the rear. The scene looked like the Charge of the Light Brigade as performed by Age Concern. The occupants were swathed in blankets and anoraks. Some waved at me as they passed, while others seemed impossibly caught up in thoughts at which I could only guess.

Behind followed thousands more pilgrims carrying illuminated signs and decorative banners. In among the French, a contingent of Scotsmen in matching tartan kilts from the diocese of Motherwell strode past, followed by another in slacks and T-shirts from Salford, then a gathering in garish robes from Kenya.

They were followed by a fair selection of the country's 22,000 priests, then more from Italy and Eastern Europe, more nuns, teenagers in cycling shorts, yet more invalids, troops of Scouts and Guides, and, bringing up the rear, thousands more anonymous pedestrians: families, parents with sleeping toddlers, backpackers, tourists and locals.

Many carried photographs or tiny flags announcing the name of the family member whose circumstances had brought them here. So many were processing that by the time those at the rear had reached me, the ones in the front had already processed back to the basilica and were driving off in motor coaches towards their hotels.

It was an extraordinary scene. On and on it went, until I realised it was nearly dark. I'd been here well over an hour and still they came. The scene now more resembled something out of Narnia: countless pea bulbs shimmered towards me on one side of the esplanade before curling away back towards the steps of the basilica whence they'd come. Up on the battlements, thousands more gathered on walkways and balconies. One young woman carrying a sleeping infant in her arms responded to the voice of the trembling priest to 'confess our sins before God' by lighting the child's candle for him. I found my eyes unexpectedly pricking with tears.

All sorts of puerile questions swirled around in my head. Where did all these people stay? What happened if the hotel elevators broke down? Where were all these carriages stashed when they weren't being used? Who starched all those nurses' pinnies every evening? And, most puzzling of all, how on earth had everybody managed to get here for such a huge one-off parade on a Monday evening? And why? Lourdes was indeed a place of miracles.

I reached into my pocket to retrieve my notebook and

brushed against a young woman standing next to me. 'Sorry,' I said without thinking.

'It's very beautiful,' she replied. That brief phrase immediately betrayed my companion as someone from near Rochdale.

'I'm only glad I was here tonight to see it,' I said.

'Oh yes,' she agreed. 'They always put on a good spread. Mind you, it was better last night. Warmer.'

'Last night?'

'At the torchlight procession. It happens every evening about now, summer or winter. Is this your first time?'

I admitted it was. She nodded and we watched in silence for some moments. I remarked how powerful the sight of so much faith and devotion was to a casual spectator, and all the more so if indeed this was a nightly occurrence. Yet not always in quite these numbers, surely?

'Oh yes,' she replied. 'In fact, this evening's a bit down. The rain, you see.'

This was her fourth trip to watch the parade in as many days. This simple fact presaged a deluge of statistics. It was her forty-eighth pilgrimage, the Pope's imminent visit would be her forty-ninth, and she'd be back at Christmas for the big five-oh. 'It just gets to you,' she concluded.

We watched again, lost in our thoughts, the only sound the padding of sensible footwear and the squeaking of axles overlaid by hushed singing. I asked my companion what it was about Lourdes that appealed to her.

'It's very special. It's as if Bernadette was standing next to me. You'll see what I mean if you visit the grotto. And whatever you do, don't miss the early morning mass. That's marvellous. You'll find the Way of the Cross is a wonderful experience too: you can collect stickers along the course and if you complete the circuit it counts as an indulgence. It's very special.' She ended our conversation by inviting me to accompany her in joining the end of the procession. Instead I shook her hand and wished her a peaceful trip.

As she left she reached into her bag and produced a small paperback guide, which she pressed into my hand.

'Whatever you do, bathe in the spring. It has miraculous powers. God bless.' With that, she melded into the processors.

I SAT UP long into the night reading her impromptu gift. The wind had got up and was slapping the window shutters back and forth, and what with the heavy furniture and the panel of ancient cardinals scrutinising me from the walls, it was an eerie interlude. The book was part religious tract, part gazetteer; it explained everything, from the location of disabled toilets to some of life's most profound unanswered questions.

Chapter two was particularly interesting, defining the necessary criteria for a miracle and explaining the complex procedure by which the authorities ensure they don't mistake divine intervention for simply a period in remission. In fact, a new category of 'authentic healing' is being contemplated – or 'miracle-lite' as it has become known – by which those who benefit from startling recovery can share their spiritual and physical experience without its precise cause being picked to bits by doctrinal professors.

There were so many things to do and see in Lourdes it was difficult to know how best to use my available time: tombs, crypts, services, blessings, processions, even a cinema showing continuous movies detailing the events of the young saint's life. A visit to Bernadette's grotto was de rigueur, but the attendance at Holy Mass was something that, as a non-Catholic, I was uneasy about.

A bathe in the holy waters of Lourdes, however, would be perfect and when I read that the temperature of the water is extremely cold, 'rarely rising above 15 degrees centigrade', that decided it. Given the fact it takes me nearly fifteen minutes to pluck up courage to get into my local swimming baths at Swiss Cottage, a dip in these chilling depths would be the nearest thing to a penance I could imagine.

At breakfast the next morning my only companions were a family of Mexicans. One of their number, by the look of her the parents' eldest daughter, had obviously suffered some incapacity and sat motionless as her parents fed her croissants piece by piece, washed down with tiny sips of coffee from a special flask administered by her mother.

The plight of this beautiful girl and her anxious parents was all too manifest. Despite her obvious torpor she was beautifully dressed in brand new garments and shoes, one of them even with the price tag still on the back, while her newly washed hair hung down in luxurious ringlets. The father too wore a crisply pressed suit and his hair was heavily pomaded.

This was palpably a huge day for them, one on which they were pinning many months – perhaps even years – of hopes. As they passed me, the daughter labouring along with difficulty supported by her siblings, I found myself smiling at them and nodding my head in acknowledgement of their plight. The father grimaced nervously back, and I tried to convey some fatuous expression of tacit hope for their prayers to be answered.

Outside it was a beautiful day. I took a circuitous route through the town, feeling the warm sunshine on my back and enjoying the sense of quiet purpose. Even at this early hour the cafés were full and in the distance a tiny funicular railway was already grinding up a hillside towards a distant summit with a cargo of excited picnickers.

Eventually my steps took me back to where I'd stood the previous night, a spot known as the Domaine, and ambled along the same esplanade towards the basilica. Groups of pilgrims were having their photos taken, while on an open-air stage a group of senior French bishops administered the sacrament to an army of Girl Guides. One of the clerics had already succumbed to the warm sunshine, his mitre lying drunkenly across his forehead as he dozed.

I joined a long queue standing in the shadow of a huge rocky outcrop. Unless there was the mother of all ice-cream vans round the corner, this was obviously the end of the queue to see the grotto.

Patrice was from Grenoble. Like me, he was waiting to see the place where the original apparition occurred, but unlike me he was here by default. He'd come because his grandmother hadn't been able to make the journey herself and he'd decided it would be a pity to waste the ticket. I explained somewhat awkwardly that I was a Lourdes virgin, and asked what I might expect at the grotto, but he seemed nonplussed by my question and began riffling through his own gazetteer as if looking for the answer.

Our destination was still lost from view, though in front of it a man wearing dungarees on a stepladder was removing hundreds of guttering votive candles from a huge wrought-iron candelabra and replacing them with fresh ones: carefully sweeping out the wax drippings with an old-fashioned dustpan and brush before lighting their replacements with an automatic barbecue lighter. From somewhere the sound of gentle choral singing carried on the breeze, but as we drew nearer the murmur of voices stilled until, with only a few yards to go, an overwhelming sense of silence fell upon everyone, the only sounds the distant tolling of a church bell and the scuffing of the cleaner's brush.

As we rounded the bend beneath the overhang, those in front of me seemed overwhelmed. Some kissed the rock, some touched it reverentially, while one woman in front of me simply ran her fingers along the fissures as if searching for a billet-doux.

Thirty feet above us, framed by foliage, and hardly big enough for a child to sit in, was the grotto itself where the mysterious apparition of the lady had first appeared. It was not so much a cave as a shallow alcove, but in case we were in any doubt, a plaster statue of the Virgin Mary had been plonked at the lip of the opening behind a dusty pane of glass.

It seemed a pity, a throwback to the Joan of Arc museum, as if the authorities lacked confidence in our powers of imagination. Below the effigy, a tiny rivulet of water was trickling down the rock face, and many in front of me scooped up droplets of it and anointed themselves on the forehead before making the sign of the cross.

A brief moment to gape up at it all and we were back out in the sunshine. I took a seat among some benches facing the statue, and watched the procession as it shuffled ever forwards. A woman sitting next to me was carrying a garish reproduction encased in bubble wrap. Her lower lip was trembling. The atmosphere was an odd one, almost mild euphoria, something I hadn't felt before.

Or had I? Was my misty remembrance of something similar an indication of a previous existence? I sat trying to recall when I'd felt like this before: the flowers, the incense, the candle wax, the vast yet silent crowds, the sense of patient forbearance, of waiting for something to happen, knowing all eventually would unfold. Then I realised: it was the eve of Princess Diana's funeral.

That week of collective mayhem, when the whole world was knee-deep in flowers and lachrymose reflection. I'd succumbed to it myself, spending much of the Friday night in Hyde Park with my own little candle, and howling uncontrollably at the television coverage the next morning. I'd even hurried up to the Finchley Road after the ceremony to strew some flowers on her funeral cortege as it trundled towards the M1. All this for a woman I'd lampooned for her vacuous and self-serving lifestyle. If I could become so entranced by something so fleeting back then, then goodness knows the power of suggestion at work within these illustrious precincts.

It was time to bathe. A signpost directed me towards the piscines, and I followed a party of Americans wearing T-shirts declaring 'Welcome To Butterfield City' as they pushed their formidable stomachs through the crowds.

At Lourdes, queuing is all part of the spiritual practice. So many are here that everything takes hours to sample, from waiting for a café table to attending the major sites. Here too, in front of the piscines, a queue of men already stood waiting at a metal gate. The baths were closed for lunch and wouldn't even be open for nearly an hour, yet more were joining at every minute.

I stood patiently in the sunshine reading the gazetteer. There were apparently seventeen baths, with the water coming directly from a holy spring at a rate of nine gallons a minute. 'Such is demand, it is very unlikely the casual caller will be able to participate' warned the literature. Oh well, I had no other plans anyway.

At 2 p.m. sharp the barriers were swung back and we crowded through, zigzagging between a series of barriers to a long line of wooden benches in the shade. I found myself next to Frank, an amiable Irishman from Galway with thinning hair, dressed in a short-sleeve shirt and slacks and with his feet encased in both sandals and socks.

Frank had that sort of Forrest Gump innocence whereby you couldn't decide if he was a profound philosopher or merely a sticker short of an indulgence. He assured me I'd better prepare myself for a long wait. 'You may not be gettin' in at all,' he warned. 'There are lots of poorly folk and they're brought to the head of the queue. I waited here eight and a half hours on Monday and only just got in as they were closin'.'

'You've done this before?'

'Oh, I always take the immersin',' he said mildly. 'This'll be my third time this week.'

I asked him why he felt the need to bathe with such frequency.

He considered for a moment. 'It passes the time,' he concluded.

'At any event it must be a marvellous experience.'

'Well, I don't know about that,' he replied.

We sat in the shade. He offered me a square of his Kinder Ballisto chocolate and we sat munching in silence. The seats around us were now crammed to bursting with men from all countries, fat Italian grandfathers, swarthy Spanish peasants, American businessmen, backpackers, all talking quietly or lost in thought. Some pushed worry beads back and forth between their fingers. Each time a fresh contingent of supplicants was ushered through into the baths, we stood and shoved up a bit like some giant party game. As we neared our turn, Frank sensed I was becoming anxious.

'You've a good weight on yer,' he said reassuringly. 'You'll survive.' But as he spoke a contingent of the sickest-looking men I'd ever seen was wheeled past us on creaking trolleys and placed at the head of the queue. An inscription on the back of one announced, 'In loving memory of Timothy O'Leary.' What on earth were these individuals doing allowing themselves to be dunked in freezing water on a beautiful day like this?

But of course I already knew the answer. The baths are the epicentre of what Lourdes has to offer. And God knows there was plenty of evidence to suggest that immense good might come from my experience.

The spring's first and most famous success was a certain Gabriel Gargam, a postal sorter who, as a result of a train crash, lay wounded and bleeding for seven hours in a snowdrift. Within weeks he was a living skeleton, taking nourishment only by tube and with an advanced case of gangrene. He was taken to the very baths I sat before now, and so ill was he that on the way back up the esplanade after bathing he was given the last rites. Yet within a hundred yards he'd sat upright, climbed from the stretcher and walked back to his hotel, whereupon he demolished a hearty meal for the first time in two years.

We Brits have achieved even more spectacular success. Most famously in the case of John Traynor, a Royal Marine, who had the affliction that has been the saviour of many a music hall act, in that he was shot in the Dardanelles. By the time he arrived at Lourdes in 1923 for his own miracle, his condition made the aforementioned Gargam look like Charles Atlas, Traynor being completely disabled 'with an inch-wide hole in the skull through which the brain could be seen pulsating'.

Nonetheless, having bathed no less than nine separate times, he leapt from his hospital bed later that night and ran full tilt back to the grotto to give thanks to God. He ended up as a coal merchant, lifting 200-pound bags of nutty slack as if they were feather pillows. Nine times, eh? Perhaps my companion, the mild-mannered Frank, had more wisdom than I'd given him credit for.

As I read all these intriguing anecdotes I tried to think good thoughts. Yet the fact was, whatever magical properties surrounded these baths and however obvious the piety and integrity of the army of helpers ministering to the sick and dying, dread and shameful thoughts were beginning to rise within me.

I simply didn't want to share a bath of water, holy or otherwise, with people suffering such manifest infirmity. Surely these individuals needed urgent medical help, not plunging in freezing water. Yet a sense of profound guilt for nursing such shallow sentiments overwhelmed me. I turned nervously to Frank and asked him to reiterate what was likely to happen.

'Well now…' he said thoughtfully, 'you'll be inside quite quickly now. You strip, after which you'll be led down into the water. They're very gentle.'

'Naked?'

'Well, you sort of keep your pants on. They're very discreet.' He chuckled to himself. 'Of course there are no towels, so you are proper wet when you come out. But it's an odd thing; you're not really wet. I mean, you're wet but somehow you don't feel it. It's difficult to explain. You just put your clothes on and come out again. That's all there is to it.'

Progress seemed impossibly slow. The sheer weight of numbers was extraordinary. Yet just when I thought I was going to be lucky or unlucky, according to how you view such things, all at once events gathered pace. A man dressed as a swimming-pool lifeguard beckoned for another batch, and I suddenly found myself inside.

I was standing in a dank corridor that was clad in white ceramic tiles. Facing me were a number of shower curtains stretched across individual booths, and other lifeguards were already dispensing people through into the interiors in ones and twos. From somewhere I could hear the sound of sloshing water and trolleys being disassembled. A strangled voice cried out in pain, and further along somebody shouted, 'Holy Mary Mother of God!' in a shrill tone.

I caught a brief glimpse of Frank at the far end: he was already unbuckling his trouser belt. Before I could call out I was shepherded into a tiny changing room housing a number of glum, desiccated-looking men. Some were disrobing, others sat quietly dripping, while others were clambering gingerly back into their jeans, huge damp stains already spreading underneath their shirtfronts.

I hung up my own clothes as best I could and sat sheepishly in my underwear. From somewhere the sound of singing now mixed with the violent gurgling of water escaping though complaining pipework.

The attendant beckoned me forward. I stood up, picked my way across the floor and stepped through a vinyl curtain. On the other side was a small chamber about the size of a small garage. Before me, set into the floor, was a mini version of the sort of communal bath in which you normally see frolicking rugby players. The water looked murky and chill. My only companions, apart from a tiny statue of the Divine Apparition on a shelf at the far end, were three teenage boys in smocks and aprons who stood around the perimeter of the bath.

The leader looked about fourteen and had a startling resemblance to a young Andy Murray. He stepped towards me holding out an already sopping towel. 'Please, take off your slip,' he said simply.

I gripped the elastic of my Y-fronts, bent over and pulled them down, the pious discretion of my young helper's discreet head-turn only adding to my embarrassment. For a split second I stood there, foolishly naked. The assistant took the garment from my outstretched hand, while simultaneously one of his colleagues wrapped the sodden towel round me like a winding sheet. It was wet, cold and deeply unappealing.

'Please, now you bathe,' he said, indicating the cloudy depths. I took a deep breath and, still wrapped in the towel, waded down the steps. It was icy. My young mentor followed me in and stood facing me, the water now sloshing over our thighs. 'Please. You sit.'

I slumped down heavily on my buttocks, causing a mini tidal wave that slapped against the far end of the bath. The water was now round my neck, grey and cloudy. Before I could protest two hands were gripping my shoulders and pressing gently but firmly down. Instantly I was underwater, and just as suddenly came up spluttering. Even as I framed the words, 'Thanks, I'll be certain to tell all my friends,' I was submerged again. And a third time. Then strong arms reached underneath me, lifted me up and I was on my feet once more.

'Now you say a prayer if you wish.' All three teenagers indicated the statue and looked at me expectantly. Say a prayer? What prayer? It may have been the extreme cold, but the only incantation my fuddled brain could think of was 'Izzy wizzy, let's get busy'. Yet their look of benign anticipation brooked no argument. I couldn't disappoint.

I launched into a whispered jumble of rhubarb and tried not to catch the Apparition's eye. This is how John Redwood must have felt at the Welsh Conservative conference that time he was invited to sing their Cym Rhonda and was left mouthing helplessly like a goldfish. Throughout I found myself avoiding the statue's glassy gaze. I was out of my depth in more ways than one, and I was abashed to be busking so disrespectfully in such circumstances.

Thankfully my furtive murmurings seemed to satisfy my hosts, and within seconds I was out and forcing my sopping limbs back through the leg holes. My Y-fronts immediately went transparent and my carefully held-in paunch was now flopping uselessly over the top of the waist. Moments later I was back in the anteroom.

The act of scrambling, still soaking wet, into my day clothes would have been the most disagreeable incident of my trip to date if it hadn't just been beaten into second place. Whatever Frank had said about the water not feeling wet afterwards was just one of many mystic singularities about the place that seemed to have passed me by. I escaped as quickly as I could and within seconds was gently steaming in the sunshine.

Pushing between the wheelchairs and the nurses, apologising curtly and hating myself more than I could recall for cursing the occupants and their blundering contraptions, I lunged ever forwards towards some open space and fresh air. I'd had enough. I'd had enough of illness and death and hope and pretending to be a supplicant while all the time I hadn't the first clue as to what I was doing.

It was disrespectful to them, and somehow also to me. The wonderfully stoic optimism and belief in things beyond our power was something I'd hoped to pick up by being among them for a few hours, but now I realised it was the wrong way round. Lourdes only had resonance if you had some idea of what it and you were here for.

And yet my frustration was tinged with disappointment. As Diana's funeral had shown, or Circus Bouglione, or any rerun of *Brief Encounter* on afternoon telly, I was at heart an old romantic who yielded willingly to anything a bit mystical or heartfelt. I'd even burst into tears at my first sight of the Taj Mahal. And today I'd wanted to be transported into whatever it was that held so many others in its thrall: yet I remained inexorably on the outside, as if peering in through a window.

The fortitude and cheerfulness of so many of the ill and elderly gathered round me was profoundly moving in itself, of course, and I was humbled and impressed by their faith: but these were single vignettes, the indomitable force of the human spirit in difficult circumstances that you could see in almost any place on earth. I could marvel and be moved by the steadfastness of these people's gaze. But I couldn't pretend to know what they were looking at.

That evening I found the liveliest bar I could manage, one near the weir with pavement tables and bustling waiters. Football was playing on a large satellite screen and the place was full to bursting with Scouts and Guides, now in their civvies and enjoying a few drinks and a flirt and a good laugh. The energy around me was fortifying, and I couldn't envisage either them or me ever needing to come back forty-eight times. Of course, I had no need of divine intervention, or at least not yet. It might one day come. But in the meantime I wanted to move on.

I set about following the example of those lucky few who had received unexpected benefit from their endeavours here, by sampling a hearty meal, and I was just tackling a large slice of *tarte aux pommes à la crème fraîche* when I received a call from Julia.

She'd just opened that day's post. Among it was a cheque forwarded via my agent for the sale of a long-forgotten BBC TV kids series in which I'd once appeared. It seemed Australia and

New Zealand had been blessed with my 24 episodes of Mister Grumble the Park-keeper.

For which I'd apparently been blessed with an unexpected cheque for just under two thousand quid.

Hide and Chic

ONE OF THE most dismaying things about being both English and male is suffering continual derogatory comparisons with our Gallic cousins. The average Englishman has a genetic reputation for both sporting and sexual incompetence leavened by stoicism, necessarily in that order. The French, by contrast, do not.

When we triumph on the field it's usually a result of grinding out a narrow win against the run of play. 'It wasn't pretty but I gave it my all. I was here to smother their natural game and come away with a point.' And our sporting metaphors equally apply in the bedroom.

The principal components of French sporting manhood are flair, élan and amour propre. Englishmen always somehow manage to look like a conference of middle-management quantity surveyors on a team-building exercise. Could anything be more explicit than Tim Henman's fist clench after each successful point over many weary years of Wimbledon failure? Heartfelt and meaningful in its own way, but inevitably more in keeping with a sixth-former completing a particularly difficult jigsaw than a testosterone-fuelled inter-national sporting superstar.

Even our names seemed to be parodies of the sort of charac-ters in a *Carry On* film: Crouch, Grewcock, Sidebottom. Names redolent of balding men with overfull bedpans shuffling up and down hospital corridors in flannel pyjamas.

But the French? Hearing John Inverdale reading out the names of the French Rugby Union team before a recent international was in itself enough to provoke the nearest thing to arousal I'd known for some time: Dusautoir, Bonnaire, Harinordoquy… images of chiselled poets with five o'clock shadows smoking Gitanes while they waited for their lovers to arrive with a bottle of absinthe and an unsheathed stiletto.

The Roman city of Arles in the Camargue is famous for being where Vincent van Gogh cut off his ear and the birthplace of the Gipsy Kings, but I was going there to sample the most daring manifestation of French manliness: the Course Camarguaise, or bull racing. The sport is a first cousin of the more famous Spanish version, but whereas in Spain the protagonists are preening dandies who demonstrate their virility by plunging vicious swords into hapless beasts already weakened beforehand, the bull-racing *raseteurs* of the Camargue compete on equal terms.

Dressed only in T-shirts and jeans, their aim is simply to get close enough to the charging beast to pluck the small woollen tassels attached to its horns without getting half a metre of compressed hair driven through their upper bowel. At one time all sorts of items used to be suspended from the creatures, including, at one point in the development of the sport, strings of sausages.

The only weapon these daring young *hommes* have at their disposal, apart from their agility and speed, is a small hooked metal *crochet*, resembling a knuckleduster, with which they cut the ribbons holding the tassels.

Arles can claim to be the true home of the sport. It began as a simple farm game when workers and staff enjoyed teasing and fighting with the bulls, although the earliest recorded official tournament took place in 1402 with a race to honour Count Louis II of Provence. Unlike Spanish bulls, which are heavy, slow-moving creatures bred so their horns are turned downwards, allowing easy access to the cranium for plunging steel, Camargue bulls are quick, agile, intelligent, and have horns pointing directly at your midriff. They're also bred to be murderously cheesed off by the time they enter the ring. Some, like the legendary Goya, the greatest denim-ripper of them all, have statues erected to their memory when they eventually peg out. Game on.

The rewards for the tassel-pluckers are a few hundred euros. Failure, on the other hand, can easily result in serious injury or even paralysis, as witnessed by the case of Didier Abellan, once an undoubted superstar of the sport but now confined to a wheelchair after being skewered in the spine during a tourney at nearby Nîmes.

Such is the reputation of the leading exponents that they're worshipped locally as much as Formula One racing drivers, with access to the best restaurant tables and the prettiest girlfriends. Their exploits are daring, brave, chic and utterly Gallic: and I wanted to see for myself. With luck there may even be a half-day course I could join, even if it were a few goes at picking fluff off a nice piece of sirloin steak.

MY COMPANIONS FOR the three-hour journey on the TGV towards Arles were nothing if not cosmopolitan. Andre from San Francisco was on his way to a three-week-long Buddhist retreat, and sharing the compartment with us were an exquisitely beautiful young couple, Delphine from Poitiers and her boyfriend Bertrand from Brussels.

We'd no sooner struck up conversation than we were joined by a pert young Hawaiian girl named Waleila (meaning peaceful river), who seemed desperate for some English-speaking company after several weeks on the road by herself.

It was a chance remark by Andre that started the ball rolling. Hearing I was an actor (I somehow appear to have dropped it into the conversation soon after looking into Delphine's huge, almond eyes), he asked what shows he should check out when visiting London later in the month. My suggestion that he take in the imminent revival of the musical *Piaf* at the Donmar Warehouse spawned a discussion about which individual most represented their country's national characteristics in the eyes of the rest of the world.

I assumed the Little Sparrow of Pigalle would be a certainty for France, but Delphine giggled when I suggested her, as if I were some old uncle reminiscing about Gracie Fields. Her boyfriend Bertrand hadn't even heard of the woman. In the end they settled for a split decision between Zinedine Zidane and a TV presenter I hadn't come across called Michel Drucker.

For Belgium's icon it turned into a close-run thing between Tintin, Jacques Brel and Hercule Poirot, although without the candidacy of several leading paedophiles it was difficult to think of anyone else to put in contention. Then we got to the United States. Despite Waleila's forceful advocacy for Wal-Mart (I had an idea she wasn't the brightest button in the box), Andre pronounced it to be Ronald McDonald, though he expected Barack Obama to overtake him if we had the same conversation next year.

And what of dear old Blighty? Winston Churchill had recently won a BBC poll as the greatest Briton, but if anything his name provoked blanker faces than Piaf. Waleila even asked if he was a member of Oasis. In the end I was outvoted as the others agreed it was a combination of Amy Winehouse and the Queen. I pride myself on a vivid imagination, but even I was silenced by that one.

Waleila got off at Nîmes, and Andre at Montpellier. The others fell into a fitful doze, and I turned to watch the countryside unfold in the afternoon sunshine. Verdant fields gave way to plains of stagnant water. We sped along a high ridge with the countryside spread before us like a scene in a model railway exhibition: neat fields, lines of vivid trees and tiny matchbox vans pottering along country highways. I wouldn't have been surprised if a pair of celestial hands had appeared through the clouds clutching a giant soldering iron.

I WAS ALREADY prepared for the fact that the *office de tourisme* would have closed fifteen minutes before I arrived at Arles – it was obviously an ancient custom designed to test the fortitude of visitors to their country – but outside the station things were even bleaker: no taxis, no buses, nobody to assist except a road sweeper dozing under a nearby tree.

My attempts to communicate with him ('Ou est la vache?') while miming the action of a charging bull had him reaching anxiously for his sweeping brush and I was forced to retreat. All I could see were sections of half-finished roads leading to a distant roundabout, which itself offered nothing but access to a sweltering car park. Whatever I was looking for, I wasn't going to find it here.

It's funny the way your luck can change. Just as I was about to abandon my scheme and take refuge in the nearest bar, I ran into Paulina and Yannis. She was from Lyon but lived in America and spoke English with an attractive lilt, while her boyfriend, a large cumbersome young man with a lantern jaw, sported an exotic dialect, part Greek, part Texan. Try to imagine Demis Roussos impersonating George W. Bush. When I asked them where they were going, she simply put her fingers above her forehead. 'We've come to see the bull racing.'

Her intervention soon brought results I could only have dreamt of. The road sweeper assured her that not only was there an event this very evening, but that if we were quick we'd catch the second half. We hurried off.

On the far side of the roundabout stood a huge and impossibly ancient archway, beyond which I glimpsed something out of the back lot for *I, Claudius*. We were soon climbing a narrow street, surrounded by crumbling alleyways and baking courtyards. I half expected to see Brian Blessed in a toga approaching round every street corner, but I was keeping my fingers crossed: after all, it was now all going so well.

And then we heard it. A scratchy, heavily amplified LP blaring out 'March of the Toreador' at full volume over the rooftops. The steep alleyway we were ascending was funnelled up a flight of honey-coloured steps. There, at the top, was a vast Roman amphitheatre. A moment later the roar of ten thousand ecstatic spectators shouting '**TORRO!!!**' billowed out through its open windows, sending flocks of pigeons scattering into the air.

But the crowd was already streaming out. '*La fin, la fin?*' I asked desperately as they pushed past. For one terrible moment it seemed we'd missed the whole caboodle, but again Paulina came to my aid, quickly establishing it was only the interval and that there were still three more races to come. All we had to do now was get a ticket.

A burly steward smoking a roll-up and with a mobile phone clamped to his ear stood between us and our goal. He was deep in conversation and responded to our request for directions to the ticket office by grunting and waving generally round the perimeter. His gesticulations suggested the booth was on the far side of the arena, so we set off enthusiastically round the exterior wall.

Four and a half minutes later we found ourselves back at the gate. He was still on the phone, except his roll-up was shorter and the crowds were now streaming back in. 'I'm so sorry, could you just clarify–' I began.

The man scowled and gesticulated again with even more vehemence, his arm gestures indicating the ticket booth might in fact be as far away as Paris. We set off once more. Five and a half minutes later and with me now holding one of the wheels of my suitcase, we arrived back at the gate again.

There's nothing like a bit of misunderstanding in tense circumstances to test the fragile bond of the Entente Cordiale. Taking my cultural lead from Timbo Henman, I launched into a series of platitudes straight from my local Conservative Club. Among the phrases I used to try to establish the whereabouts of the booth were: 'Now look here', 'This simply isn't good enough' and, although Paulina assured me she didn't hear it, I fear I may have used, 'I ought to warn you I sometimes write travel pieces for London newspapers.' If so, I'm profoundly sorry: but with cries from thousands of ecstatic fans echoing round the walls and a rousing rendition of the 'March From Scipio' thrown in for good measure, the sense of frustrated desire was turning me into what is known in the acting trade as a knobhead.

At the third time of asking we spotted what he was pointing at. The booth was a mere four feet away, near enough for our friend the steward to have taken our euros and performed the transaction himself – though I realise that would have spoilt his fun. Although to call it a ticket office would have been overstating the case: a single, ancient, clawed hand stretching out a couple of bony fingers from the darkness of a hole set into the wall.

In my experience there isn't any situation that cannot be remedied by a bottle of pop and a bag of peanuts. If you can throw in a tiny cairn terrier in a tartan harness to pat occasionally on the seat next to you, you're in about as perfect a situation as it's possible to find on this earth. Within minutes I had all three.

THE SIGHT INSIDE the arena was definitely one Van Gogh would have fancied tackling, particularly if somebody had made off with much of his paint box, as it came in only four available colours: blue sky, white seats, brown ring and ominous blood-red wooden perimeter. Charlton Heston would have happily ridden round this lot. Although it has been used for bull-racing only since the fifteenth century, the structure was being given its finishing touches about the same time as Mary and Joseph were bedding down in the cattle shed. How on earth had the Romans ever built something as huge as this? Originally designed to hold 20,000, even on a weekday evening there were nearly half that number roasting in the heat.

Down in the ring, and dressed simply in white T-shirts and white denims, stood the *raseteurs*, looking like a gathering of painters and decorators who'd stumbled in through the wrong entrance. Reputedly fearless, proud, devil-may-care and inured to the dangers they face, the only clues to their identity were the names printed on the backs of their T-shirts: Villiers, Luciterne, Debussy.

They seemed relaxed enough about their impending ordeal, loitering against the sides or talking to friends in the crowd. Then there was a blast from a trumpet, a bull trotted in from a gate on the far side, and they all stood up straight.

I never realised until now how much bulls behaved to type. For some moments the creature stood looking back and forth as if judging when best to cross a busy motorway, while the *raseteurs* watched gingerly from a distance. Then, realising it was supposed to be in a contest, it remembered its lines and started hamming it up like a bovine Donald Wolfit. From being the sort of animal you'd want to tickle under the chin and feed Cadbury's chocolate buttons, it began snorting furiously, flicking its tail, lowering its horns in the direction of the nearest target and even pawing at the ground with one of its front hooves.

It was, frankly, a bit overdone. Less is more, my old drama tutor used to say. That bull could have done with some one-to-one with Lee Strasberg.

Then it was off, as if fired from a cannon, hurling itself madly in the direction of the nearest pair of white denims. At first the spectacle most resembled members of a cricket team attempting to punch a bull on the head – an event I've actually witnessed when a farmer left a gate open while my team were playing Pyecombe II's in an adjoining field. Now the bull careered towards the chosen victim as if its life depended on it. After a furious pursuit, and just as it was about to add a major item of hosiery to its private collection, the fleeing *raseteur* vaulted spectacularly over the top of the enclosing fence before landing in the front row of the audience, where he clung like Spiderman. It was a heart-stopping manoeuvre.

The bull shuddered to a halt, clattering against the partition and throwing up clouds of dust. Other *raseteurs* were already converging from all sides. The bull set off again, this time chasing each and every one of them in the same mazy circuit, while its collective quarry jinked and ducked, desperate hands clutching wildly at the top of the animal's head whenever it got within goring distance.

Eventually one of them snatched the woollen *ficelle* from between the bull's horns and leapfrogged to safety over the fence, where he landed among a party of schoolchildren and nearly ruined the marriage prospects of a man selling sunhats. Cheering wildly, the victor raised his tiny trophy aloft and the crowd broke into ecstatic applause.

The arrival of the second bull was followed by a burst of commentary, from which Paulina learned the creature was called Horatio. In addition, it seemed one of the *raseteurs* was a local boy made good who needed to pluck only one more *cocarde* to have a chance of lifting the Trophée des As, rewarded to the leading exponent at the end of the season. Paulina was evidently something of an expert on the young *raseteurs* of the Camargue.

Horatio proved to be a Mike Tyson of a beast, and it was no surprise that no one so much as laid a finger on him. After fifteen minutes the animal was allowed to depart with both his balls (at least the woollen ones) and his reputation intact.

As we waited for the final bout to commence, Pauline told me a little about herself. She was doing business studies in Boston but wasn't enjoying the experience. 'America is too concerned with money,' she insisted. 'Everything there is money. Even the air you breathe is money. I miss France.' She gave Yannis's thigh a squeeze and he smiled contentedly.

She had a point. The further I advanced round this country, the more I sensed they might have got the work–life balance just about correct. Here, for instance: there was no mass merchandising, no grinning stewards marching up and down the aisles selling glossy programmes or trays of beer. As in everything French, the pervading sense of quiet formality ensured that you could sit back and enjoy yourself without worrying about how much it would cost to have your car parked or whether you should buy the commemorative DVD at the end of the evening. And all in a 2,000-year-old stadium.

After several blissful minutes feeding peanuts to the terrier on the next seat, it was time for the final round. Another vast animal appeared, whose name Pauline didn't catch but who was obviously the bovine equivalent of Grant Mitchell. Even before he was through the gate it was obvious he was determined to cause mayhem.

The local favourite seemed to hold a particular fascination for the beast, and after one murderous chase during which our hero appeared to stumble, it seemed we might be in for a genuine gorefest. But at the last moment the young *raseteur* hurled himself over the top of the partition and into a narrow passageway between the ring and the front seats. But at least he was safe.

Except he wasn't. Mitchell launched itself at the barrier and, to the accompaniment of splintering wood, somehow managed to get its front hooves over the top, where it lay, breathless, its back legs kicking furiously in thin air. A final effort, and it catapulted over and landed on all fours in the circular passageway in which our hero was sheltering.

Mitchell was one of the legendary 'jumpers'. Few beasts can perform this Herculean task, but Mitchell wasn't topping the bill for nothing. Scenting possible carnage, it sped off along the circular passageway with Paulina's hero only inches in front.

But the effort of jumping five feet of timber fencing had taken its toll, and by the time it found its way back into the ring via the entrance gate it was starting to tire. Our hero took his chance and, in a blur of dust and sweat and snot and ripping denim, he successfully cut a *cocarde* and made off for the safety of the walls immediately in front of our seats, where he brandished his trophy high in the air.

The look of smouldering enchantment in Paulina's eyes as she gazed down upon her sweating champion was something I'd not witnessed in womanhood since Dawn French was unexpectedly snogged by George Clooney on live TV. I suspected lantern-jawed Yannis was going to have his work cut out in the weeks ahead.

After our hero's final wave to the crowd the event was over: no quasi-martial parade or preening histrionics or dragging the body of the poor defeated beast along by a tractor. Mitchell, realising it had lost this particular bout, merely clattered back down the tunnel for an isotonic drink and a debrief with its trainer before returning to its *manade*; while after a brief ovation for the departing gladiators and a final adieu from the announcer, everyone got up to leave.

Afterwards we wandered through the town and stopped for a drink at a café. The premises had an old-fashioned stereogram in the front porch from which customers could select their own choice of vinyl, and I put on some Jacques Brel – 'La Chanson des Vieux Amants' – before standing my new friends a glass of Ricard and some pastries selected from a menu written in Tippex on the chest of an adjacent tailor's dummy.

What was it about the participants, I pondered, that made them so masculine in their curious, unadorned fashion? Was it their youth? The risks they took in pursuit of the prize?

Paulina had a faraway look in her eye. She was adamant the appeal was their sheer athleticism. The ability to run a hundred-metre dash thirty or forty times in the brutal sunshine of a summer's afternoon and then to jump a solid five-foot fence only to splatter yourself against a sheer concrete wall, and all of it with half a ton of live bull bearing down on you, was, she assured me, the epitome of what she looked for in a man. Particularly if it came gift-wrapped in white denim. 'Forget Zidane and Ronaldo,' she ended dreamily, 'those are real men.'

She was right. In some ways the *raseteurs* were the French equivalent of the old-fashioned English Corinthian: super-fit, sleek, doing it just for the glory and the chance of their name in the newspaper. These were guys who, when not fleeing charging bulls, spent their time fixing cars and delivering the mail. Once upon a time in Britain, rugby, athletics, even the boat race had had the same pure quality. But no longer.

It was time to take our leave, Paulina and Yannis to the station, me to check into a small hotel in the main square. As evening fell I sat on my balcony gazing down at the bustle below. It was the sort of heady evening that only high summer in an ancient Roman town could offer up, something timeless and burnished, and the quiet murmur of conversation and laughter mingling with the twittering of birds in the foliage seemed like the sweetest sound in the world.

The bull-racing had felt an authentic spectacle, and not just because of the lack of tourists in the crowd, nor even because of the advertising prohibition on the participants' shirts. It was the sense of witnessing events in a structure older than Christmas which provided a sensory frisson and hard-wired the event back through French history. What on earth had happened to such structures and events back in Britain, if indeed we had ever possessed any? Apart from Hadrian's Wall I could hardly think of a single building of similar dimensions that still represented anything like the original architect's plans. Medieval castles, I suppose: but when did you see anything so appropriate presented in them? Russell Watson singing highlights from *Cats* at Hatfield House hardly counts.

God knows how many of these awe-inspiring venues still stood in this part of France, or how they had survived in such extraordinarily good condition, but whatever the reason, they'd been taken care of over the centuries, or at least left well alone.

The potent blend of ancient surroundings and blissful weather provided much of the magic to this country. Arles had the feeling of a settlement that had been baked in the sun since time immemorial. No need here for alternative plans, rainproof marquees or insurance policies in case of cancellation due to flood or tempest. The sun would shine because the very gods for whom the buildings had been dedicated had decreed it should be so. Of course the tourist office would always be closed while people took two-hour lunch breaks: who wouldn't, when you could enjoy such surroundings and such temperatures?

And as for bull-racing, I promised myself I'd have a go one day if ever the opportunity arose. Even if it was only wresting a cable-knit sweater from one of Bouglione's tame heifers while Dandrine held it by the head.

Boule and Bouche

BOULES – OR PÉTANQUE, to give it its fancier name, by which most Englishmen know it – is France's national game. A tough, chain-smoking, bastardised half-brother of its poncey English equivalent, it has no time for refinement or club etiquette or old dodderers in white caps waving their hankies about to indicate potential approach routes for the next roll.

Au contraire, everything about boules speaks of rough and ready. Unlike the carefully polished woods used by their English counterparts, the Gallic implements are made of brutish cast metal and weigh nearly two pounds: enough to kill a man if injudiciously used. And instead of manicured lawns and prim clubhouses, the French version is played on any old bit of tree-shaded ground, usually one littered with gravel, stones and discarded twigs.

The sport is both a male preserve and bastion of working-class sensibilities, involving men with hands freshly begrimed by axle grease relaxing with their friends before returning home to the wife and a hearty meal that no doubt involves meat and potatoes. As for accoutrements, the only polish applied to a boule is a mixture of phlegm, spittle and sweat.

Perhaps because of that, boules is part of the national psyche. Thus the quickest way to raise a Frenchman's blood pressure is to suggest that it's no more than a derivative of the original invented by England's own Sir Francis Drake on the hoe at Plymouth: which is, of course, exactly why it's such fun to drop it into the conversation so often.

During my travels I'd frequently spotted tournaments – with some 17 million people playing it nationally, it's difficult to miss – but I'd discounted it as a proper sport, believing it to be a byword for pastoral conviviality among spry retirees, a perfect low-energy pastime suitable for sultry summer evenings. Yet the next morning's breakfast news bulletin left me in no doubt: if I wanted thrills 'n' spills, I need look no further.

According to the bulletin, a game of boules the previous evening had resulted in a player being killed. So serious was the incident that the police had been called and an investigation started. The word manslaughter was even being bandied about. Far from the glorified marbles I'd envisaged, the game was obviously a life-and-death struggle.

The incident sounded like something out of *The Fast Show*. The player in question, one Frank Hourcade, had apparently been bending over to examine the jack when one of his teammates threw his ball at it, hitting the unfortunate victim broadsides on the temple and killing him on the spot.

To add insult to injury, the victim was head of tourism for Lourdes airport, the one town where you would have thought you'd be safe from acts of such cosmic malevolence. A witness to the tragedy was quoted as saying Mr Hourcade was fit with no medical problems: perhaps forgetting in his grief that regular attendance at the gym is scant security against being clobbered in the side of the head at close range by a huge great metal ball.

The item also hinted at darker forces abroad. Apparently the authorities had already been forced to clamp down on physical and verbal abuse on several occasions, a new and unsettling phenomenon dubbed 'bouliganisme'. Indeed, some club matches had allegedly been banned in the Nièvres region after a series of unseemly brawls.

It seemed I might have dismissed it too soon.

Thankfully the proprietor of my hotel was able to give me some tips on the sport and how I might find a nearby game. Monsieur Pellerey was something of an Anglophile, and needed no second invitation to practise his excellent if somewhat halting English. Over a glass of Healey's Cornish Rattler, a lethal West Country cider he kept for just such encounters with willing Rosbifs, he provided precise directions to a nearby square fringed by plane trees where boules was traditionally played each evening during the summer months. If I turned up about 6 p.m., he was sure I'd be able to find a game.

'But one word of warning,' he concluded. 'Please ensure you join in a French game. Don't ask to join in with the Muslims. The two don't mix, and they won't take kindly to being asked. You might find …' His words tailed off in the air.

I wrote the word 'Muslim' on the back of my hand to show willing, and finishing my tumbler of Cornish Rattler, thanked him for his help and set off. All I had to do now was kill some time till early evening. Perhaps I'd start by sourcing a crash helmet.

Arles was a delightful city to wander round. There was a Roman baths and a necropolis, after which I had a quick look in the Van Gogh museum, followed by a visit to some open-air flamenco dancing, predictably to Romano-funk from the Gipsy Kings. I ended up back at the café I'd visited the previous evening, where the proprietor, a delightful girl named Eleanor, served up huge portions of both Charles Aznavour LPs and cherry cheesecake. She, too, assured me I'd find a game of boules before the end of my stay, although her advice too contained general vague warnings against falling in with the wrong crowd.

I arrived just after six. The square was deserted – or nearly so. There was indeed a game being played with some vigour, but even at a hundred paces I could see that the group lobbing metal balls back and forth in the dust were about as French as burger and fries. I may not be an international traveller, but even I know that you don't get that size of backside anywhere else but among the Yanks.

A huge man with a square head like Herman Munster, wearing the traditional American-tourist-in-Europe garb of baseball cap, pressed shorts and sneakers with white sports socks, was tossing the telltale metal balls uncertainly in the direction of a tiny wooden jack, or *cochonnet*, scrutinised by a couple of appreciative women, both sporting spectacular sun visors.

Watching from a nearby bench was Megan. A brittle young thing from Oregon, she explained that the players were her mom and pop, and that they were receiving instruction from their tour guide as part of the all-inclusive two-week cruise package with Sundowner Tours down the river Rhone, a holiday which her sullen features indicated had eaten up most of her parents' life savings and possibly her legacy once they popped their sneakers. She seemed pretty unhappy about it.

We watched in silence. A woman dressed entirely in brown Dralon was instructing Pop in the rules of the sport by consulting a sheaf of papers. She seemed no more certain of what they were supposed to be doing than he did. Nonetheless Pop was having a high old time, tossing the balls gently into the air as if lobbing hand grenades in the hope the pin wouldn't come loose. 'Gee, that was neat,' he said after his final throw. 'I had a lot of fun there.' His wife applauded happily.

While he sat down heavily on the bench next to us and began massaging his ankles, I wandered over to introduce myself and ask if I might join in. The instructor replied to my halting request in a perfect cut-glass English accent. A sort of Camilla Parker-Boules.

Eve was actually from Lucerne in Switzerland. Her knowledge of the game was somewhat sketchy – her real speciality was the paintings of Titian, Giorgione and Italian Masters of the Renaissance – but her job spec as principal tour guide for Sundowner Tours demanded she allow her charges forty-five minutes of instruction in France's national game in the final week of the trip. Pop, Megan and Mom were the only ones who'd put their names down on the noticeboard.

'I think you're supposed to try and get the big balls as near to the little ball as you can without actually hitting it,' she explained warily. 'And the winning total is thirteen points. That much I'm sure of. I'd happily allow you to try your hand but we've got dinner back on the boat in ten minutes followed by a lecture on the poetry of Voltaire.' She indicated the Rhone, which wound its majestic way along one side of the square in a long lazy curve. Just peeking over the top of the embankment was the top deck of some vast pleasure cruiser, its engine whirring noisily in the evening stillness.

'Anyway, you've come to the right place,' she continued. 'Just hang around here and a game will crop up sooner or later, and you're likely to be welcomed, particularly if you offer to stand the players a glass of pastis at the conclusion of the match. It's the traditional end to any social event around here, they love that sort of gesture. But be careful,' she added darkly as she waited for Pop to retie his sneakers. 'There are French games and Muslim games. Whatever you do, don't ask to join in the Muslim games.

They won't like it. Particularly if you offer a drink. It's considered the badge of the infidel. Let sleeping dogs lie, that's my tip. You'll easily be able to tell them apart. Good luck.'

With that she tapped the side of her nose conspiratorially, gathered up her charges and wandered off in the direction of the boat.

These constant yet discreet references were faintly worrying. I knew that racial sensibilities ran high in this region of France, and that nearby Marseilles was a stronghold of Jean-Marie Le Pen's National Front Party, which I recalled had come an impressive fourth in the first round of last year's general election. Yet all was sweetness and light in this part of Provence. Or was it? I promised myself to ask Monsieur Pellerey about the matter of racial and religious integration over a glass of Rattler when I got back to the hotel. In the meantime, I'd keep my wits about me.

Eve was right about one thing. Within minutes of her departure a gaggle of middle-aged bouligans began arriving in ones and twos and converging beneath a set of trees on the far side of the square. They were the sort of players I'd expected: salt-of-the-earth fellows, with straining waistlines, frayed shirts and droopy moustaches. I rubbed my hands in some loose earth, undid a button or two and wandered over to try my luck.

IT WAS ABOUT ten minutes later, and just as I was about to throw my first ever competitive boule – in fact, precisely at the moment when I heard one of my teammates referring to another as Abdul – that I realised I may have made a bum choice.

I'd been wondering for some minutes why I couldn't understand any of what was being said. I'd assumed that perhaps it was some dialect specific to the plains of the Camargue, but now it was only too obvious that these curious gurgling vowels, tumbling over one another as if trying make a sound in order to amuse a newborn baby, were Arabic.

'Ahhalleleerrabbelle!' The eldest member of the group pushed me roughly towards the centre of the square. He dug the heel of his shoe in the ground, described a rough semi-circle in the dust and pointed irritably for me to stand inside it.

There had been other indications too: ones which, if I hadn't been so deliriously happy to be invited to join in the first place, I might have noticed. The fact that one of them was wearing a djellaba, for instance. Or that, of my five fellow-players, four of them had still failed to register my existence.

I smiled hopefully at the one who'd dug the circle, an elderly Arab looking like a tanned Wilfrid Bramble, who I suspected was the captain of the opposing team. In truth, the divvying up of the two sides had passed in a blur: I knew that we were three a side, but beyond that I was none too sure who was 'us' and who was 'them': although I fancied that, unless I was careful, they all might become 'us' and I might find myself the sole representative of 'them'.

'Alluufftyhuuuhhyaa!' The one who'd first allowed me to join in was pointing to the jack, lying about fifteen yards away across the ground. With crinkly hair and a row of frightening gold teeth set into a look of intense irritation, my sponsor was a swarthier version of ex-Governor of the Bank of England, Eddie George. I stepped up and hurled the ball in the direction of the tiny *cochonnet*. The ball landed with a dull thud about a yard too long.

'Allanabaeelallarl.' Eddie George bounced his hands up and down in the air as if testing the springiness of a mattress or trying to calm a rabid dog. My lobbing was obviously too forceful. But even as I prepared to toss my second boule, Wilfrid Bramble pushed me out of the dust ring and took my place.

In addition to Wilfrid Bramble, Abdul and Eddie George, there were two others, one of whom bore a striking resemblance to Oliver Postgate's Nogbad the Bad, and another who, in poor light, could be mistaken for Private Walker in *Dad's Army*. They all appeared equally unsettled by my participation. By now I was wishing I'd never seen that bloody newsflash about the bloke being clobbered in the temple. It made me jumpy. And that had been a match between fellow Catholics: these men may have had brothers and cousins walled up in Abu Ghraib, perhaps the very ones cowering in those photographs while Lindy English stood on their naked backs with a cigarette in one hand and a rabid Alsatian in the other. Any unexpected incident involving my brains being dashed out in a misunderstanding about whose turn it was would be treated with the utmost compassion in the current febrile political climate.

My only hope for salvation lay with my sponsor, Eddie. I'd approached him initially after spotting him unpacking his boules from a square of dirty oilcloth. He'd responded to my entreaty to be allowed to participate with all the glee of a man studying his tax returns, but had eventually extended a brusque invitation by shoving three spare balls from his holdall into my hands and pointing for me to wait under the plane trees until further directed. Only with him could I find protection.

Blindly, like a puppy desperately searching its master's face for indications of where and when it was supposed to have a shit, I stood blindly transfixed on my reluctant sponsor. Without him I was sunk.

The next twenty minutes were among the most tense since I left home. I'm not claiming that my ordeal qualifies me as the natural heir to Terry Waite or John McCarthy, but there was a simmering aggression among my hosts that was undoubtedly in part caused by my presence.

Or so I'd convinced myself. After all, I hadn't a clue about the rules, or whose side I was on, and with the balls all looking the same once they'd landed, it was impossible to determine which to avoid and which to knock out of the way. I secretly cursed this stupid foreign pastime and the twits who played it. No wonder we didn't bother with it back in Britain.

But muttering oaths wasn't going to help me now. I dare not bail out, yet whatever I threw, each new effort seemed to lead to a new argument, accompanied by ever more gesticulating, most of it in my direction.

Wilfrid Bramble in particular seemed to be outraged by my presence and was sounding off to Eddie about every three minutes. I say it was about me, but it could just as easily have been about the tactics for winning the game, or where they were going for dinner. There was simply no way of knowing, but the cumulative effect of their vehement shouting was beginning to prey on my nerves. 'Hostage is a man hanging by his fingernails over the edge of chaos, feeling his fingers slowly straightening,' said Brian Keenan. Now I knew what he meant.

Whatever else, my hosts were certainly no slouches at the game. Each of them possessed an impressive array of half lobs, full lobs and shooters, all of which betrayed many long years of practice. Nogbad in particular had a happy knack of bunging his ball so that it hit those of his opponents smack on the full, splitting the pack and sending them all spinning to oblivion while his dropped like a stone in their place. It was an impressive trick.

By contrast I could offer up nothing. Each time I tried, my half lob was too short or my full lob too long. After forty minutes or so I could sense my efforts beginning to drag my team down.

Abdul's crowd were now neuf–quatre in front, and with thirteen the magic number at the finishing tape, it was clear my ineptitude was proving a handicap. Eddie's irritable encouragement of the first few games had given way to a sullen acceptance.

But things were about to change. On the eighth game a typically wayward offering of mine hit a loose pebble and jagged off at nearly 90 degrees, causing it not only to hit the jack, but dribble away with it to untenanted ground, well away from the balls previously clustered around it.

I instinctively turned to apologise, but Eddie was smiling at me. 'Bueno,' he said simply, patting me lightly on the shoulder. It was the first vaguely intelligible word I'd heard since the game commenced.

It seemed to do the trick. My lucky shot won my first point, and with Eddie and Private Walker also weighing in after me, our total suddenly leapt to six. I scored again in successive games, and before I knew it the contest was thrillingly placed at douze all. By now a small crowd had gathered and was watching with interest.

At this point Eddie took me to one side. He splayed his fingers to indicate the score, then mimed cutting his throat with one hand: whether to indicate the sudden-death element or what might happen to me if I screwed things up for him, I couldn't tell. 'La belle, la belle,' he kept saying. All I knew was one more point would win the match. It's all I needed to know. This was going to be a nail-biter.

With the order of throwing altering without apparent reason, it was impossible to predict when it might be my turn. Thus it was only once the ground was carpeted with everyone else's efforts that I realised I was to have the final throw of the match.

By now everybody was gathered at the far end by the jack. I

looked across at Eddie. He nodded solemnly and performed his mattress-testing mime once more. I stepped into the ring and tried to concentrate, but by now my palms were sweaty and it was difficult to get a grip. I wiped my hands on the back of my shorts, took a deep breath, picked up my first boule and prepared for launch.

My first two offerings were as bad as anything I'd managed all evening, one of them nearly taking off a slice of Abdul's left foot. This really was no place for open-toed sandals. But my final delivery, an attempt to replicate Nogbad's coconut-splitting technique, landed smack in the middle, sending the others scattering in all directions. The others hurried across and gathered round. After an agony of pointing, all but two were kicked away. The remaining items were equidistant from the jack. And one of them was mine.

For some minutes they stood around debating the result. Eddie seemed convinced we'd shaded it. Nogbad evidently thought it was his. Eddie insisted the game was won and stooped down to retrieve the ball and claim victory, but Nogbad pulled his arm back: an action that set off another fevered discussion.

After much dispute, Abdul was deputed to go to the hedge and fetch a twig to measure the distance, but it proved inconclusive and debate broke out afresh. The babble was growing in volume with every second. A couple of spectators, obviously friends and workmates of the protagonists, were slowly drawn into the argument. Voices became shriller, the gesticulating wilder. Whatever my final ball had done, it had thrown the game into turmoil.

I was powerless to intervene. Before my eyes the dispute was escalating, like one of those news items where a peaceful parade suddenly toboggans into mindless violence before anything can be done. With Nogbad now poking his index finger in Eddie's chest, it occurred to me there might be latent cultural differences between individual players. They were all obviously from the same culture and faith, but who knows: more complex dynamics might be at play here. Eddie was brushing away the offending finger and doing his mattress-testing gesture again. There certainly seemed no love lost between them.

Perhaps some were Sunni and others were Shiite?

It was descending into a full-scale argument. The prospect of being on Megan's boat eating burgers and learning about Voltaire suddenly seemed attractive. I looked over at the distant lights. The craft was at least 500 metres away. Could I leg it over there if things got nasty? Impossible. I'd never make it through the hedge.

Then, just as quickly as it had flared, the argument stopped. As one, everyone turned to look at me. Wilfrid Bramble said something to Eddie George in a low murmur: he seemed to be instructing him to take decisive action. But Eddie seemed reluctant. He stood motionless, his gold teeth glinting at me through stretched lips.

One of the hangers-on, a bloke in a motorcycle jacket with Elvis Presley sideburns, pointed towards me and uttered some new decree. Eddie shook his head. Nogbad joined in, then Private Walker, until everyone in the square seemed to be whispering to him at once. Still he remained silent. What were they asking him to do? And why was I involved? His implacable stare suggested a private conflict I could only guess at.

Then he reached into his coat pocket.

My blood ran cold. Don't mix with the Muslims, they'd all

said. The maître d', Eleanor at the café, Eve the tour guide. These were people who knew only too well the dangers facing the unwary traveller. I even had an insight into the fear and terror many Muslims must experience themselves in this strange land where the National Front can come fourth in the polls and nobody bats an eyelid. There was nothing Sunni about this moment.

In fact, I felt like Shiite.

Eddie was slowly removing his hand. In his clenched fist something glinted. Something with a handle and a blade. He looked at it sadly. Then he pointed it straight at me and began to advance.

IF YOU'D SAID to me six weeks ago that the proudest moment of my entire trip would be the moment when I was offered a builder's tape measure and asked to perform the solemn task of arbitrating a game of boules, I'd have assumed you were mad. But Eddie was handing me a device with a spring-loaded retraction system, the sort that workmen use, and was indicating for me to kneel and judge who had won.

I took it in both hands and crouched down. Ten pairs of gimlet eyes bored into me as I held it gingerly between the offending balls. Nobody spoke. It was impossibly close. Yet it was up to me to make the correct call. I felt a heady mixture of responsibility, relief and pride. But which one had prevailed? Mine, or theirs?

The distance was no more than a millimetre. I checked and rechecked several times. The only noise was the distant humming of the engines of the river cruiser. Finally I made my decision and pointed to the winning ball. God knows whose it was. Eddie came over and helped me back up. The glint from his molars was blinding. It was mine. We'd won by a single point.

The game was over. Eddie pumped both arms in the air with delight. 'Bueno, très bien,' he shouted, extending both hands in my direction. He clasped me warmly to his bosom, and the air was filled with the sound of multiple backslapping.

Even before we'd disengaged, others were lining up to shake my hand: Private Walker, Abdul, Wilfrid Bramble; even Nogbad the Bad was nodding warmly in appreciation. I suddenly felt wretched at my earlier instinctive supposition that they were the local branch of Al Qaeda.

It was now time to return their faith. I bowed low, then asked if I might have a photograph. 'Ah, a photo, mon capitaine,' shouted Eddie, breaking into peals of laughter. 'Mon captaine,' chorused Wilfrid Bramble, lining up beside him. 'Mon capitaine,' shrieked Nogbad, kneeling down in front. 'Mon capitaine,' yelled Walker. I scurried over to my bag and found my camera.

I took a snap of my five colleagues all shouting 'Mon capitaine' as the shutter clicked. Then Abdul took one of me and Eddie with our boules displayed in outstretched hands, then Eddie took one of me and Wilfrid Bramble, and finally the bloke in the motorcycle jacket took one of both teams with me in the middle, an arm round Eddie and Abdul. 'Bueno!' he shouted as he pressed the shutter.

We chorused back as one. 'BUENO!'

As I collected my bag from the bench they were already marking out another game, but all stopped to give me a final rousing cheer. My path back towards the hotel took me alongside the river, where I stopped to scan back through the photographs on my viewfinder. On board the nearby cruiser the lights were on, and through the blinds in the dining lounge I could make out the hunched figures of elderly Americans enjoying their evening supper.

Funny. Only a matter of weeks ago I recalled glimpsing a similar craft on the Seine at Rouen, and thinking how lovely it looked: lounging on a luxury sundeck, being served sumptuous meals and waiting for the next town to appear round the bend in the river. And best of all, a guide to take care of everything, explain the history of the settlement, point out interesting sites, recommend restaurants, arrange for a game of boules and generally forestall any unexpected surprises.

No longer. I sincerely thanked the stars I was a lone traveller and not a prisoner of the Sundowners' daily tour schedule. My route may be less luxurious, and was certainly filled with more uncertainty: but tonight I'd played a match for real with a group of Frenchmen, who had lent me their ceremonial tape measure and trusted me to call the result as I saw it.

Back at the Hôtel Rabelais the bar was in full swing. I ordered a tumbler of pastis and sat quietly in the corner where I finished the morning newspaper, and toasted the memory of poor Frank Hourcade, my new friends and my own unlikely triumph.

Fools rush in, so the saying goes. Three separate times in this city I'd been warned away from crossing the cultural and racial divide, yet this fool had been utterly embraced by a group who would have no reason to be especially generous to middle-aged twats wading in and messing up their precious hour's R&R. The experience had been all the more memorable because of it.

I could have gone on pondering like this in the downstairs bar for many hours, but Monsieur Pellerey had noticed my glass was empty, and was already wandering over with the remains of his Healey's Rattler.

No thanks, Monsieur Pellerey. I'd already drunk more than

enough, and even I wasn't fool enough to mix my drinks this late in the evening. Who knows what might occur if I had this on top of the native brew?

I might end up with a Cornish pastis.

Dips and Crudités

IF THERE'S ONE thing above all that differentiates us from French, it's our relationships with our bodies.

When the French want to celebrate their sexuality, they have Brigitte Bardot and Serge Gainsbourg entwining in erotic luxury beneath a burning sun. We have Robin Askwith pretending to be a window cleaner while John Junkin pursues him with a clipboard. Truffaut ends his films with a lingering kiss. We end ours with everyone getting sprayed by a fire extinguisher.

In my entire fifty-one years on this planet I'd only once been naked in public: and this was briefly in a play at a fringe venue above a pub in Dalston. The premises closed soon afterwards. Consequently much of my body is still the same colour as it was on 4 February, 1957: a sort of creamy white, reminiscent of the microwaveable porridge so favoured by time-stressed parents nowadays.

I knew a bit about naturism, of course. Indeed, my home town of Brighton had introduced Britain's first nudist beach on a stretch of windswept shingle in the early 1970s. But instead of the continental image depicted in the promotional literature, the reality was a single foreign-exchange student sitting in a topless bikini while rows of men in raincoats ogled her with binoculars from a safe distance.

Health and Efficiency, British Naturism: these were required reading for any teenager growing up in the 1970s, but the magazines themselves made no sense. British naturists seemed to have only one recreational pursuit, that of cooking sausages. Whatever the weather, there'd be identical blokes in specs wearing nothing but a chef's hat and a pinny, holding up great forkfuls of spitting chipolatas, while behind them young things aimlessly threw beach balls around.

Naturism in France, by contrast, was, and is still, big business, employing 3,000 people and bringing in 250 million euros a year: an inevitable consequence of life in such a glorious climate and surroundings. The industry owes much of its success to the magnificently named Albert LeCoq, who founded the Club Gymnique in 1933 and the first naturist holiday centre on the Atlantic coast the following year. Initially considered as a social curiosity, French naturism nowadays is a celebration of joie de vivre and spontaneity.

For someone like me who waits until the mercury reaches 30 before I'll even remove my tie, these qualities have been profoundly absent. Yet the whole point of coming to France was to break free from social conditionings that still held me back. If I was really serious about becoming one with the sea, the sun and the wind, it would surely be better to try my luck here rather than wait till I was back in Cleethorpes.

THE DADDY OF all nudist camps is Cap d'Agde in the Languedoc. It's about as far from the British image of a nudist camp as you can get. Known throughout France simply as Espace Naturiste, or the Naked City, it's the world's biggest nudist centre, a sprawling temple to the wonders of God's greatest creation. Covering nearly three kilometres of pristine Mediterranean coastline, it can accommodate up to 40,000 individuals during peak season.

It was not to be toyed with. Surrounded by steel gates, barbed wire and a ten-kilometre-long wire fence, there were also dark rumours about compulsory medical check-ups before being allowed in. Fortunately I had a local contact to explain the intricacies. Ruby, the sister of an acquaintance of mine in London, sold real estate in Agde old town, and in return for dinner agreed to give me a few tips.

We dined al fresco on the towpath outside my hotel on a steamy Friday evening, and in between batting away blood-starved mosquitoes, chit-chatted about life in this part of France. It wasn't until we got to dessert that I mentioned my scheme to spend the whole of the next day at the Espace Naturiste, and when I did so she stopped eating for a moment and wiped her mouth with a napkin. I asked her what was wrong.

'Nothing, nothing,' she assured me playfully. '*C'est bon*. You will have the best time.' She even confessed to having visited it herself a few times, and described crystal-clear water, a laid-back approach, and, as long as I obeyed the few simple rules, an enjoyable and relaxed environment.

'What rules are those?'

'Well, no photography, of course. And total nudity at all times. And it is best not to giggle or finger point. They take their recreation very seriously. But you will enjoy.'

I hadn't intended to take my camera anyway, and if there was any giggling or finger pointing to be done I fully expected to be the subject rather than the perpetrator. 'Anything else?'

'Are you staying the night?'

'I hadn't thought about it. Should I?'

She poured herself some coffee while she considered her response. Cap d'Agde was a curious hybrid of a place, she explained. As well as a naturist centre, it also catered for – and here I had to do some rough translating for her – 'swingers'. Parallel to, and in tandem with, the vast majority of dedicated nudists, Espace Naturiste also welcomed a more eclectic clientele, ones who combined nudity by day with exotic sexual practices by night: exhibitionists, libertines and 'swappers of wives' as she put it. The needs of this piquant minority were supplied by an array of on-site nightclubs that offered everything a dedicated swinger could ask for, including chandeliers.

Surely the task of persuading naturists to rub along with individuals whose aim was to enjoy sex with multiple partners would tax the diplomatic powers of the Secretary of the UN himself. Or was I just old-fashioned?

'I know, it seems odd,' she agreed wistfully. 'And yet until recently...'

Of late there had been tension between the two groups. Although swingers only made up about 10 per cent of the clientele, some committed naturists were now complaining that the swingers' needs were overwhelming the founding tenets of the project.

Ruby's description of the situation as 'tension' was something of a euphemism. In recent months the two most notorious nightclubs had burnt down in mysterious circumstances. Arson was suspected and the police were investigating, but as far as Ruby knew, nobody had yet been prosecuted.

The 10 per cent were in no doubt that the mainstream 'mullahs of nudism' were behind these attacks, while the 90 per cent countered these claims by declaring they were happy to coexist, as long as the libertines didn't start doing it in the street and frightening the horses. Yet resentment still simmered between the factions.

Had Ruby experienced any of this 'tension' herself? She shook her head. 'No, not this summer. In previous years many times, but now… I think I wait to see who has started the fires before I return. There are many other nice beaches on the coast.'

We parted soon after 10 p.m. As we said goodbye, I asked her if she had any other advice to offer.

'Be sure to use plenty of sunscreen,' she replied. 'Some parts of your body will never have seen a day like this.'

NAKED CITY WAS nothing if not remote. Situated on a spur of land some miles from the town, it required an uncomfortable hour-long trip through a wasteland of urban sprawl choked with cars. My heart sank, particularly when my driver pulled over in the worryingly titled rue Clappe and announced this was my stop.

I retrieved my bag from the overhead rack and squeezed my way down the aisle. Was that clicking noise the buckled wheel on my suitcase or the sound of my fellow passengers' disapproval?

I joined an assortment of backpackers and couples with matching suitcases outside the entrance block, and soon found myself at the front desk, staring across at a woman who had obviously taken her fashion lead from the Aeroflot cabin crew handbook circa 1976. Huge, rouge-cheeked, with Daisy the panto cow eyelashes, she sat behind a grille stapling bits of paper. I explained that I wanted to stay for the night.

She shook her head. It was impossible: did I not realise it was August, the busiest time of the year for nudists? The one hotel was full to bursting, and even the campsite was booked out months in advance. I must come back in October.

Disappointment mixed with intense relief surged over me and I began to go. But then she asked me back. Had I heard of the day pass? For only nine euros I could enjoy the facility until eight o'clock. Would that do? Moments later I was squeezing through a turnstile in the perimeter fence behind a posse of tottering cyclists in swimming trunks.

Now what?

A middle-aged couple wearing nothing but flip-flops strolled past me with a bag containing their weekly shopping; there were some baguettes poking out and what seemed to be a collection of fresh peaches in a mesh net. The arrangement of their groceries may have been accidental, but now everything teemed with hidden meaning. '**Total nudity is obligatory within the quarter**' stated my information sheet.

The only problem was there was nowhere to change: not even a changing block, let alone cubicles or a safety deposit box. There was nothing for it. For the first and I imagine the last time in my life, I stripped naked in broad daylight in the middle of a mini-roundabout.

I set off down the Boulevard des Matelots towards the sea with my shoulder bag slung as carelessly over my shoulder as I could manage. The size of the complex was staggering. A mini marina with upwards of thirty boats shimmered in the heat, next to what appeared to be a full-sized boatyard and chandlers' stores. Beyond stretched endless apartment complexes. I walked onwards, whistling tunelessly.

Eventually tarmac gave way to some gentle dunes. On the other side the scene that greeted me was stupefying. Naked bodies stretched as far as the eye could see, reclining on sun loungers or dozing under beach umbrellas. Thousands more were swimming in a crystal sea, while yet others capered about in the surf hitting tiny rubber balls to each other with table-tennis bats.

Apart from the obvious, it could be a scene from any French resort in high season. Yet old habits don't disappear overnight. It was still too soon to be running around starkers. Luckily a small wooden walkway led to some sun beds that offered a little privacy, and I hurried over.

Recliner 122 offered both privacy and a parasol. But I'd obviously picked a popular spot. Next to me a sleek older woman was sitting astride recliner 123 reading a copy of *Paris Match*, looking much as one might expect apart from a large gold chain suspended from both ends of her labia. Such were its dimensions that I momentarily wondered if she might be the local Lady Mayor.

I turned over on my left side so as to face the other way. But the view was even more unsettling. Recliner 121 was occupied by a middle-aged German, complete with blubbering stomach and handlebar moustache, applying copious amounts of sun cream to his midriff. Catching my look, he introduced himself as Jörgen.

I sat up and tried to fix my gaze on the sea, but wherever I turned, quivering things filled my eye line. The sight of one old man kneeling on all fours in front me while he tried to assemble a picnic table was enough to put all thoughts of lunch out of my head, possibly for life. Although it did remind me that the curtain pulls back in London needed dry-cleaning.

If I wanted to give myself time to get used to all this nakedness, there was only one place to hide. Moments later I was doggy-paddling out in the sea.

For the first time since I'd arrived a sense of wellbeing began to replace my anxiety, and I splashed about for some while drinking in this new strange new world. There was something indeed wondrous about seeing so many people with so few hang-ups, and gazing back at them from the water, I could truly begin to appreciate the appeal of Mr LeCoq's noble concept. The sensation of swimming in the nude was immeasurably lovely, and I cursed my stunted outlook that it had taken me so long to experience it. And to top it all, it was strangely, reassuringly, unsexy.

'No lewd behaviour in the family area will be tolerated' blared a sign at the entrance; but as any man will tell you, erections are difficult to predict. They can be spontaneously activated by extreme cold or warmth, the need to empty your bladder, and all sorts of unlikely stimuli it would be difficult to justify in a magistrates' court. Most pertinently, they can be ignited with devastating speed by sudden immersion in water. But today, at least, I was immune.

Or so I thought.

By the time I'd emerged from my dip I'd drifted several hundred yards down the beachfront, and my route back along the strand took me past a secluded cove in which a man was fooling about in an inflatable dinghy. I sat down to watch. It was only then that I noticed the figure of another sun-worshipper clambering up the rocks towards me.

A tall, wafer-thin woman, she ticked all the boxes for what you'd look for in feminine iconography if you knew you'd never have to justify your tastes to Jo Brand or Germaine Greer. Elegant, stick-thin, with two enormous collagen-enhanced lips, she also sported bleached pigtails that poked out from gaps in a pink baseball cap.

But her pièces de résistance were two of the most stupendous breasts I'd ever seen outside the top shelf of my local newsagent's. They were not so much breasts as a child's drawing of them, the sort of items that not only defied the natural laws of gravity but were also, until the advent of plastic surgery, physically impossible to possess.

Her natural élan was set off by a set of wedged espadrilles and a small white poodle that trailed behind her on a spangly lead. Normally this sort of blatant porno-meets-Hollywood eye candy wouldn't float my bateau at all – but my tossle had other ideas. Every dog has its day, so the saying goes, and my dog was definitely not returning to its master's whistle.

Even as she approached, something was beginning to rise towards the horizontal, and I knew I was in imminent danger of violating one of the central dictats of the resort.

It was about four hundred yards back to the shelter of my beach recliner – thirty seconds if I turned and ran. My last sight of her was of a sad little smile, as if this was the sort of thing she had to face every day at Espace Naturiste. Which I'm sure it was. And I doubt she would have wanted it any other way.

ESPACE NATURISTE WAS indeed a complete home from home. There were no fewer than four separate mini-villages within the compound, each with their own apartment blocks, launderettes and mini-supermarkets where you could buy anything from mop and bucket sets through to stuffed olives. I passed bakeries, jewellery outlets, even a post office.

Ruby hadn't lied when she'd described it as a virtual town. If you could forgive the unattractive 1950s civic architecture, all cement walkways and stained concrete arcades, it could almost be Center Parcs.

Each turn of the corner brought new oddities. Skirting round the side of a huge complex called Heliopolis, I stumbled across a naked boules tournament in full swing, with twelve games simultaneously in progress and a silver trophy standing proudly on a side table for the eventual winner. If I'd closed my eyes I could have imagined myself back in Tunbridge Wells, the only sound that of convivial chatter and clacking balls.

The only thing that betrayed Espace Naturiste's other identity was the shops themselves. For every outlet offering washing-up liquid or feta cheese was another specialising in bondage gear and crotchless panties. I wandered into one in which naked couples were browsing through sets of nurses' uniforms and comparing different types of vibrators. Here you could purchase a dizzying range of garments, including rubber suits you could have used to clean the inside of a septic tank with. I suppose when removing your clothes has ceased to be sexy, you have to get your kicks by finding ways of putting them back on again.

It was time to eat. Something in me fancied scallops, and I took a seat at an elegant seafood restaurant beside a miniature swimming pool in which families were sploshing about. The eatery boasted silver cutlery, linen tablecloths and waiters wearing starched white aprons round their midriffs, itself a Godsend in a place specialising in the preparation of fresh food-stuffs.

It was as I was scanning the menu that I noticed my first nightclub. Situated on the far side of the pool, and adorned with a couple of cement sphinxes in the porch, the entrance had a shuttered, boarded-up look to it, and the sign was no longer legible. Telltale scorch marks flecked the awning. This surely must be one the casualties of the mystery arsonists. I resolved to do some proper sleuthing once lunch was over.

But even getting something to eat proved a stressful interlude. At an adjoining table, an elegant nude with breasts almost touching her dinner plate was prising open a selection of crust-aceans with an oyster pick. I found myself continually crossing and uncrossing my legs, so in the end I cancelled the scallops and set off to find a vegetarian option.

My change of location paid dividends. An elderly couple sitting at the next table in the prosaically named Café Melrose assured me there was an internet terminal in a bar back down by the beach. Hopefully the powers of Google would open up some of this campus's secrets.

The bar in question was situated on a natural rock formation overlooking the main beach. Out on the sun terrace, expensive-looking couples in wicker chairs drank from bottles of champagne nestling in silver pails, while inside the restaurant bronzed revellers sprawled on sofas watching the final practice round of the Brazilian Grand Prix on a giant plasma screen.

When I arrived a young couple were already at the computer, conversing in excited undertones as they jotted notes down in an exercise book. Eventually they paid up and moved away to a nearby table and I took their place. But what words to key in? I decided to start with 'swinging'.

But the computer beat me to it. Whatever I was attempting to sniff out, the couple before me had already been there, because I'd no sooner keyed S and W than a cookie completed the process for me and the screen was filled with the words SWINGING SAFARI – CAP d'AGDE.

Almost every other establishment in this complex seemed to be dedicated to sauna-ists, swingers or swappers. Deux by Deux, for instance, situated barely yards from where I was sitting, offered a maze of subterranean dance floors and dungeons, plus 'ample supplies of useful peepholes handily situated at crotch height'.

Le Phraeon, a club I'd already spotted across the concourse from the post office, specialised in 'gang bangs on Wednesday afternoons', while Exotic Dreams promised 'a sex club and water beds'. One establishment guaranteed 'two consummations' in the admission price. Whose job it was to adjudicate was anybody's guess, although I imagine Eddie George's tape measure would have come in handy. There were parties for enthusiasts of rubber, of pierced genitalia, even a Hot Chocolate tribute group. The subterranean floor plans looked substantial enough to withstand a nuclear attack.

'No one knows what goes on behind closed doors,' sang Charlie Rich. Never was a truer word spoken than here. Gazing about at the thousands enjoying the sunshine or watching Jenson Button having his tyres changed, it was impossible to tell who was who, or what was what. Perhaps herein lay its success to date.

The previous occupants of the computer, for instance, now sharing a dessert at an adjoining table. The boy was chattering nineteen to the dozen while his young partner looked on distractedly and waited to be fed gobbets of ice cream from a long spoon. Would these mild-mannered youths be hard at it through peepholes less than six hours from now? Or were they the ones stashing the bottles of fuel propellant and old rags in their apartment wardrobe? Most likely they were neither.

Yet now I looked more closely, there was a hint of sadness about the girl's features. Her button nose had a suspicious curve to it that smacked of surgical intervention, and the area around her eyes seemed to be gently suppurating, as if some lengthy invasive procedure was still deciding whether to settle. Was she a less than enthusiastic party to the demimonde of the 8 p.m. watershed, a reluctant convert accepting both physical and cosmetic compromise in order to keep her boyfriend? Who knew: it was all too easy to let your imagination run riot in Naked City.

I spent the rest of the afternoon walking barefoot in the surf along the beach. My walk took me along three kilometres of the most beautiful beachfront imaginable, pale wet sand imperceptibly sloping down into clear warm sea; and several times during my stroll I simply plunged into the water, each time enjoying the new-found freedom. Apart from a couple of men sitting in distant dunes sheepishly reading motorcycle magazines, Cap d'Agde was as innocent as *Rebecca of Sunnybrook Farm*.

It was only when I noticed that people were wearing swimsuits once more that I realised I'd strayed past the official boundary and was now ambling among the denizens of the neighbouring public beach. Yet even here, France displayed its greater maturity towards the human body. Anybody blundering unawares in similar circumstances back in England would have been followed home by an angry mob wielding banners and stoving in their front windows before demanding action from the council. Yet here my mistake was viewed with tolerance bordering on indifference. One sunbather even asked me if I'd mind venturing further into the surf to retrieve her tennis ball.

By the time I returned to my recliner, Jörgen had departed and the Lady Mayor was asleep. In the fog of my initial anxiety I'd foolishly forgotten Ruby's advice about sun cream and my buttocks were now like two braised pork chops, but otherwise I felt ten years younger. I ordered a sandwich from the beach bar and considered my options. With barely an hour left till chucking-out time, one aspect of Cap d'Agde – naturism and the naturist deal – had won me over utterly. Yet the other remained stubbornly beyond my grasp. How best to use my remaining time?

Just then I heard the strangled shrieks of the Bee Gees drifting in the breeze. I roused myself and followed the sounds over to a large building set some way back, from where their hit song 'Tragedy' was pouring out. A group of nudists was clustered round the entrance, while others were already on their way out, flecked with gobbets of soapy bubbles as if they'd just stepped out of a luxurious bath.

'Glamour-Puss Foam-n-Mousse Disco Extravaganza' screamed a Day-Glo sign pinned to the door.

A foam 'n' mousse disco would almost certainly be as near to sampling actual swinging as I might get, or indeed desire. I decided to take a peek inside. But a muscle-bound bouncer barred my way. He pointed to the bottom sentence. 'Strictly non-Solo' it read. My calm assurances in fractured French got precisely nowhere.

Then I noticed her: an elderly woman, possibly in her late sixties or early seventies, resembling a retired primary school teacher, her thinning hair an exotic medley of grey and bright pink, standing by herself a few yards away. She, too, seemed anxious to gain entrance, and like me seemed uncertain whether or not to brave the clipboard Himmler. We looked like Billy and Tilly No-Mates.

I don't quite know how we managed it. One moment we were apart, just a middle-aged man and an elderly woman standing forlornly outside a guarded doorway, then the next, without a word being spoken, we were converging simultaneously on the entrance. We timed our arrival perfectly. By now the steward was taking a call on his mobile phone, and we were waved through with barely a glance.

I found myself in a cavernous space illuminated by wheeling disco lights. In the centre of the floor a number of leathery individuals stood around, dancing in a desultory manner, while a machine attached to the wall spewed out cascades of lumpen foam, most of which was dropping straight to the floor. There were no writhing bodies, no acts of exotic hedonism, no sexual gymnastics: just a load of peeling Germans jogging up and down like revellers at a disco to celebrate someone's fiftieth birthday. And, as Robert Helpmann once observed, the trouble with nude dancing is, once the music stops, nothing else does.

Then I spotted Jörgen. He was rocking back and forth in a pair of orange jellies to 'How Deep Is Your Love', eyes closed, his huge belly like a hula skirt around his thighs and his Bobby Charlton comb-over hanging listlessly down like seaweed. He spotted me, raised his cocktail in salute and started shimmying across. It was time to go.

Were these customers regular naturists dipping their toes in the water of libertinism, or libertines who couldn't wait until the evening? It was impossible to tell. But of one thing I was quite sure: I'd seen enough. I could get this sort of thing at any Rotary Club dinner-dance back in Britain, and probably with an all-you-can-eat carvery thrown in for good measure. In any case, a siren was already sounding the half-hour warning bell for the closing of the gates.

Whatever else, I was now a firm convert to the naturist ideal. The starched, sniggering mentality I'd arrived with had dissolved under the bucolic magic of life in the raw. Nudity, far from being something out of the pages of *Viz*, now seemed the most natural thing in the world.

Of course the weather was everything, and it was difficult to see it ever taking off back home apart from in steamy, purpose-built indoor centres with integral climate control. But again France had shown me a way of approaching the good things in life without having to overdo it, send it up, trash it or run screaming in fear.

Regarding the other strand of this curious establishment, the jury was out. It had obviously once been the jewel in the naturist crown: yet Naked City risked losing all by hitching its star to a leisure pursuit that, for all its efforts to appear mainstream, was psychologically incompatible with the status quo.

The statistics spoke for themselves. Fewer naturists were now spending their time here, particularly those with young children, and the contingents from Germany and the Netherlands were being supplanted by visitors from America with only one aim in view. And what a view. Each new arson attack would further confirm Cap d'Agde's decline from the ideals of naturism still espoused in the publicity material. It would soon have to make a choice.

My final action was made purely on impulse. What better way to finish my day trip than by calling Ju? She'd be tickled to death to know where I'd been. And what a tale I had to tell. I slipped on my clothes at my favourite mini-roundabout, retrieved my phone from my shorts and called home.

It turned out I'd rung at a bad time. She was just sitting down to watch the semi-finals of *Britain's Got Talent*.

Well, this would lighten her humour. I told her of my exotic day spent among the swingers and sun-worshippers of Naked City. I regaled her with my encounter with Jörgen. I listed the incident of the woman with the oyster pick and the unfeasible blonde with her poodle. I detailed my expedition among the sex shops and ended up by laughing again with the recollection of dancing naked to the Bee Gees next to a German businessman among cascading bubble bath.

Finally I assured her that by the time they'd be cavorting on leather sofas with complete strangers and shining up their clitoris chains with anybody within buffing distance, I would be safely tucked up in bed. What's more, I was looking forward to it.

Julia?

Julia, are you still there?

Mini Marathon

ONE OF THE things that baffled me as kid was why the French always beat us in *Jeux Sans Frontières*.

Jeux Sans Frontières, you may recall, was the international arm of the BBC's popular domestic game show, *It's a Knockout*. Described variously as 'school sports day for adults' or 'the zany Olympics', the tournament featured teams from different towns, usually dressed in outlandish outfits, competing to perform tasks in absurd games that featured lengths of elastic, inflatable swimming pools and custard pies.

Inching along greasy poles with trays of wine glasses while your competitors bombard you with wet sponges in the hope of upending you into tubs of freezing water is something we Brits should have cakewalked. After all, summer fetes and carnivals consist of little else.

Yet we didn't. From the very first pan-national contest in the summer of 1967, when France's Nogent-sur-Marne came first and gallant little Bridlington came a lousy last, it was always the French teams who seemed to triumph. How could we, a nation steeped in the civic lunacy of rag weeks and begetter of *The Goons* and *Monty Python's Flying Circus*, lose so badly to a country we'd bailed out only thirty years before, particularly one so notoriously dismissive of anything smacking of civic silliness?

In fact – shock horror – it turns out *Jeux Sans Frontières* was not an English invention at all. The original concept had been dreamt up by none other than my dad's personal antichrist, Charles de Gaulle himself, some time in the early 1960s. The French president had first sketched out the notion as a means of fostering 'better relations between French and German youths', following the damage done to peace and harmony during the war.

Whatever the cause, my Friday-night viewing always ended with the French *tricolore* being waved by teams of ecstatic Frenchmen, while Lytham St Annes or Woking sat in the background smarting with impotence and shame. It all seemed so unfair.

I'd already noticed various flyers for the Trophée du Languedoc throughout Agde. The adverts depicted men in straw hats and hooped T-shirts apparently trying to skewer one another with giant cocktail sticks. It appeared less an episode of *Jeux Sans Frontières* and more Gilbert and Sullivan's *The Gondoliers* as directed by Sam Peckinpah.

But over a leisurely breakfast at my hotel, the proprietor, Monsieur Lessaud, was able to provide a full tabletop demonstration of what I could expect to see if I were prepared to hang around until the Sunday afternoon.

If there's one thing the French love, it's a historical re-enactment. Almost every town and village seems to have their own version of some long-forgotten conflict they feel they might have won if only it could have been the best-of-three, usually advertised by illustrations of people in doublet and hose gnawing on chicken bones or riding about in gleaming armour. But the Trophée du Languedoc, organised and managed by the magnificently named Société Nautique des Jouteurs Agathois (itself celebrating its hundred and fifth year), was palpably as good an example of the genre as I could stumble upon, and a must-see for any student of things Gallic.

In this case, two identical rowing boats (butter dishes), each powered by twelve oarsmen (sugar cubes), repeatedly hurl themselves towards each other on a section of river. The prow of each boat curves upwards into a wooden platform high above the water on which stands a single warrior (prune stone) who, armed only with a wooden lance and shield, attempts to spear, poleaxe, gouge or topple his competitor into the water as the boats surge past. Monsieur Lessaud was confident this once a year event would be right up my rue.

I SPENT SUNDAY morning playing with his charming two-year-old daughter, who sat gurgling happily on the floor of the foyer and trying to pull at anything she could get her tiny hands on. One of my most pleasurable half-hours of the whole trip was spent watching some Italian travellers trying to correctly refold their road map of Western Europe after she'd opened the entire document while they'd queued for thirds at the orange juice dispenser.

Afterwards I killed a couple more hours wandering round the old town, investigating its narrow alleyways and ancient buildings. Julia called during my walk to tell me, in case I wanted to know, that Michael Vaughan had just resigned as England cricket captain. It was the first piece of home news I'd had for some weeks.

Funny: before setting off on my trip I couldn't go more than a couple of minutes without a fix of John Humphrys or *Face the Facts*; I'd even downloaded some episodes of *In Our Time* onto my iPod in case I found life insupportable without Melvyn Bragg. But now it all seemed strangely peripheral and irrelevant. Political events seem a lot less important when the alternative is watching fully grown men on rowing boats trying to impale each other with lances.

I SUPPOSE IF you want to be summoned to a tournament of water jousting there's no better way than to hear a brass band playing 'La Marseillaise'. That's what I was beginning to love about the French. They didn't monkey about with ethnic inclusivity and the need to represent youth and cultural minorities; they just strap somebody into a tuba, rig up the *tricolore* and start bellowing about ferocious soldiers coming to slaughter our sons and wives, and we all know where we stand.

By the time I'd arrived at the riverbank, things were already cranking up. The towpath on both sides was crammed with spectators, with more lined up on the parapet of the bridge. I elbowed my way through until I found a berth right behind the judges' table.

Already marching towards us behind the band was one of the oddest processions I'd seen in recent years: a phalanx of beefy individuals in white uniforms and natty boaters, followed by a contingent of elderly women in knitted shawls and mob caps, and bringing up the rear, in clacking stilettos, what appeared to be debutantes out of the pages of the *Tatler* circa 1960.

At last everyone was settled, whereupon a line of senior elders and former champions took their places at a long trestle table placed on the towpath, headed by the *grand fromage* himself, the venerable Eternal President. On the table in front of him stood a statue in bronze of a muscular winged god wrestling with a lion, presumably the prize for the victorious jouster.

At 3 p.m. precisely, the president grabbed a microphone and asked everyone to stand. The town fell silent. A lone cornet player began a doleful lament, something melancholy and regretful in the vein of the theme from *Coronation Street*. For nearly a minute we stood in complete silence, the only distraction being the elderly maids discreetly handing bottles of water to one another from a large cardboard container. They looked like a remake of *Cranford* as sponsored by Evian.

No sooner had the lament died in the air than the entire band struck up the most unlikely sequel: Tony Christie's classic 1960s pop anthem, 'Yellow River'. Already hurtling towards each other on the river, and destined to collide in front of the judges' table, were two large rowing boats, being propelled by crews of straining oarsmen.

It was just as Monsieur Lessaud had depicted with his prune stones. Perched precariously on the elevated platform at the prow of each craft stood a hulking specimen of French manhood. Each was gripping a small wooden shield in one hand while swinging a lance in a laborious arc above his head with the other.

All I could make out from the frenzied commentary was that the contestant in the *bleu* boat was called Didier and the one in the *rouge* boat Philippe. Even as the Eternal President was adjusting the volume knob on his loudspeaker console from 'loud' to 'deafening', the two boats were ploughing furiously towards mutual oblivion. All it needed to complete the scene was Eddie Waring in a stripy blazer and Hush Puppies running around with a whistle. But there was nothing friendly about what occurred next.

As the boats passed within inches of one another, each jouster lifted his lance, aimed it straight at his opponent's ribcage, as if seeking to pin a butterfly on a giant piece of card, and braced himself for the impact. The collision was heart-stopping. A sound of splintering wood, curses and grunts from the two contestants, and next moment both of them somersaulted into the water and disappeared between the waves.

An anxious moment later, their heads appeared above the surface, Didier now bleeding profusely from a gash on his cheek. In between ingesting a fair portion of the river, he started shrieking complaints of foul play to the judges, who immediately began consulting ancient ledgers stacked on the table in front of them.

Didier couldn't wait. So incensed had he become that he took matters into his own hands, swimming across to Philippe and thumping him directly on the top of his head. This sparked a violent brawl that was only stopped by the intervention of a couple of swimmers from the referees' motorboat.

After much conferring, the Eternal President announced that the manoeuvre had been within the permitted rules of water jousting and that Philippe was therefore the winner. But by now the boats had been turned round to face the opposite direction, two new competitors were on the perches and the whole process began again.

This curious ritual was to be repeated endlessly over the next two hours, each time with different combatants. With every approach the process began afresh: plashing oars, rolling drums, Tony Christie hits, cheering crowds, splintering wood, curses, and the proclamation of a successful contestant through to the next round. A glance at the programme being studied by a German woman next to me suggested there were no fewer than eighty-eight candidates: until it was reduced to a single victor, this curious ceremony looked likely to continue for some time, possibly into next week.

By 5 p.m. we were barely a third of the way though the card. In truth, once you'd seen one water joust you'd seen them all, yet the crowd on the towpath appeared rapt. Everyone seemed to know or be related to one or other of the combatants. I kept expecting somebody to come round with a collection box for some local hospice or cancer charity, but having a communal laugh in order to raise funds for needy causes was not part of the mission statement of the Société Nautique des Jouteurs Agathois, Something far graver was at stake: civic assertion.

What clinched my decision to take a break from the spectacle was the German woman in the adjoining seat. First, she complained when I lit up my cigar, then she complained that I was reading her programme over her shoulder, then that my bag was taking up too much room under her seat. I suspected if I hung around much longer she'd start mentioning our bombing of Dresden. As it was, I squeezed past her as inelegantly as I could, and wandered into town for something to eat.

But the town had shut. Bars that a few hours before had been humming with customers were shuttered and closed, and restaurants I'd picked out as being likely venues for my evening meal had notices pinned to the doors reading 'back at eight due to exceptional circumstances'. Everyone in Agde, it seemed, was at the towpath.

In the end I took refuge in the only available option, the Four Aces kebab shop, a dog-eared takeaway located in an alleyway by the town hall. A couple of tired-looking Eastern Europeans were behind the counter, superintending a drooling hunk of pensioner's leg on a rotary spit.

With its greasy wall tiles, sticky floor and calendars advertising local breaker's yards, the place had exactly that look of despair that signifies similar establishments the length and breadth of urban Britain. I'd been hoping to get through my trip without ever eating somewhere like this: but it was Sunday, Agde was closed for the holidays and I was hungry. The chicken at least might be edible. Perhaps just this once.

But instead of the flaccid meat surrounded by shredded cabbage served up in a polystyrene tray that would normally be the result back home, I was rewarded with a place at a plastic table out on the pavement covered by a fresh paper tablecloth, and a delicious roast chicken dinner with baked onions, roast potatoes and salad with fresh vinaigrette, accompanied by a basket of delicious fresh bread and a *pichet* of cool water.

I sat in the shade of the town hall, listening to the distant sounds of cheering mixed with 'Billy Don't Be A Hero' drifting on the breeze. Even in these unpropitious circumstances provincial France seemed to be able to summon up a touch of pomp and occasion.

It was just as I was about to tuck into the baked onions that I spotted a man furiously beckoning to me from a plastic table on the other side of the doorway. He seemed insistent that I join him. I gathered up my plate and went over to see what the fuss was.

I was about to meet Agde's answer to Stuart Hall.

JEAN-PAUL GREETED my arrival at his table as if it were the final piece in some celestial jigsaw. Once formal introductions had been completed, he sat down, poured me a glass of rosé, despite my attempt to decline the offer, and welcomed me to his town.

Jean-Paul was a philosopher. I knew this much, because he told me so himself. A curious, animated little man with bushy eyebrows and an expression like a ventriloquist's dummy, his conversation came in spurts between mouthfuls of sausage. As he ate he explained his view of life, which was based on three central tenets:

1. He only had three years to live.
2. The inhabitants of Agde were cretins.
3. French cooking was unsurpassed throughout the world.

His conversation would have been almost engaging if it weren't for the fact he was completely pissed. I tried to steer the conversation towards general pleasantries by observing what a wonderful place Agde was, and how tasty the food, but my attempts to big up his home town seemed to momentarily enrage him.

'I am talking on things I am great expert. I know about cooking, my mother she was excellent cook.' His eyes filled with tears, and he took another mouthful of sausage as if to dull the pain.

'You know my signature meal?'

I confessed I didn't. He shrugged philosophically to indicate he didn't hold my ignorance against me, then launched into an explanation of how to cook beef with carrots and fried aubergines along with – and this, he was anxious to impress upon me, was the pièce de résistance – 'sauce of the cranberry'.

I agreed it sounded wonderful. He leaned over and grinned lasciviously. Would I have another drink? I assured him I hadn't even started this one yet. He considered my reply, then announced, as if it was the only feasible response, that his problem in life was that he had always 'wanted to go Scottish'.

I didn't know it was possible for such a primitive body movement to contain such nuance, but in Jean-Paul's hands the shrug was an instrument of infinite delicacy, indicating in this instance the cosmic unfairness of a world that forbade going Scottish to such a rabid enthusiast as himself.

I tried to catch the eye of the youths at the till, but they were serving a party of Italian teenagers. My only option was to endure.

'You like Scottish?' he asked.

I admitted I did as long as it was the right time and place. He nodded thoughtfully and took another glug of wine before launching into a story about a young woman from the Highlands he'd met while at catering college and how he'd finally lost her to a trawlerman from Stromness. He struggled for some moments to extricate his wallet from his back pocket, where presumably lay a dog-eared photo of his amour. Eventually he gave up the struggle and stared moodily at the table.

'You play chess?' he hissed suddenly. I replied that I did. The news delighted him. He had spent some time in Australia, he explained, during which he had found himself playing a game with Russian dissident Garry Kasparov.

'What is more, I beat him!'

'No!'

'YES!!' He let out a shriek of triumph that would scarcely have been bettered by the Eternal President. 'I beat Garry Kasparov! You know how? I play the Irish Gambit! You know what he offer me as prize?'

'No, tell me.'

He let out another cackle, before halting abruptly and putting his finger to his lips. 'Shhhhh. I tell you.' He turned my head to the side with the fingers of one hand and whispered in my ear.

'His wife.'

This confession sent him rocking with such horrified delight his eyebrows nearly disappeared beneath his hairline. 'HE OFFER ME HIS WIFE! She very beautiful, with, you know...' He cupped his hands in front of him to indicate her bust measurement, and ended by describing a classic hourglass figure in the air. Then silence descended once more.

'Chess is game where elephant may bathe and gnat may drink,' he concluded.

I asked him about the Trophée itself.

'C'est magnifique,' he answered spiritedly. 'In Trophée you witness the true spirit of the real France. Mimi Castaldo, you know him?'

I replied sadly not.

'Mimi win the Trophée three years in the run, four in total.' At this point he held up five fingers to prove his point. 'My mother, she know him. She cook for him. I play chess with him. The winner of the Trophée is God here in Agde. He sleep with most beautiful women, he has access to best tables in restaurants.'

'Including here?'

He dismissed the efforts of the Four Aces kebab shop with a theatrical swipe of his hand and by spitting in the direction of the doorway. 'This place is shit. The food is for the pigs; I wouldn't feed it for my dog.'

This final exhortation seemed to tire him and he fell moodily silent once more. I gobbled down the last of the *poulet* and paid up. Seeing my departure, he tottered to his feet and expressed the hope we would meet again. I hoped so too, adding my belief that one day he would fulfil his wish to go Scottish.

He shrugged again, indicating he was already fortified against the possibility it may never happen. Finally he handed me his business card, extracting a solemn promise to call him if I was ever again in the area. We shook hands and I was allowed to leave.

Before I had gone ten paces I heard him calling once more. But this time his exhortations were to the Italian students sitting on the nearby steps of the town hall. Like me, politeness got the better of them and they wandered over to join him. I suspected beef with carrots and sauce of cranberry was going to get several more airings before the evening was over.

The coup de grâce of my meeting with Jean-Paul at the Four Aces kebab shop was when I inspected his card on my way back to the river. He turned out to be the proprietor.

BACK ON THE river bank the cathedral bell was sounding the advent of evening mass and the tourney was approaching its climax. In the time I'd been away, the original eighty-eight had been whittled down to the finalists, and as I resumed my seat they were being heaved towards each other for the decider. Yet even now it was far from over.

So knackered were the rowers, and so afraid of falling at the final tilt were the participants, that it took nine more approaches before the larger of the two, a cherubic beefcake named Aurélien Evangelisti, was declared the victor, though sadly it was over a technicality rather than with the grandstand finish of skewering his opponent against the parapet of the bridge.

But if the finish was anticlimactic, the celebrations weren't. The ecstatic victor was ferried back to the shore where he accepted the bronze statue from a breathless Eternal President to a rousing rendering of the Beatles' 'Can't Buy Me Love'. No sooner had he lifted it in triumph than he was engulfed by well-wishers: blood-flecked opponents, blushing beauty queens, old maids, wizened gondoliers and members of the judging panel, along with hundreds of friends and supporters. Being the champion really seemed to matter in these parts.

And guess what? It was time for another procession. It always is in France. Now carrying the trophy on his shoulder and serenaded by another reprise of 'La Marseillaise', the victor was shepherded to the head of the crowd and invited to lead the entire congregation over the bridge and into the town, presumably for a king-sized knees-up. I was just tucking in at the back of the procession when my phone rang.

It was Julia. She'd run out of petrol on the North Circular and couldn't get the automatic petrol cap open. I withdrew from the procession and spent some minutes explaining the whereabouts of the releasing mechanism under the dashboard and where the emergency call-out number might be located on her AA membership card. By the time I'd finished, the riverbank was deserted and I was alone.

I hurried across the bridge and into the maze of empty streets surrounding the cathedral, yet the town seemed to have swallowed them up. But then the sound of martial music echoing from an upstairs window of the town hall showed me the way forward. The front doors were wide open, and from the burble of chatter spilling out from the first-floor windows, it was obvious the entire town had decanted upstairs: in fact, to the very room beneath which I'd dined less than an hour ago.

But there was a problem. Jean-Paul was still at his table, directly opposite the entrance. Now alone, he was pushing crumbs of bread and curling lettuce around the tabletop with a plastic fork, presumably in an attempt to relive his Irish Gambit that had proved so successful back in Australia.

I sneaked behind a pillar at the bottom of the steps and watched for some minutes. At last his eyelids closed and he fell into a fragile doze. I hopped past him, skipped up the front steps, into the entrance hall, up an ornate marble staircase decorated with frescoes, and seconds later was reunited with the Trophée du Languedoc and the inhabitants of Agde.

The room they'd shipped up in was obviously an official council chamber used for civic functions: ornate tapestries hung from the walls, and scenes of naval battles interspersed with sculpted angels bedecked the ceiling. Someone had set up an impromptu bar, from which glasses of wine and orange juice were being dispensed. At the very front of the throng stood the champion, still with his prize clamped to his right ear and beaming at each new compliment. Here was liberté, égalité et fraternité made manifest. As if to prove the point, one of the contestants pushed a tumbler of squash into my hand.

It seemed wherever I went in this strange land, sooner or later I rubbed up against civic pride in all its municipal glory. Local tradition and identity were still something to be cherished and celebrated. There is an expression over here, *la règle*, which, roughly translated, means everything done at the right time and in the right way. These might be unfashionable qualities in today's 'just-do-it' world, but I had a feeling the benefits of *la règle* far outweighed its shortcomings.

I'd come to the Trophée thinking it was all a bit of fun, something to attract tourists to the town and give the local papers a nice photo op for their front page. But far from an excuse for a bit of tin rattling, events such as these kept the fabric of small-town society from fraying at the edges. I envied them their sashes and their protocol and their sense of belonging.

As the entire room joined in a third (or was it a fourth?) reprise of 'La Marseillaise', my thoughts drifted back to *Jeux Sans Frontières*. The expression of civic identity through anachronistic sporting endeavour may have been dreamt up as a foreign policy initiative in the corridors of the Elysée Palace, but it had already been happening throughout France for hundreds of years. All you needed today was to replace the T-shirts and boaters with giant duck outfits, and you could have filmed it there and then.

No wonder they always won. Sneaky *bâtards*.

Barrière Reef

IF YOU ASKED a Frenchman the way to the French Riviera, he couldn't tell you. Not out of native obtuseness or because it is a particularly highly guarded secret, but because the name is an Anglo-Saxon invention.

For the French it is the Côte d'Azur, the azure coast, glittering blue of sea and sky, where the sun shines for more than 320 days a year. But it has an English moniker because for centuries it has been a place of pilgrimage for us Brits: or at least, for those who can afford it.

Ever since it was dragged up from ancient Mediterranean olive groves and fishing villages, it has been a playground of exclusivity. A fifty-mile stretch of winding hairpin coastline dropping precipitously to the sea, made forever famous by Cary Grant and Grace Kelly motoring so glamorously and recklessly through it in Hitchcock's *To Catch a Thief*. From St Tropez in the west to the principality of Monaco and the Italian border in the east, the names in between run like a litany of stylish promise: Cap Ferrat, Antibes, Cannes, Nice. Early British travel writers promoted the region's climate as a cure for consumption, and in the wake of their grudging praise, the Riviera became not only a diversion, but also a destination.

When the railways came in the 1860s, so did the sponsorship

of European royalty. In 1872 the Prince of Wales started coming for three weeks every spring in the royal yacht *Britannia*, and the sport of outdoing your peers with the size of your boat has never looked back.

By the twentieth century, the Americans had joined the party and it began to resemble a kind of Mediterranean Stella Street where, if you found the right grand hotel bar in the 1930s, you might enjoy a sing-song around the piano with Edward VII, Somerset Maugham and Scott Fitzgerald, or perhaps a dance round the handbags at the Discothèque Quatre-Saisons with Edith Wharton, Isadora Duncan and Coco Chanel.

The tourist industry hereabouts owes a great debt to Coco. It is claimed she invented the vogue for sunbathing when she acquired a tan on the Côte in 1923, and on returning to Paris made it all the rage. Add to that the first appearance of Brigitte Bardot on Cannes's famous beachfront in that bikini in 1953, and the Côte d'Azur's reputation as the place to see and be seen was confirmed.

Now the Americans and English have largely been replaced as *chiens suprêmes* by the new royalty – Arab princes, Russian oligarchs and the super-rich of Hollywood, who still come here for the film festival.

And now I was coming too.

FOR ANYONE WITH acting pretensions, Cannes is the ultimate European destination. Arriving by helicopter on the famous Croisette for the premiere of your latest movie, this is the dream of every jobbing actor.

I had to acknowledge it was never going to happen. Although I'd been happy enough with my one line in the recent Hollywood blockbuster *V for Vendetta* ('Send more troops immediately to

Sector Four'), I recognised that by itself it was unlikely to propel me across the red carpet or win the coveted Palm d'Or.

No matter: at least I could pretend. I could have my photograph taken on the carpet, or gambol on the beach – even loll by a trillion-pound yacht, as long as I didn't actually set foot on the gangplank. A vivid imagination would suffice in all respects, except one. If I wanted to experience the movie-star life in Cannes, there was one experience I couldn't fake. I had to stay at the Majestic.

The Majestic – or, to give it its full title, the Majestic Barrière – is one of the two or three hotels you always see on the movie round-ups, usually with Gary Cooper or Bruce Willis standing in a tux with a lighted cigarette in one hand and a smouldering blonde in the other. A palatial art-deco structure, it occupies the prime spot on the Croisette, directly facing both the famous beachfront and the Palais des Festivals, epicentre of the annual film beano.

Whether you sit on its impressive sun deck gawping as Madonna and Clint Eastwood sweep past, or lounge in one of its discreet deluxe suites on the top floor, the Majestic offers an experience described in one guidebook as 'criminally posh'. It's easy to run up a bill the size of the French national debt if you're not careful. No wonder film stars only venture here when someone else is paying for it.

In addition to traditional French décor and black marble bathrooms, the hotel also allegedly boasts a heated outdoor pool, a fitness centre, five tennis courts, multilingual staff, barbecue grills, soundproofing, climate controls, hairdryers, pet-sitting services, toiletries, slippers, DVD players and cribs. I wasn't sure I'd need many of them, but it was nice to know they were there in case of an emergency.

But if the facilities were mouth-watering, the cost of them was eye-watering. Don't even ask, I told myself as I dialled the reservation desk. Instead, my faux-confident demand for a room seemed to have the desired effect. Instead of asking for a fax outlining my family's heraldic shield and the phone number of my hedge-fund manager, the voice paused just a few moments before answering, 'Would that be a standard or a sea view, monsieur?'

And I was in. It was simple as that. One of the most luxurious hotels in the entire country was expecting me with open arms.

I MAY HAVE daydreamed about dropping into Cannes by private helicopter, but in the event my choice of transport was a comedy of errors. Presuming the August trains on the Côte would be full to bursting, I succumbed to the allure of the one-euro bus ride along the Riviera, thinking it would be the better bet. In fact, the journey, a half-hour sprint by train, took nearly four hours by bus.

We crawled through endless resorts in a slow-moving crocodile of holiday traffic, stopping every few minutes to let on scores of tourists, none of whom had the correct change. In addition, every other one clambered on with either suitcases or giant inflatable lilos in the shape of popular cartoon characters, requiring the driver to get out and rearrange the luggage compartments every ten minutes. Kipling called Cannes 'a music hall review', P.G. Wodehouse called it 'a loathly hole', while the French writer Guy de Maupassant felt so depressed during his stay here that he cut his own throat. By the time I hobbled off the coach just after 2 p.m., I was ready to agree with all three.

The Majestic, at least, was hard to miss. It dominated the front like a colossus. Even the drive to the entrance was long enough to merit a Little Chef halfway up. Lamborghinis jostled with Lotuses and Ferraris for the attention of the porters, the sort of vehicles usually reserved for transporting Mafia bosses to their local barbers. Nearly all of the number plates were in Russian or Arabic.

The revolving door into the interior would itself have happily done me for a couple of nights. Once through I found myself dwarfed by a foyer decorated in gold leaf and supported by impressive columns, at the base of which were fastened display cases of exquisite jewellery. Black leather sofas and designer boutiques fringed the area, while bellhops looking like refugees from *Cinderella* scurried about with lizard-skin suitcases. It was quite a place.

A starchy concierge, all pressed waistcoat and pearl cufflinks, looked up and gave me a courtly smile.

'Monsieur?'

'Checking in. Name of Simkins.' I was determined not to stand there drooling at the ceiling.

'Ah yes. Room 545. Suite overlooking the sea. Could I trouble you for your credit card, sir?'

I fished in my pocket and pulled out my wallet. A one-euro bus ticket fluttered down onto the desk in front of him.

'Yours, I think,' he said, picking it up gingerly and handing it back. He took the card from my trembling hand and inserted it into the terminal on the desktop.

As the machine whirred and clicked, I felt a rising sense of excitement. I rarely, if ever, allowed myself treats such as this, but I justified my decision as reward for six weeks of relative slumming it. With all these fabulous extras on offer and less than a day to enjoy them, I was intending to hit the ground running. In fact, I could do with a dip now after the misery of that ride. I asked where I might find the heated open-air swimming pool.

'The swimming pool is closed, sir.'

'Closed? The swimming pool?'

'I'm afraid so, monsieur. We are currently undergoing an extensive refurbishment and renovation, and although the building work has ceased for the summer the pool has to remain closed for reasons of safety.'

Oh well. I'd have to spend a bit more time in the fitness centre.

'That, too, is closed, I'm afraid, sir.'

'Closed? The fitness centre?'

'I'm afraid so, sir. We have arranged for a few of the smaller machines to be placed in one of the conference rooms, but obviously this may not meet your requirements.'

My deluxe experience was beginning to turn into something less than memorable. I made a final effort.

'Well, at least tell me where I can find the health spa.' If nothing else, I could relax in a warm Jacuzzi and then steam away some of the grime of the trip in the sauna, apparently one of Europe's finest.

'Once again, sir...' He gave a shrug and pressed the button to complete the transaction. The machine whirred for a few seconds and began to spew out a receipt. Too late.

'Your card,' he said, handing it back to me. Was it my imagination or had it shrunk?

Oh well. Damage done. With the entire building apparently being rebuilt about my head, there was nothing for it but to freshen up in my room. The way things were going it might be the only part of the hotel still open.

'Your room is not ready yet, sir.'

'Not ready?' It may have been the effects of sitting in that bus next to a giant inflatable Spongepants for much of the day, but the reception was swimming before my eyes.

'I'm afraid not, sir. Check-in is customarily not until fifteen hundred hours.'

'Fifteen hundred hours?'

'We will do all we can, sir, but it is stipulated in the terms and conditions.' He indicated a glossy leaflet at the side of the desk. 'In the meantime, may I suggest you leave your luggage with our concierge, after which you may like to take a walk along the Croisette, and my colleague will telephone you on your mobile as soon as it ready.' He tore off the printout emerging from the terminal and handed it over.

'Jesus!'

'Pardon?'

'Nothing.' I'd caught sight of the total. It was staggering. Over eight hundred quid, even before local taxes and whatever fiendish ways they could think of to break me, and I still hadn't got inside the door. You could stay at the Hôtel des Lapins in Bordeaux for nearly four weeks for that sum, and you'd get your own stash of heroin on top of the wardrobe thrown in.

I planted myself on a nearby sofa to recover. On the other side of an onyx coffee table sat a sulky teenager in a designer sarong, holding a gold-encrusted Gameboy with one hand and texting on her mobile with the other; while in a far corner a terrified Filipino nanny struggled to maintain control of a couple of young children who were kicking a beach ball between the chairs. A woman in her sixties with a face sculpted by Myton or Taylor Woodrow sat at the far end, distractedly reading a newspaper. I hadn't seen a pair of lips like hers since I'd last visited the London aquarium.

I needed a drink. But the bar menu had yet more bad news. At nearly a tenner for a glass of Heineken, and even a Cola-lite weighing in at over a fiver, my carefully planned budget was haemorrhaging with each minute.

Instead I sat drinking in the atmosphere. You could certainly imagine Brad or Tom being at home here. Most of the residents were dressed in the customary garb of the modern über-rich: designer jeans, bespoke espadrilles, ornate sunglasses, with cashmere sweaters draped carefully round their shoulders. They stood about in ones and twos, distractedly studying the jewellery cases as they waited for their Porsches to be retrieved from the carport.

Eventually my room was ready. As we waited for the elevator, the concierge explained that some of the facilities were still available, including a stretch of private beach exclusively for residents directly opposite the hotel. I didn't even need to show my room card, just state my name and enjoy the facilities.

Room 545 was certainly impressive. With a view out over the building works towards the esplanade and the sea beyond, it had its own bathroom with gold taps, a separate dressing room, and in the main living area itself a double bed the size of Rutland. Bottles of luxury shower gel decorated the washbasin, and a folder of elegant stationery with the hotel's logo was laid out on a padded desktop.

Other touches included personalised tissues, your own bath robe and the ubiquitous trouser press. A nice feature, explained the concierge, was a set of electronic venetian blinds that could be operated remotely from a switch by the side of the bed. He demonstrated the movement and bade me a very happy stay.

After he'd left I undressed and lay on my back in just my pants, playing with the venetian blind mechanism. There was something agreeable about it, the way they went up at a flick of the index finger, and then came back down again.

Part of their fascination was that, by contrast with the TV programmes on offer, watching the blinds going up and down was as absorbing as *Indiana Jones and the Temple of Doom*. Of the twenty-three available channels, the first eleven were Arabic. All of them seemed to offer versions of someone looking like former health minister Frank Dobson in a djellaba, sitting on a garish sofa. The twelfth was a demonstration featuring eight-year-olds in traditional Arab gear throwing knives at one another.

The thirteenth and fourteenth were devoted to something called Dubai Lifestyle. On one, five bling-encrusted teenagers were conducting a fevered discussion in Los Angeles English about the pressure exerted on film stars in Qatar to succumb to plastic surgery. On the other, the same quintet were grooming tiny dogs on their laps and discussing the best type of diamond-studded colour to go with the pet's personality.

It got worse: vividly coloured soap operas with gibbering actors slamming doors and bursting into tears, government announcements on oil production (Frank Dobson having changed into a suit), before we got to channel nineteen and the relative sophistication of TV Ukraine showing a live demonstration of synchronised marching. Eventually *BBC News 24* appeared, and I've never been more pleased to see Peter Sissons in my life.

The next problem was hunger. I couldn't go out as the porter still hadn't arrived with my case, and my only pair of shorts was now soaking in the bathroom sink.

Then I remembered. On my way to the room I'd noticed a silver trolley parked a dozen or so yards further down the corridor. God knows I never thought I'd do this, but if these channels were any indication of the tastes of the clientele, they probably weren't the sort who were used to the 'eat it all up, there are children starving in Africa' school of gourmandising. With luck they'd be at the local Mercedes dealership ordering something convertible for the evening. There was sure to be something on offer.

I put on the handy dressing gown that was hanging on the bedroom door and looked out. The trolley was still there. I hurried along to the far end, past framed photographs of Richard Chamberlain and Jack Nicholson arriving for some long-forgotten bun fight. I remember auditioning for this sort of caper once. I think it was an advert for breakfast cereal where the desperate hotel guest ends up sitting in his underpants on the bottom tier of the trolley still eating Crunchy Nut Cornflakes as it's wheeled back to the lifts. I hadn't got the advert, but I didn't intend to fail a second time.

I lifted the serviette. Underneath was a small wicker basket containing two uneaten bread rolls and some cheese. I stuffed the contents into my pockets of my gown and hurried back.

I was midway through this impromptu feast when the door burst open and the porter marched in unannounced with my case. Lying on a bed dressed only in pants and eating stale bread rolls while watching Arab children throw knives at each other could have had landed me in gaol, but thankfully the porter had been under the misapprehension I was still cruising the Croisette, and was so abashed at his intrusion he left without even hanging about the doorway with his hand open for a tip.

It was nearly four by the time I was ready to venture out. I crossed the Croisette, four lanes of angry traffic separated by a central reservation planted with swaying palms, shimmied between a children's merry-go-round and a café selling glutinous croque-monsieurs, and approached the beach. A smart flag with the hotel logo was fluttering by the top of a flight of wooden steps. The sea looked inviting, confirming the reports by celebrated visitors over the centuries of turquoise water and cloudless skies. Now, at last, I could enjoy my own slice of chic for a couple of hours.

I hurried down the decking staircase and flashed a smile at the attendant.

'Simkins, room 545,' I said brightly.

'Thank you, sir. Welcome to the Majestic Barrière beach, enjoy your stay...' He ticked off my name on a computerised checklist and indicated an area of sand at the foot of the steps. In truth, to call it a private beach was something of an overstatement – I'd seen larger children's sandpits from B&Q. There was room for barely three individuals all changing their trunks at the same time, and much of it had been claimed by a huge woman on a sun lounger with a Yorkshire terrier on her lap.

The attendant sensed my hesitation. 'Of course, you can always use the pontoon, sir, that's for your enjoyment as well.' He pointed me towards a handsome structure gently bobbing up and down, at the end of which were more recliners. Several overweight business types were sprawled on them, tapping away on laptops perched on their stomachs, while at the far end some dudes were playing an impromptu game of volleyball.

'Your credit card, please, sir?'

'My credit card?'

'Yes, sir. Or you can put it on your room bill if you prefer.'

'My room bill?'

Word had obviously been passed down from the concierge that the English bloke in the green crocs with a weakness for Arab boys throwing knives was a bit slow on the uptake. He smiled graciously. 'Yes, sir, there is a charge for the facilities.'

'How much?'

'The beach area is thirty-six euros a day or twenty-eight for a half day, and use of the residents' platform is fifty-six euros per day or forty-six for the afternoon. Recliners are, of course, included and beach towels are available.' He seemed to anticipate my next question. 'Beach towels are five euros.'

The businessman J.P. Morgan once wrote, 'If you have to ask how much it costs, you can't afford it.' I may have decided to throw caution to the wind when I made the booking but this was surely taking the mickey.

I sat squashed and unhappy on the public beach, surrounded on all sides by squabbling families. Barely two feet away, on the other side of the flimsiest piece of trellis I've ever seen, was an area of real estate that I considered rightfully mine. I was close enough to hear the woman slurping her cocktails up through a straw. Yet it might as well have been fifty miles away in Monaco.

And as for the pontoon: it seemed even more enticing now I wasn't prepared to pay for it. Through my murderous haze it seemed everyone was a possible celebrity. The fat woman with the dog looked uncannily like Vanessa Feltz, now I looked closely. And wasn't that portly American blowing up his kid's beach ball Richard Dreyfuss? And what about that guy covered in body oil and wearing a thong, playing volleyball with a load of mincing acolytes. John Barrowman, surely?

I felt mugged. Apart from coshing me over the head and making off with my wallet, the Majestic Barrière couldn't have demonstrated a more perfect example of daylight robbery. But this was no good. Perhaps a swim would cheer me up. I plodded determinedly out into the water.

In truth the sea made for greasy bathing, though whether it was the amount of sun oil on the backs of the other swimmers or the number of motor launches puttering about, it was impossible to say. At one point something floated past in the water, which, after a colossal act of will, I was able to persuade myself was the remains of a breakfast roll. At least I could take comfort from the fact that those poseurs on the pontoon would have to share the same disagreeable water as me. Nature is no heeder of man's footling attempts at annexation.

It was this realisation that gave me my idea. I swum round into the bit of sea that would also have been prohibited if the Majestic had only possessed a long enough piece of trellis, until my feet felt sand. A few more strokes and my stomach scraped the seabed.

I stood up in water barely ankle-deep and grinned smugly at the hotel attendant and the lady with the dog. As long as I didn't actually remove my feet from the sea, I was untouchable. I freely admit it was one of the most pointless, adolescent and time-wasting things I have ever attempted, but it made me feel better. What with this and the impromptu meal I was beginning to claw back some of my initial expenditure. Isobel at the Biarritz casino would have been proud of me.

It was time to take a look at what had brought my wife here nearly forty years ago as an au pair. Might as well start with the epicentre of the movies, the celebrated Palais des Festivals.

THE CANNES FILM festival, as in most things French, only began life as a protest gesture. So incensed was the indigenous film industry at the decision by the judges at the 1938 Venice film festival to bow to fascist pressure and award its top prize to a German documentary that the idea of a home-grown alternative was born.

Hitler was never one to take that sort of thing lying down, and on the eve of the opening ceremony in 1939 he upstaged it in spectacular style by invading Poland, an act that forced several leading movie stars of the day, including Mae West, Tyrone Power and George Raft, to turn back without even having their yachts valet-parked.

Nowadays, of course, its reputation as the world's leading film marketplace is assured. I'd been looking forward to a sight of the famous red carpet, but the mighty Palais des Festivals proved one of the most dismal buildings I'd ever witnessed: and you're talking here to somebody who visited the Millennium Dome. Built in 1982 specifically to house the rapidly expanding film festival, it was nicknamed 'the bunker' even before it was finished, and it didn't take a minute this afternoon to see why.

Built from what appeared to be pre-distressed concrete, it looked like something designed by Stalin for provincial Siberia and left here by mistake: enormous, threatening, unattractive and forbidding in equal measure, it squatted like a huge toad in the middle of the Croisette, forcing everyone to sidestep round it or turn back.

Even the famous carpeted staircase was apparently an architectural cock-up. Following incidents in which several leading celebrities stumbled during their festival ascent, an intermediate landing was hastily inserted halfway up the twenty-four steps, so that today it has a heavy, lumbering look to it.

Nonetheless, the treads were occupied by the usual gaggle of tourists and star-struck movie buffs having their photos taken. A couple from Germany asked me to take their snap, and as someone had left an assortment of life-size cardboard cut-outs of movie icons for the purpose, I persuaded them to pose with their arms draped round Daniel Craig as 007. From somewhere inside a rock concert was tuning up, and the air was rent with curious screeches and thumps. I was anxious to be away.

My real destination was the marina, centrepiece of Cannes's cosmopolitan reputation and a place where my wife had first interfaced with the French. She spent some months on a yacht here in the mid-1970s as a nanny to an aristocrat's children, partly to broaden her cultural horizons, partly to escape the attentions of a man from the Wigan branch of New World gas cookers who'd developed a crush on her.

He apparently turned up at the yacht some weeks after her arrival, having cycled all the way across France to find her: adding he'd just have to leave his wife and everything would be hunky-dory. No wonder she was so traumatised by the experience.

It wasn't difficult to find the Port Vieux. Just follow the masts. The pontoons were nose to tail in luxury motor cruisers, each of which could have managed the entire Dunkirk evacuation without government help. Even the smallest vessels were huge, while the bigger ones seemed like ocean liners.

Julia had described her time here as like being inside a gilded prison. It should have been paradise, she said, but the experience was made hell by being forced to share it with people you'd cross the street to avoid – were it not for the fact you were being paid to look after their brattish children.

It seemed little had changed.

The entrance to the marina wasn't actually forbidden to the public, but it was designed to make things as difficult as possible while still encouraging you to take a gander: presumably much like the celebrities onboard. The coquettish teasers employed by the port authority included curious little dogleg turnstiles that seemed to have no discernable ambition other than to hold you up, meaningless lengths of chain suspended between pillars you could easily circumvent, and signs asking you not to come on board when it was bloody obvious that nobody would dare try it without an invitation in case they were shot by a Kalashnikov.

And it was busy. Couples with small cameras and backpacks ambled up and down, gazing open-mouthed and speculating in low murmurs about how they'd cope with such a lifestyle, were fate or the national lottery to permit it.

Huge three- and four-deck ocean cruisers bobbed cheek by jowl, their protective buoys squealing in complaint as they squashed against their neighbours. Every craft sported spacious open-air dining areas at the rear, furnished in teak and mahogany. Glass chandeliers hung over gleaming dining tables decorated with vases stuffed with sunflowers, and crowning the top of each boat was enough radar and sonar tracking equipment to keep NASA happy for a year. From all sides, jet skis hung like giant pieces of jewellery. How could Julia possibly have been so unhappy living on one of these deluxe behemoths?

Many of the boats seemed to be registered in Nassau or Georgetown. Their names suggested long leisurely days at sea sipping the finest champagne and swimming with tuna-friendly dolphins: *Lady Lisa*, *Galaxy*, *Arabesque* and *Sunny Dream*. It was impossible to estimate how much the bigger ones might cost simply because I can't count that high.

By the time I'd wandered along the various pontoons a few times it was early evening, and many of the rich and glamorous of the jet set had finished their meals on deck and had departed for the casino or some modish nightclub. Cabin doors swung idly on their hinges while weary staff in gleaming white uniforms cleared away dinner plates and mopped deserted decks. Lights blazed, huge wraparound televisions blared pop videos into opulent lounges devoid of viewers, laptops lay discarded on sofas. The *Conan O'Brien Show* was playing on one satellite TV screen the size of my local multiplex, the canned laughter echoing through the empty boat and out into the night.

At the end of one particularly imposing pier stood a craft that dwarfed all the rest, appropriately named *Don't Touch Me*. It was simply colossal. Add a few gun emplacements and you could have subdued a small country with this boat, a towering monstrosity in gleaming blue and gold with six decks and enough motorised dinghies stashed on the poop to mount an invasion.

A small crowd of sightseers was gathered in front of it, taking pictures and talking in hushed tones as if in church. This craft, too, was deserted, but sitting on the bollard to which it was tethered was a young man in his early twenties, kitted out in official *Don't Touch Me* livery of white uniform with blue trimming.

Yussef was having a crafty fag and obviously enjoying a few minutes sitting down while his owners were away enjoying themselves. He looked exhausted, yet was obviously enjoying the minor celebrity status his position afforded him and seemed happy to answer inquisitive bystanders.

He spoke so softly it was impossible to hear much of what he said, but it was evident that *Don't Touch Me* was the pick of the boats. Eventually I edged near enough to ask him a question of my own. What, I enquired, were the dimensions of the craft from front to back? He smiled sheepishly, looked around him to check he wasn't being monitored, and quietly informed me it was fifty-six feet. No fewer than twenty-six crew members were required in order to function at full capacity.

'And guests?'

He puffed quietly on a cigarette before answering. *Don't Touch Me* could happily accommodate twenty-two passengers in supreme comfort. By my reckoning that meant nearly fifty people could happily coexist without having to queue for the chemical toilet. I've been in hotels smaller than that.

Eventually the other bystanders wandered off, and I happily accepted his offer of a fag. There was something sad and beautiful about Yussef, and we stood in silence for some moments, the only sound the gentle lapping of water beneath the pontoon and the occasional throaty roar of some jet-powered Ferrari inching its way along the Croisette. I ventured that many people wandering along the harbourside would envy him his job.

Yussef agreed he was one of the lucky ones. He enjoyed his work. He'd started out in commercial shipping but the work was hard and the pay uncertain, whereas this gave him regular hours and a sense of status. Although wages were low, they were guaranteed, and it gave him extra satisfaction knowing that it benefited his family in the Yemen, who were very poor and relied heavily on his monthly contribution.

Did he get home much?

'My father is very sick,' he said simply. 'I cannot visit home, but he needs much medicine and the money I am earning here will help to keep him alive.' He threw his fag end into the inky water and watched it sink below the surface. 'Perhaps one day I will see him again,' he added softly.

When I asked him if *Don't Touch Me* was capable of sailing on the ocean, he smiled as if I'd asked him whether it would safely make it across to the other side of the harbour. In fact, the journey they were about to commence would take them right across the Atlantic to Bermuda. 'Many days at sea,' he said.

So what happened if the weather was bad?

'No problem.' He shrugged. 'We load the boat onto to a larger boat which makes the journey for us.' A 'dog express', the procedure was apparently called. Yussef assured me the larger boats did it all the time.

When I asked him how much this little baby cost, his smile widened. This was obviously the question he was most frequently asked, presumably hundreds of times a fag break. 'Forty million dollars, fifty million?' he estimated with a shrug.

'Fifty million?'

'Sure, why not?'

I could think of plenty of reasons, but instead asked him how he got on with his employers. This had always been the aspect of shipboard living Julia recalled with least fondness.

'They're OK,' he replied warily. 'It all depends. Sometimes it can be tough, but this is their boat, not ours. These people are very rich, very...' He invited me to complete the sentence and it hung in the air. 'Once you are at sea you have to work as hard as they require. But–'

'YUSSEF!'

A woman of middle years had arrived behind us and was already walking up the gangplank towards the stateroom. She was dressed expensively with glittering earrings and carefully coiffed hair decorating a permatan. In the darkness she'd caught us both unawares.

Yussef shot up as if stung by a cattle prod. The woman barked a furious reprimand at him in French, made worse by the fact that she didn't bother to look at either of us as she thundered past. I didn't need my *Instructions for British Servicemen* to know what she was saying, all I needed to do was to watch Yussef's features. It was something along the lines of: 'You bloody slacker, do you think I pay you good money to fritter your time away yakking to a grubby tourist when you're supposed to be on duty all evening and ready to stand to attention whenever I come within saluting distance!'

Whatever its nuance, Yussef was unravelling before my eyes. He glanced back at me with a terrified look, desperate for reassurance that it didn't look as bad as he feared, that her words weren't as harsh as he'd imagined, that his job wasn't going to be terminated just as soon as the woman's husband got to hear about it.

I could offer no comfort. The woman had already disappeared inside, slamming a galley door just in case her message wasn't explicit enough. He scuttled back up the gangplank behind her, picked up the nearest squeegee and began mopping the deck furiously as if trying to erase his error. He looked horror-stricken. And I can't say I blame him. I too would be horror-stricken at the notion of spending my time trapped on board any boat named *Don't Touch Me* with such a hard-faced banshee for weeks on end. However big the boat was, it wouldn't be big enough for me.

I wished him a discreet au revoir: but even if I'd fetched John Barrowman in his thong from the pontoon and asked him to do three choruses of 'I'd Do Anything,' I doubt I'd have regained Yussef's attention. I strolled off back in the direction of the Majestic and my six-hundred-quid kip.

Poor Yussef.

Back along the Croisette, the road was lined in furiously revving sports cars with parties to go to and not an inch of tarmac available between them. The rock concert was now in full swing in the bowels of the Palais to the accompaniment of laser lights probing the sky. My final diversion before heading back to the hotel was to stand on the red carpet and have my own photo taken by a couple of giggling Koreans. I asked if I could be snapped with a celebrity cut-out.

'Which one you like?' asked the eldest of the girls, tittering nervously. It seemed the other options besides Daniel Craig were J-Lo and Chewbacca from *Star Wars*.

In the end I plumped for Chewbacca. If that woman on the boat was still around, I would need all the help I could get.

I ENDED MY evening in the open-air restaurant at the hotel. It was a beautiful starlit night, and the smell of succulent meat from a sumptuous charcoal grill mingled with the scent of flowers. Sour-faced couples sat at candlelit tables toying stonily with glasses of champagne, while a female singer accompanied by a lone guitarist serenaded the diners with Astrud Gilberto hits.

It was a hard old battle for the poor girl. Quite apart from the distant roar of car engines, somebody back at the concert venue had obviously turned up the volume, because the best efforts of the rock band were echoing crisply off the walls of the Majestic's east wing and landing, pitch-perfect, directly in our soup.

When I ordered up the cheapest item on the menu, a simple bowl of pasta with fresh tomato sauce, I instinctively found myself adding a 'sorry about that', as if my very choice of meal had exposed me as a cheapskate Brit who wasn't playing the game. Yet the waiter seemed to warm to my blurted apology and kept returning to ask if I was enjoying my meal. I got the impression smiles were thin on the ground for the hotel staff among the denizens of the Majestic Barrière.

'Criminally posh' was how it had been described. But that could have applied just as well to the entire town. Cannes, I suspected, had once been, and probably still was, a splendid location: after all, visitors as varied as the Prince of Wales, Kipling and Rupert Brooke had all described its elegant promenade, its shimmering sea and, above all, its graceful and picturesque architecture. Even the curmudgeonly Wodehouse had eventually been won over. Yet I couldn't forget poor old Yussef.

His plight this evening seemed to sum up the problem with the place. It was tyrannised by people with too much money. The seafront and cafés may be crowded with revellers, but there was an air of joylessness – or, rather, a sulkiness – as if the ability to appreciate the finer things in life has been dulled due to long years of familiarity. Hopefully the rest of the Côte d'Azur would wear its natural riches with a lighter touch.

WHEN I RETURNED to the marina the next morning, *Don't Touch Me* had disappeared. If Yussef was correct it was probably already halfway to Bermuda. I hope for both his and his father's sake that Yussef kept his job on the craft, and that somewhere in the world he's still swabbing decks and polishing surfaces.

At least, I think I do.

Mmmmm ... Bistro

CHARLES DE GAULLE once complained, 'How can you govern a country that has 246 different types of cheese?' His claim was a gross distortion: there are estimated to be more than 1,000 kinds, and the average Frenchman consumes nearly 50 pounds of the stuff a year.

What is it about French and food? The consumption of calories over here has been turned from basic instinct into the beautiful game. France's immersion in the pleasures life has to offer is probably at its fullest expression when it comes to grub. To the French, food is sacrament, the taking in of the body of France in all her rich bounty. Their cuisine is a badge of national and local identity, and the reverence with which it is handled both a genuflection to their ancestors and a living example to their children.

While the French have worshipped at the dining table for millennia, one man's name and reputation rings clear above the cacophony of table chatter: Auguste Escoffier (1846–1935), the emperor of French cuisine, who took the ornate but cumbersome tradition of cooking for the toffs and turned it into the food of Everyman. During a prodigious career at some of the greatest restaurants and hotels in Europe, he codified and modernised French food, culminating in the mighty *Guide Culinaire*, published in 1903 and containing over 5,000 recipes, including sixty-two for tournedos of beef, 104 for sole and a recipe for oxtail soup which takes five hours.

While it's a source of some piffling comfort to Englishmen to know that his most creative period occurred while at the Savoy Hotel in London, it's best not to mention it over here unless you want a plate of *poires et figues chaudes à la cannelle* tipped over your head. What it undeniable is that during his tenure in England's capital city, he produced some of his most illustrious dishes: including peach Melba in honour of the Australian soprano and tournedos Rossini in favour of the Italian composer.

That he ended up being dismissed for taking backhanders from suppliers proved a tragedy for Rosbifs everywhere, as he merely returned to his homeland to refine and reduce his genius over a low heat rather than bestow his benison on Victorian Britain. As a result, French cooking is synonymous with Michelin stars while ours is more redolent of their tyres. If Escoffier is France's culinary Godhead, ours is surely Saint Bernard Matthews. They live to eat, while in England we eat to give ourselves something to soak up the booze while we're watching *Match of the Day*.

It's our loss. The French still seem to care about how they raise every farm animal, and encourage every asparagus spear with amour. Never mind the local boulangerie and charcuterie, even at your local supermarket 90 per cent of the produce will be from within a thirty-kilometre radius, and just in case anyone tries pulling a fast one, the average French housewife questions her butcher or grocer like a well-honed Gestapo officer, demanding to inspect the family tree of every last leg and leaf.

My French education was clearly unthinkable without

sampling the best cuisine France could offer: regional, bespoke, unfussy, seasonal, reasonably priced and, if possible, served with a smile. It should have been a doddle – after all, it's impossible to eat a bad meal in France… or so everyone kept telling me. Yet until now my experience had suggested otherwise.

The novelist Norman Douglas may have avowed that 'the French could produce an excellent and nutritious substitute out of cigar stumps and empty matchboxes', but at some of the places I'd eaten during my trip the chef had obviously taken him at his word: from the *salade au fromage de chèvre chaud* in the café at Nantes station that reminded me of the joke 'I can't take that back now, sir, you've bent it', right through to stewed turkey and haricot beans near Bernadette's grotto in Lourdes that even divine intervention wouldn't have saved.

Perhaps I shouldn't have been surprised. 'We are no longer eating like the French,' one leading chef had recently complained in response to rising sales of convenience foods and ready-made sauces. 'We're eating like the English.' In France it doesn't get much worse than that.

And yet wonderful food was still everywhere I looked: on market stalls, in the windows of delicatessens, in shopping baskets on every street, and on the plates of virtually every half-decent restaurant I passed. And if I wanted to sample the true taste of France, authentic and home-cooked, neither the chilly opulence of Michelin nor the modish nouvelle cuisine of too little on your plate and too much on your bill – it might as well be here, in Provence.

In any case, although Cannes might have been the unwelcoming maître d' at the front door, my next destination was allegedly the culinary equivalent of Maurice Chevalier: warm, welcoming, authentic and with a song in its heart. It was also the place where the young Auguste Escoffier was born and began his culinary education. Now I hoped to follow suit.

And after all – as everyone knows who's ever seen *The Boy Friend* – 'it's so much nicer in Nice'.

I'D ALWAYS REGARDED Sandy Wilson's 1920s feel-good musical pastiche as something of a cliché, with its bright young things in tennis shorts all falling in love *sur la plage* and its stereotypical French maids all talking like *zeeeees* and saying 'Ooh-la-la' at every flick of their duster. Yet such is the city's reputation that even that most jaundiced of Francophobes Smollett was captivated by the place, staying for two years and even trying to get himself elected as British Consul.

Once Smollett had given it the thumbs-up, the British followed in such numbers that the locals, who hadn't yet acquired a word for 'tourist', named all foreign arrivals 'anglais', including Germans and French. Dickens came here by steamer and Stephenson by donkey; Hans Christian Andersen and Chekov strolled on the prom; Oscar Wilde sought solace following his release from Reading gaol; H.G. Wells conducted a torrid affair in the mighty Negresco Hotel on the seafront (designed by Gustave Eiffel), and Harpo Marx loved the place so much that in 1928 he offered his services as chauffeur to George Bernard Shaw just so he could hang out here for free.

Most famously Isadora Duncan danced here barefoot with a reptile, shortly before being strangled when her scarf caught in the wheels of her sports car. Indeed, it was the British community here who funded the town's seafront-cum-boulevard, the raffish Promenade des Anglais.

In fact, Nice proved even more hospitable than I'd hoped, not only holding the door open for me but offering me a drink and somewhere to hang my coat as well. The city may be the fifth biggest in France, but it felt more like Torquay with sunshine. The *soleil brille*, the *mer est bleu* and the *crêpes dans les cafés sont formidables*. The famous promenade was both unpretentious and pleasing, with a succession of public beaches each falling over themselves to look more inviting than the last, even down to the stylish 1930s signs in wrought iron announcing their presence. Up on the prom, joggers and rollerbladers weaved in between dog-walkers or couples dozing in the sun, while below, bathers performed looping dives off wooden pontoons or meandered about in pedalos. Further out, squealing teenagers bumped along behind speedboats on inflatable bananas, while an antique biplane puttered above the shore towing an advertising banner in its wake. With each hour I spent here, Sandy Wilson's original musical seemed less a theatrical satire and more a gritty documentary.

But I wasn't here to enjoy myself. My aim was to sample the best that French gastronomy could offer. Yet there were so many restaurants both ancient and modern, Posh and Becks, it was impossible to know where to turn. I either needed a local expert or a chance encounter with Michael Winner. Luckily fate was on my side.

CARMEL HAD BEEN living in Nice for the past fourteen years. Originally from Eastbourne (she emigrated to the Canadian prairies in search of excitement), she'd moved to France in the early 1990s to pursue her dream of learning French cooking the Escoffier way. She'd obviously taken to it like a duck to orange, as nowadays she's one of Provence's most celebrated restaurant critics, a trusted and trenchant expert whose mere presence at the front door could turn swaggering proprietors pale with fear.

We met in a coffee bar overlooking Nice's picturesque flower and fruit market and discussed France's obsession with food. Far from the celebrity status afforded it around the restaurant tables of the world nowadays, French cuisine was born of the stark necessities of subsistence farming. 'With food so scarce, you either found a way of serving up brains and stomach lining or eventually went hungry once you'd eaten the rest of the beast,' she explained. Anything that could be eaten was, and anything that couldn't was rendered swallowable by the addition of increasingly sophisticated sauces and *jus*.

In that sense, she maintained, Provençal cooking was atypical. It uses fish and vegetables, ingredients less prized elsewhere in France where meat is still king. 'French cooks still regard vegetables as little more than garnish, whereas here...' She described an arc with her hand: all around us stalls were laden with fresh produce – artichokes, asparagus, aubergines, and on through the alphabet – while each stallholder found himself besieged by customers scrutinising the produce as if searching for fingerprints. But the items on display here had cast-iron alibis: with their glossy skins and plump expressions they were the vegetable equivalent of model citizens.

We walked round the market, Carmel patiently identifying the flavours and colours essential for great French food. Mushrooms and red peppers were particularly popular in these parts, as were tomatoes and courgettes, and particularly chard, which she assured me was a local speciality and used widely in cooking throughout the region due to its plentiful supply. 'You'll find virtually every accompanying vegetable served up is chard,' she explained.

I assured her it was something I was already used to with my wife's cooking.

So where should I go to sample French cuisine at its best? I'd already made a reservation at La Petite Maison, one of the area's most famous restaurants and with an A-list reputation for celeb-spotting during the summer months – President Sarkozy himself had already visited it only recently.

'Avoid it like the plague,' she insisted. 'The food is good but the service is foul. They don't admit as much but take it from me, it's unofficial policy. If you're a local somebody – film star, or member of the local legislature, you'll be treated well, but otherwise you should stay away. They regard their behaviour as a way of discouraging riff-raff and no-hopers.'

Carmel held to the view that the true spirit of Escoffier was nowadays to be found in the bistro tradition: a single chef, a marble counter, joined-up cooking and local produce. She thought for a moment as she idly flicked through my guidebook at the various restaurant reviews, most of which she confessed she'd written herself. Then she clapped her hands in triumph. 'Of course!'

The eatery in question was a family-run establishment near by. 'Actually it's only a stone's throw from where the great chef himself began as a kitchen hand,' she explained. 'He started here as a boy of just twelve in a tiny backstreet restaurant run by his uncle François. The rest, as they say, is history. And the place I have in mind will be very similar in some ways. It's French cuisine at its best – I'd go so far as to say it's virtually impossible to have a bad meal there.'

So what should I order?

'Trust that to the chef,' she replied. 'Simply ask for the daily special, whatever it is. There's only ever one, you'll see it displayed on a blackboard on the wall, and it's always magnific-ent. The ingredients will be sourced this morning both here and at the meat market so it'll be the freshest dish on the menu. If you want a taste of true France you needn't look any further.'

Which is why eight hours later I found myself staring at plate of fresh cows' tongues surrounded by pickled onions.

IT HAD ALL been going so well. The restaurant was exactly what I'd hoped to find, a secluded little place tucked away in among the narrow alleyways and dark courtyards that formed Vieux Nice, the old town. The front windows had pleasing red and white gingham half-curtains, and inside both the décor and the staff were equally unpretentious: just sufficient copper pans and decorative lobster pots to suggest authenticity, and a fine example of Carmel's much-treasured 'bistro-style' counter lined with ancient soda siphons in pastel hues.

It was easy to see why this place would be popular with one half of the human species: the waiters who greeted me were two of the most jaw-droppingly handsome young men I'd ever seen outside the Chippendales roadshow. Yet far from a cunning publicity stunt to attract middle-aged spinsters straight off easyJet, they turned out to be grandsons of the original proprietor, a fact confirmed by a clutch of ancient sepia prints of their similarly square-jawed ancestor standing at the very bar in 1927.

Henri and his brother now assisted waiting tables, and would eventually take over the business from their mother, an elegant woman in a woollen stole who stood by the cash till with the permanent expression of someone who'd stayed in all day for a delivery man who hadn't turned up.

The starter had been, to use the patois of the Sunday papers, immense: a home-made fish soup that came with enough accessories and rituals to warrant its own instruction booklet, including a basket of warm croutons, a dish of fresh mustard-mayonnaise infused with chilli and wild herbs and finally a clove of garlic big enough to break your toe.

Henri took some time to explain the required ritual: rubbing the garlic on the bread as if buffing a pair of shoes, then balancing a huge smear of mustard-mayonnaise on the top and finally giving the whole thing a good soaking in the soup before wrestling it into my mouth. Bathtime was never this much fun. I sat happily dunking, bobbing, sinking and devouring my tiny playthings for many minutes. Several times the sopping croutons fell off my spoon and splashed noisily back into the bowl, showering the top of my trousers with soup, fish, oil and chilli, but by now I was too happy to care. This was obviously why the French preferred to take such time enjoying their meal: the ritual was so wonderfully complicated.

So when the second course arrived I'd been somewhat nonplussed. I'd only understood one word of the blackboard – boeuf – so assumed that *langue de boeuf sauce Ravigote et pommes vapeur* would be some succulent steak, perhaps with a green salad and some fries, like the meal being devoured at the table next to me by a couple of divorcees out on a hesitant date. But Henri assured me that cows' tongues were the speciality of the house. 'This is a traditional French dish,' he insisted. 'We cook them for many hours in a sauce including fresh capers and shredded tarragon and these baby shallots. I think you will enjoy. Bon appétit!'

After his departure I sat staring at the tongues for some minutes. Now I knew what it must be like to be a contestant facing one of those ghastly challenges on *I'm A Celebrity Get Me Out Of Here*. Even the boiled potatoes looked like Paul Burrell.

The problem was their appearance. If cows' tongues had been served up back in Britain their provenance would undoubtedly have been concealed to avoid offending sensibilities: chopped and shaped into reassuring cutlet shapes, possibly with breadcrumbs and perhaps even a ham 'n' cheese filling in the middle. But there was no mistaking these things. About nine inches long, they looked as if they'd simply been ripped out of the animal with a pair of pliers and slapped on a plate.

There were suckery-looking things all along the surface, presumably taste buds, and that cleft running directly down the middle I recognised only too well from my own shaving mirror each morning. Worse still, as they flattened and extended out towards the root there were sinewy bits and fibrous strings of gristle hanging over the side of my plate that presumably had once stretched deep down into the animal's throat. Apart from that nothing, except potatoes, pickled onions and a tepid sauce to help me out.

It's odd how the brain works. I dimly recall my brother Pete telling me of a particularly boozy trip to France during his brief time with the Reconquer France For Britain Society in the 1960s. It was at the time the country was just dipping its collective toe in the waters of foreign cuisine – Neapolitan ice cream, vichyssoise, melon segments with glacé cherries, that sort of thing – and in Dieppe he'd been offered a new dish smothered in garlic and fresh lemon juice which he'd vastly enjoyed and wolfed down with enormous gusto. Five minutes after the final mouthful he was informed by the waiter he'd just had his first taste of octopus, and was promptly sick.

So what should I do now? Cut one of them up? Ask for a blindfold? Pick a sample and suck the end? I had the feeling it wouldn't go down too well with my neighbours, even if they had similar designs on each other for later in the evening.

I looked across. The woman was enjoying a plate of veal

escalope, while her companion was tucking simultaneously into his steak with one hand and a bowl of fresh pasta with the other. Both meals looked sublime – the pasta especially so. But of course it would – here in Nice we were barely a penalty dive's distance from the Italian border.

I had to trust. The starter had been without doubt the most beautiful example of the genre I'd ever had in my life: even now my own taste buds were still luxuriating in gently fizzing chilli, while an intoxicating aroma of fresh garlic wafted up from my finger ends every time I moved them. I had to trust Carmel, I had to trust Henri, and above all I had to trust France.

I closed my eyes and tried to imagine myself at Pizza Hut, cutting into something deep and crisp. I sliced the very end of the first tongue off just before the tip, slathered it in potatoes and sauce and onions and anything else to hand, harpooned it with the tines of my fork and inserted it carefully into my mouth.

It was delicious. Sublime, a sweet, succulent taste and texture, the gentle sugary content of this tenderest of meat set off against the tartness of the tiny onions and the piquant subtlety of the capers. Here, moist, yielding and rolled in fresh parsley, even the boiled potatoes had been raised to an art form.

Thirty minutes later I pushed my plate away, sat luxuriously back in my chair and discreetly belched. With my plate wiped clean with crusty baguette and my stomach now as full as an egg, this was what pure contentment must feel like. Henri at once hurried across. 'C'était bien?' he asked. My mouth was still full of bread in caper sauce, but I nodded energetically and gave a 'C'est bon' sign by pressing my thumb and forefinger together. If I'd been Michael Winner instead of Michael Simkins, I'd have not only given the meal five stars but offered Henri and his brother a contract to star in *Death Wish 23*.

The meal ended with another piece of oral heaven. Although I'd already set my heart on the chocolate truffle ice cream, Henri insisted I try the house speciality: *poire Louis Bonne* cooked in orange wine. The pears were a specific variety, he explained, and the favourite fruit of Louis XIV: skinned and then cooked on a low heat in a juice of white wine, fresh oranges and miniature apricots, and served in a tiny cauldron.

They arrived. I lifted the lid. A scent of pure late summer assailed my nostrils, alcohol infused with mellow fruits and sugar. The pears – again, three of them, pale fleshy and exquisite – sat obediently upright on their bases in the sauce: moist enough to yield to cutting with the side of a dessertspoon yet firm enough to wait till safely in my mouth before gently falling apart.

I left the restaurant just after 11 p.m. sublimely happy. Although I'm not claiming it had much to beat, the meal had been by some way the most memorable of my adult life: quirky, succulent, plentiful and sublimely cooked. The whole caboodle had come to something under forty quid, fifty including the superb half-bottle of Provençal Château Coussin Sainte Victoire wine I'd allowed myself to go with it.

Now at least I knew what the French were on about. No wonder they took so much care and time over each meal. Wouldn't you if you could have that sort of experience three times a day? My plan to have a one-on-one with classic French food had been realised beyond my wildest dreams, and now I could move on: but not before solemnly promising to return within a year to enrol in one of Carmel's own celebrated weekly cookery courses. I could get used to this.

Sandy Wilson had got it right after all. It was indeed so much nicer in Nice. Even the German philosopher Friedrich Nietzsche, not a man known for his gay badinage, had written of the city:

'Here, in Nice, I grow like a plant in the sunshine.' He was right. Bustling, saucy, and above all full of energy and light, Nice was everything you could wish for. If there had been any more of the Riviera to travel on towards I'd happily have done so, possibly for ever – but the sight on my bedroom TV of an overweight Italian tenor with a spray-on tan and dyed thinning hair singing 'Volare' to a group of bikini-clad lovelies reminded me the border was only twenty-three miles away. Unless I turned left quick sharp I might end up among them, and that would never do.

I headed for my bathroom with the infusions of *langue*, chillies, capers, orange juice and fresh garlic still dancing a jig in the recesses of my mouth. It was almost as if they would never leave. It had been a perfect evening.

Nearly perfect. It was then I realised I'd left my toothbrush back at the Majestic in Cannes.

Veni, Vidi, Vichy

THERE ARE MANY reasons to visit this queen of spa towns, located in the ravishing countryside of the Auvergne, slap bang in the middle of France. Some of them I am even prepared to talk about. Most celebrated is its reputation as the supreme example of La Belle Epoch, the period between Napoleon and the Great War when France, and Vichy, were at their cultural zenith.

This small city on the Allier river has been known since Roman times for its hot and cold springs, and reputed cures for rheumatism, arthritis and digestive complaints. The celebrated letter-writer Madame de Sevigne and the daughters of Louis XV came here in the late seventeenth and eighteenth centuries – the former comparing the showers to 'a rehearsal for Purgatory' – and the subsequent visits of Napoleon III in the 1860s put Vichy on the map and made taking the waters fashionable.

It soon became synonymous with courtly grandeur, sprouting opera houses, private health complexes, casinos, a public bandstand and any number of stylish hotels. By the outbreak of the Great War this graceful town was attracting nearly 100,000 visitors a year.

Although the average age of the visitors nowadays probably exceeds that of an old people's home, it's reputed still to be one of the most charming and civilised resorts in France. Just to prove it, this year it even hosted the world Scrabble championships.

But there were other, more practical reasons for my wanting to visit. I was in need of some TLC myself, and Vichy's world-famous private spa treatments were reputed to be among the best in Europe. You'll get an idea how badly I needed it if I tell you I was beginning to resemble my passport photo.

But if I still had any lingering doubts about whether it was worth the detour, a game of Kerplunk soon settled the issue.

KERPLUNK IS ONE of the few leisure activities not previously ascribed to this imperial resort, but six-year-old Edmund was about to change all that. When you're sharing a table on a long-haul train to Lyons with a middle-aged woman and her over-energetic son who needs constant diversion, a game or seventy can do wonders in passing the time. So they were playing Kerplunk, and, pretty soon, so was I.

Pascal was travelling home after a summer spent with her in-laws on the Côte d'Azur. An intense and intelligent woman with smoker's breath and salt and pepper hair scraped back into a bun, she was half-English and half-French. This not only made conversing easier, but also understanding the rules of Kerplunk.

Little Edmund wasn't the ideal candidate for a game that requires patience, dexterity and a steady hand, but as his main delight in life was to whip out the sticks holding up all thirty-two marbles and see them plunge simultaneously to their doom, it hardly mattered.

While we played, we talked. I told Pascal of my mission, going on to describe my meeting with circus folk, my attempts to become a sommelier, my sight of Barrington Hancock's testes at a local beauty spot.

She laughed guardedly as if trying to judge whether she'd sat next to a gifted raconteur or a dangerous pervert: but in between the sound of cascading marbles she started to thaw, and even took to explaining points of interest from my stories to little Edmund.

'And where are you off to now?' she asked.

I told her, adding all the wondrous things I hoped to do and see: the mineral waters, the private treatments, the world-famous bandstand, and all that evoked France at its cultural and courtly best.

'You mustn't go to Vichy,' she replied.

'Why not?'

'Because you will not understand. My parents still argue about it even now. My father is English, you see.'

'But the war was sixty years ago.'

She stared out of the window for some seconds while considering her reply. Eventually she turned and fixed me with dark, severe eyes.

'You are British,' she said. 'There is one thing that separates you from the French. You carry no sense of guilt for what you did in the war. That is why, as a nation, you will never understand Vichy.'

An awkward silence descended, broken only by little Edmund carefully stacking his marbles. Her verdict had stung me and I spent some minutes concocting a robust defence of my itinerary.

Of course, I knew what she was referring to, even though her assumptions about the true purpose of my visit were inaccurate. After all, the haze of past grandeur at Vichy is intentional. The town tethers itself to the days when its history recorded little other than the comings and goings of Napoleon III, because more recent events are too painful to contemplate.

This mild-mannered spa town became the administrative

capital of a defeated France in the days after conquest by Hitler's Germany in 1940. 'Vichy France', the area of the country conquered but left unoccupied and semi-autonomous by Hitler's troops, was only chosen in the first place because of its central location, its profusion of hotel rooms and a working telephone exchange. Yet it became synonymous with 'collaboration', at the time a non-pejorative term to describe 'working together' with the conquerors, but which quickly became a synonym for appeasement or pragmatism, according to your view.

The pitiable head of this discredited regime walled up in the opulent Hôtel du Parc was octogenarian Marshal Pétain, hero of Verdun and thus a natural figurehead for a nation craving self-respect. Imagine Tunbridge Wells being made capital of occupied Britain having lost the same conflict, with an eighty-year-old Lloyd George as PM, and you're somewhere near it. But the idea that I was travelling all this way to Vichy just to enjoy its historical discomfiture was ludicrous.

In the end I mentioned none of these things to Pascal. Instead I had another game of Kerplunk. But it seemed a pity. Why does every Frenchman assume an interest in Vichy automatically means a prurient interest in the war, when until now my thoughts had only been of its myriad other attractions? They really needed to get over it. We parted cordially enough at Lyon, but Pascal had let a Vichy-sized elephant into our corridor and it hadn't gone away.

While awaiting my connection Julia called and upended me further as only Julia still can.

'Well, good luck if you're going there,' she said. 'You'll end up being tarred and feathered if you open your gob. They're all collaborationists, aren't they?'

I was stunned. Here I was in my eleventh week and this was

the first piece of historical opinion Julia had ever come up with. Famously disinterested in dates, unless they come with stones in a nice plywood box decorated with camels, here she was suddenly going on about collaboration.

'You don't know the half, matey,' she said. 'When I was on that boat in Cannes I had flu one weekend, and in the middle of it my boss's French business partner came into my cabin, sat down on the bed beside me and asked me what my dad did in the war. He was from Vichy.'

'And what did you say?'

'What do you think? I told him the truth. That Billy was an aircraft mechanic in the RAF.'

'What did he do?'

'Well if you must know, he took my wrist and gave me a Chinese burn.'

'Did you say anything?'

'Hardly, I had a temperature of about a hundred and four, I was barely aware what was happening.'

'Was that all?'

'No, he also put his hands under my nightdress and felt my tits.'

THE PLATFORM AT Lyon gave me a chance to inspect another of France's national characteristics at first hand. They don't queue. They look as if they do, but don't be fooled.

The old dears are the worst. They sit quietly on the platform gossiping about their in-laws in that curious sing-song voice that all French women have, the one that's always on the break so it sounds like they're on the point of yodelling, but the moment a puny four-car sprinter service hoves into view they turn into the front row of the scrum at the Stade de France with only a final push-over try needed and the referee already raising the final whistle to his lips.

By the time I'd shouldered my way on board the seats had long gone, and I spent the next two hours wedged in the gangway between a girl playing hip-hop on her mobile phone and an elderly collie dog with breath like stale oxtail crisps. So desperate for a berth was one woman near me that she mimed the worst stage swoon I have ever witnessed in order to persuade a foolhardy student to offer up his seat, whereupon she instantly recovered.

Vichy looked awful in the rain. I pulled the toggles tighter on my rain hood and trudged through the sodden streets, my spirits sinking at every turn. Why on earth had I given up the barometric joys of the Riviera for such a dispiriting place?

I don't know what made me walk into the Hôtel Nottingham. Perhaps it was the name: something in me half hoped to find Brian Clough and Peter Taylor playing darts next to a cabinet of hot meat pies, with draught Bass available in the bar.

What I got was far better. The moment I stepped in through the entrance I knew I'd found the hotel I was looking for in *Monsieur Hulot's Holiday*. An aroma of savoury cooking smells such as I'd always envisaged emanating from the imaginary dining room greeted my nostrils. Through a set of glass doors I could make out people in blazers and cardigans bent over plates of soup accompanied by the sound of gently clacking cutlery.

Lights blazed, the carpet was deep, and in a corner of the foyer two old ladies in their Sunday best were dozing happily, one with her dentures half out. There was even a bell on the desk to summon the manager. Best of all, when I pressed it, it brought forth Leo.

Leo was the sort of bloke you'd want to put in your pocket to take out and rub every time you got a bit desolate. A man in his late twenties with twinkling eyes and ready smile, he resembled the sort of earnest young male dancer I've encountered in the choruses of West End musicals, the sort who never misses a show and is always first up at the karaoke party.

Having provided a cup of tea to restore my spirits even though I hadn't yet committed to staying there, he invited me to inspect my room, and clinched the deal by offering to lend me an umbrella if I decided, having seen it, I'd rather press on.

By the time I'd checked in and unpacked, the rain had stopped; the afternoon was muggy and still with a pale, apologetic sunshine. At the *office de tourisme*, a very young woman with the French for 'trainee' on a lapel badge was talking to her supervisor.

My request for a list of local places of interest led her to the ubiquitous unfolding of the tourist map and enthusiastic circling in blue biro which I'd long since come to know and love. There was Old Vichy, New Vichy, Operatic Vichy, Spa Vichy, Casino Vichy, Architectural Vichy and, needless to say, Tourist Train Vichy.

'And Pétain Vichy?'

'Pardon?'

'Pétain Vichy? The war years?'

She shook her head uncomprehendingly. 'I do not understand.'

'The war. You know, 1940 to '44. I thought I might take a look round.'

'I'm sorry, sir, we have nothing on that.'

'But–'

'You might try the bookshop. They have some history books on the town.'

'It's just that–'

'But they will, of course, be in French.' Her senior colleague moved smoothly to the desk and retrieved a small brochure from under the counter. 'I think this may be what you are looking for,' he said. On it were indeed details of a guided tour of Occupation Vichy, and what it coyly described as 'all its comings and goings', on alternate Wednesdays. I'd missed it by about three days.

'Was there anywhere in particular you were looking for, monsieur?'

I replied that the spot I most wished to view was the Hôtel du Parc, the building where Marshal Pétain and his erstwhile cabinet had set up shop and from which they ruled nearly two-thirds of the country for nigh on four years.

'You are in it, sir.'

'In it?'

'Just about. In fact, you are probably standing where they once washed the dishes. The hotel is no more, you see. The greater part of the building was converted to private apartments in the 1960s and sadly is not open to visitors.'

His young compatriot seemed as surprised to learn of its existence as I was. Obviously there wasn't much call for such information in these parts.

I pocketed the brochure, and having thanked them for their help, bade them goodbye. As I was leaving, the manager indicated a discreet memorial sited directly across the street, dedicated to the 6,500 Jews who were shipped to their death during the Vichy years. I crossed the road and spent some minutes studying it. A small marble rectangle framed by a block of granite, it was a moving, if stark, tribute to the strange shadows cast by this sunlit town.

*

MY NEXT DESTINATION was the magnificent Hall des Sources, just visible across the park among the trees, and home of the fabled mineral waters.

The hall was enclosed in a huge metal gallery, transported here lock stock and barrel from the world fair of 1889. As long as a football pitch and supported by graceful wrought-iron pillars, this immense conservatory exuded gentility and faded elegance. It was even hotter and muggier inside than it was out, a quality that only added to the sense of ennui as I ambled around its echoing arcades.

The mineral waters themselves were situated at a rectangular mosaic wall, right in the middle of the hall. For the price of a paper cup from a handy dispenser, you could sample up to six different versions, each with their own therapeutic properties. The principal bog-standard version, on constant stream from a scaly tap, is the Source Chomel, which carries the name of the doctor who first developed it. Its taste proved to be a gamey blend of bathwater mixed with farts.

For the sake of even-handedness I eventually sampled the lot: including the fluoride-rich Source Grande de l'Hôpital (Eno's with aftertaste of dishcloth), Source Lucas (Marmite) and Source du Parc (low-calorie bitter lemon mixed with Germolene).

The final one, Source Grande Grille, was recommended in small doses only, but some wheezing tourists next to me were filling entire bottles with the stuff and knocking it back as if it was going out of fashion. Which I suppose, in a sense, it is.

Thirst quenched, I followed the sound of singing echoing from the far end until I came across a woman in a golfing cap clutching sheet music and bawling into a microphone connected to a karaoke machine. This was my first proper encounter with the art of *chanson*, the rich and quintessentially French form of ballad singing that found its greatest exponent in Edith Piaf.

This woman, however, sounded more like Edith Evans. The sound was horrible. Her audience, slumped in front of her in an untidy cluster of picnic chairs, was a contingent of the frail and elderly out for the day. Their features were contorted with misery, though whether as a result of their infirmity or the enforced entertainment it was difficult to say. But if Vichy was trying to shake off its reputation for quiet suffering, this woman was doing the place no favours.

In a large glass anteroom next to her was much more fun. A tea dance was in progress. Elderly couples were foxtrotting their way round the floor in pairs to a French version of Victor Sylvester LPs, and what's more, enjoying themselves enormously. Brucie would have liked it here.

I stood and watched for some minutes before being invited to perform a stately St Bernard's waltz by a corpulent woman of uncertain years with hennaed hair and sunglasses. We clumped round the hall, enjoying the movement and the music and the genteel gyrations of our fellow dancers, and afterwards moved outside to the gardens, where she accepted my offer of a Café Crème and in return proffered me the last of a consignment of tiny Vichy pastilles from a small tin, subsequently pressed into service as an ashtray. To a soundtrack of cooing pigeons from distant boughs, we played a short game called who's worst at foreign languages.

'Il fait beau.'

'But it is hot.'

'Je suis très fatigue.'

'I have visit London.'

'France est très gentile.'

'I am too fat for dance.'

Eventually she was whisked away by a man in a pony-tail who

stopped only long enough to tell me he'd once been a second-hand record dealer in Camden.

THAT NIGHT I enjoyed a fabulous dinner prepared by Leo and his brother, who happened to be the chef: including Napoleon of smoked salmon with green lentils, scrambled egg in red sauce, all rounded off with a bottle of rosé and a platter of mouth-watering cheeses. Leo took time off from serving the other diners to explain the rules of sampling French *fromage*, which are basically that you must always commence with the mildest first and then work your way clockwise round the plate until you come, in this case, to a garlicky confection you could have used to chloroform hospital patients.

All around us the elderly bourgeoisie of France sat contentedly slurping soup up through sprawling moustaches. When I declined Leo's offer of a dessert he was having none of it. 'You are on holiday!' he gleamed as he plonked a huge slab of Bellenaves Piquenchagne in front of me. Vichy was certainly working its gentle magic.

THERMAL TREATMENTS ARE big business in France. French national health insurance is so comprehensive that it provides such benefits on tap, as it were, for anyone requiring attention. Even at such a swanky location as the Thermes de Vichy Calou, my first destination the following day, up to 100 per cent of the cost of a standard twenty-one-day cure is paid for by a combination of social security benefits and supplementary top-ups.

Not that I knew this when I arrived. But it was obvious from the queue of liverish individuals waiting to be let in that someone other was helping to fund their convalescence. The assistant at the front desk was very sorry, but virtually none of the treatments could be sampled at the Calou unless I possessed the proper documentation, plus a certificate from my local GP confirming my particular seediness.

It hadn't occurred to me that the facilities wouldn't be available for ready money: and in any case my own GP was on a walking holiday in the Trossachs. It seemed the best that France could offer – the seaweed wrap, the hot stones massage and the foot pulverisation – were beyond me.

Perhaps the assistant just took pity, but as I was turning to leave, she mentioned there were certain less intrusive treatments readily available for the casual visitor without the need for a sick note. The range was limited, but if I only had one day…

Five minutes later I was changing into my swimming trunks and awaiting my first brush with the Vichy magic: an *enveloppe de boues.*

The Calou complex, built only in 1990, was much what I'd expected of such a place, a vast modern sanatorium containing endless silent corridors fringed by identical doors and populated with figures shambling about in dressing gowns and flip-flops. I sat awaiting my appointment with a glass of myrtle tea, listening to the soft muzak and the distant sound of gently running water. It was certainly a congenial environment, with uniformed assistants gliding silently among the punters filling up the samovars and wiping down surfaces with mops.

The only anachronism in all this discreet modernity was the display of historic artefacts on every landing. It probably seemed a good idea at the time to jazz things up a bit by decorating the landings with antique contraptions from yesteryear – not only informative, they also confirmed the long and distinguished heritage of the treatments on offer in Vichy, but nonetheless the items made for uneasy viewing.

I spent several minutes inspecting machines festooned with flanges, hooks and levers, and, according to the accompanying signs, used for such vital bodily exertions as percussing the trunk, extending the bras, efflugering the abdomen and, in the case of the final exhibit, an alarming contraption sagging under the weight of suckers, leather bungs and flywheels, 'frictioning the frotters'.

I was just wondering where my own frotters might be located and whether having them frictioned would be pleasurable, when I heard my name being called. It was a woman called Nellie in a nurse's uniform.

Nellie's job was to smear my entire body in hot gunk the colour of bubble gum from a brimming plastic tank, after which to wrap both the gunk and me in clingfilm. I know some people who would pay good money for this in the backstreets of Soho, but with many others waiting for their own treatment in adjoining rooms, Nellie's brisk efficiency brooked no daydreaming. I'd no sooner been prepared than I was ordered to lie down on a table covered in kitchen roll and stay there without moving until such time as she chose to return. She closed the door behind her and I was alone.

Presumably the solitude was part of the therapeutic process. I made a conscious effort to relax my limbs, a procedure that resulted in a delicious slurping sensation, as if I'd been dipped in a vat of Baileys Irish Cream. Within minutes I was fast asleep. When I woke I was already being torn open and my contents inspected. Nellie was now encased in white slaughterman's gumboots and a plastic mac, but it was only to protect her pristine tunic while she washed me down with a garden hose. I was left to extricate any remaining particles with a watering can and a bristle brush, and with a brisk *au revoir* she was on her way. The procedure had lasted no more than forty minutes.

I finished my treatment with a conventional thermal bath, sitting in a space-age tub in an otherwise unoccupied room while submerged jets massaged my every nook and orifice. Afterwards I spent the rest of the morning nipping between the sauna and the Jacuzzi. It was certainly very relaxing. Through a glass partition at the far end I could see a small swimming pool in which a gaggle of elderly woman in floral bathing hats performed stiff-legged movements in time to piped Chopin. It was easy to imagine the nineteenth-century equivalent of the place: elegant dowagers and gouty aristocrats reclining in chairs surrounded by potted palms.

I suppose, whatever the era, this is what sophistication is all about. Having sufficient time and money to passionately pursue doing bugger all.

THE MIDDLE PART of the day I spent exploring the town. Vichy's architecture is a pleasantly odd mix of styles, with the neo-Moorish, art nouveau, neo-baroque, art deco and ultra-modern all rubbing shoulders under the dappled shadows of the plane trees that line the streets.

Grand Victorian hotels dovetailed with dainty patisseries, and everywhere the contented middle classes were walking their dogs or sitting at pavement cafés reading the papers. At every turn I was greeted by beautifully preserved remnants of the town's imperial past: casinos, arcades and a low-rise opera house straight out of Buxton or Malvern.

Of the war, little remained. The only other commemoration I discovered was a small plaque set into a wall, commemorating the eighty MPs who voted against transferring power to Pétain in

1940. And perhaps it was my fanciful nature, but there was a quietness about the place that seemed at odds with its size, as if the entire population was keeping a low profile. Cars rarely went above thirty, nobody played loud music, while even the modern curse of talking on mobile phones at full volume in public spaces seemed to have been refined into something more discreet and muted.

Was this a population who had got used to enforced confidentiality? Or just some of Nellie's pink gunk still lodged in my ears?

My second port of call was situated across the Parc. If Thermes Calou was the King of Spas, the Célestins was the Emperor, a glittering monolith in steel and glass, backing on to the broad, tranquil banks of the Allier river.

The interior was even more impressive than its rival. A huge minimalist foyer contained nothing but blue sofas shaped like giant kidney beans, while chairs suspended on chains swung listlessly under the fierce air conditioning. Men in green surgery fatigues and beige-coloured Crocs padded silently in and out of automatic doors looking like extras from ads for headache cures.

The receptionist was called Nancy. She too was very sorry that many of the treatments were not available, though not in this case because of insurance issues – this was an entirely private establishment – but simply because they were booked up many months in advance. A tub complete with effervescent carbon bubbles was on offer, but I reckoned that by combining a glass of mineral water with a hot bath I could sample the experience for free back at the hotel.

'In that case, I am afraid there is little available. It is the last week of the season, you see. Unless…?'

'Yes?'

'We have a space at 3.40 this afternoon for the jet-powered body *tonifiant*.'

'I'll take it.'

A jet-powered *tonifiant* sounded just the job. The curious ritual at the hands of Nellie earlier on had left me somewhat sluggish, and for much of the day since I'd felt curling up back at the hotel with a good book and box of chocolate brazils. But here was something that was guaranteed to leave me feeling refreshed and invigorated for the adventures still ahead.

Once more unto the swimming trunks, I sat in the foyer in a luxurious robe swinging back and forth in one of Twiggy's chairs and reading the latest brochures on skin care. My *Instructions for British Servicemen* booklet had no equivalent English translation in its glossary for jet *tonifiant*, but luckily my guidebook did.

'Jet *tonifiant*' it began. 'The experience is like being sprayed with a high-power jet of water of the sort used to disperse riots.'

Armand looked barely strong enough to lift a pressure hose, let alone operate one. Certainly you wouldn't want to rely on him in case of civil disturbance. A tall wiry individual startlingly like Louis Theroux, he led me down the ubiquitous corridor dotted with lolling businessmen into what seemed to be a white-tiled room with sluices. The only item distinguishing it from an abattoir was an industrial-strength patio cleaner that lay coiled in one corner. That, and a pair of handholds cemented into the tiles at shoulder height at the far end.

'Please, take off your gown and go and stand by the far wall,' he explained sadly. I did as requested and stood nervously facing him as he uncoiled the apparatus. 'Turn round please, and grip the rails to brace yourself,' he continued. In the best traditions of Vichy, I did what I could to prevent my environment from becoming a battleground. All I could see now were pristine white tiles an inch or two in front of my face.

How had Madame de Sevigne, the aristocrat who first put this town in the map, described her experience? 'A rehearsal for Purgatory' was how she'd described the showers. And that had been two hundred years ago.

'Ready?

I nodded mutely.

The next second I was hit by what felt like an Exocet missile. Armand's jet tonifiant caught me just below the knees, causing me to jack-knife until I was nearly squatting. I hauled myself up the tiles, but the contest was hopelessly uneven.

I yelled in shock, but the noise of the water drowned out all other intrusions, and in any case, in Vichy, no one could hear my screams. A rasping snake of pain arced up and down my body as Armand directed the jet, dwelling luxuriously on each vertebra before moving onto my shoulder blades and thence down to my buttocks, where it spiralled in concentric circles towards what, if I had any, were presumably my gluteus maximuses. It was like being massaged by the Incredible Hulk.

I stood hopelessly, teeth clenched, whimpering softly, like dogs in canine beauty parlours do when they're being dunked in icy, shampoo-filled water and having their hair pulled into impersonations of Elvis Presley by grinning assistants. Forbearance and fortitude were all I had to offer.

The jet momentarily ceased. 'Now, please, turn round and cover your abdomen.'

I did as I was told, protecting myself as best I could from the savagery that surely was to follow. I could now see Armand about twenty feet away, one hand on the main handle. A quick tug on the flow wheel and my eyes screwed tight once more.

Eventually, with a final right hook to my neck, the battering was over. When I opened my eyes again, Armand had already stashed the hose neatly in the corner and was approaching me with a large bath towel. He wrapped me tenderly like a parent embracing his son after a particularly difficult cross-country race, and with a final shy smile opened the door for me to leave. I staggered back out into the changing room. I'm just glad I only paid for five minutes' worth: I couldn't have stood much more of that.

It was only later when I stood in front of the changing-room mirror that I noticed the effect. I looked terrific. Eight weeks of sun, saltwater and railway compartments had been washed away, to be replaced by something pink, wholesome and toned. Whether it was merely the endorphins kicking in or something more profound, I was beginning to feel like conqueror of the universe.

Champions of Vichy's particular blend of sulphurous magic talk about the famous 'Vichy look'. Whatever it was, I had it too. I'd arrived here this morning looking like Marshall Pétain, and left resembling Captain Hurricane.

MY OWN FINAL act of collaboration occurred that evening when I attended the brass band concert back in the Parc des Sources opposite the Opera House.

As it turned out, Le Kiosque à Musique was every bit as special as I'd imagined. A beautiful bandstand in duck-egg blue, garlanded with wrought iron in the shape of musical staves and decorated on this gloomy evening with lanterns and tricolours, it was a vision of harmony and reason after the travails of the day.

The concert, the last of the season, wasn't due to commence till 8 p.m., by which time it was raining again and getting dark.

Summer, it seemed, was nearly over. I joined a throng of about a hundred diehards, many of them over fifty, one or two of them surely veterans of the wartime conflict itself, on the foldaway seats arranged in rows on the wet grass. Many of the audience had rain hoods and umbrellas. With the first few leaves beginning to drift gently down in ones and twos from the trees, there was something sweetly melancholic about it all.

And that was even before the music started. I don't know what it is about brass bands, but I only have to hear one to feel like crying. And now, on this dank evening, the Orchestre Harmonie de Vichy was determined to succeed where Nellie's mudpack and Armand's pressure wash had failed.

'Extraordinary how potent cheap music is,' wrote Noël Coward. And when it's played on a rainy autumnal evening on France's most beautiful bandstand, and surrounded by pensioners in rain hoods, gently nodding their heads in time to the melodies or whispering the lyrics to their grandchildren and trying to come to terms with their past...

Vichy may still be emerging from the confessional box, but now I too had a confession to make. Pascal had been entirely correct on the train when she'd accused me of cultural rubbernecking, and however vehement my denials at the time, her instincts had been on the button. Despite its many attractions – the spas, the architecture, its famed gentility – it had all along been Vichy's reputation as a town still skulking in the shadows of its past that had drawn me here. Now in the quiet confessional of this park, it was time to acknowledge, if only to myself, my dissembling.

Vichy had grown on me. I don't know what I'd been expecting, but there seemed to be a heart-breaking sense of regret about the place. The town was the civic equivalent of Lord Profumo, a natural aristocrat who has spent his years repaying past misdemeanours by doing good deeds, yet was still nervous of making too much fuss in public in case he was spotted. The resort still carried its civic history like luggage on its back.

People talk about the Vichy syndrome, the way in which generations too young to have been implicated in the war still feel guilty about what occurred: and even Leo, the young and vigorous owner of the Hôtel Nottingham, and just the sort of individual who'd surely feel no need for remorse, had stopped work and given me a look tinged with mistrust and disappointment when he'd heard me mention the name of Pétain while talking to a couple of English-language teachers earlier in the evening. His face reminded me of Pascal's warning on the train here. 'You will not understand.'

Yet I understood this much. Vichy was a memory I would recall with fondness once my trip was ended. Now, on my last night, I sat for nearly an hour, as it grew dark, listening to the sweet sad music. Strauss waltzes, modern pops, arrangements of easy-listening favourites. But the Orchestre Harmonie de Vichy was saving the best till last. With exquisite, if unintentional, irony, their final selection turned out to be a medley of songs from the British Isles.

My final moments were spent sitting in a quiet park, in France's most infamous town, tears coursing silently down my cheeks, singing 'There'll Always Be An England' with a load of pensioners in pacamacs.

Chanel Tunnel

WHO WAS IT who said, 'Paris is always a good idea'?

If it wasn't an Englishman, it should have been. For the average, trussed-up *No Sex Please We're British* Brit, Paris has always been the stuff of dreams. It's not for nothing that *La Bohème* is one of our nation's favourite operas. The story of artistic endeavour, tragic love, poverty jostling with glamour and middle-class yearning for a life fully realised is what every poor old bank clerk from Basingstoke yearns for, a displacement in time in which all that matters is life, love and art. Paris is a place in which we can forget ourselves, reinvent, expunge the dead weight of our past and discover wine, women and song, far from the twitch of net curtains.

Somerset Maugham wrote of it. Sickert painted it. And as for photography, it's impossible to take a bad picture. Robert Doisneau's studies of post-war Paris offer up irresistible images of lovers kissing on street corners, while those of his contemporary, Brassai, evoke the mood music of the capital at night – backstage at the Folies Bergère, or amorous couples entwining underneath street lamps.

Above all, Paris is the capital of chic. As in no other city, looking good on the streets is *de rigueur*, and if you don't, Parisians will soon tell you, even if it's with a toss of the head as they pass.

Rather more wonderfully for Brits, they'll probably try to strangle you with their Hermès scarf if you remind them that their city owes its entire reputation for haute couture to a portly Englishman who couldn't speak a word of their language. Yet Charles Worth, one of the unsung heroes of British enterprise and universally known as the father of Parisian fashion, was actually born in Lincolnshire and is a supreme example of the interconnectedness of our cultures.

Having started as a draper at Swan and Edgar's in London, he arrived in Paris in 1846 with only 117 francs in his pocket. Yet such was his self-possession that instead of grovelling to his patrons' every demand, as was accepted best practice at the time, he started calling the shots, telling the fashionable ladies of Parisian society what he might allow them to wear if they were awfully nice to him – and of course they lurrrrvvved it.

His skill led to all sorts of innovations we take for granted today: the use of human models, sewing his nametags onto garments and introducing the fashion parade so that his exclusive clientele might view the latest offerings in style and comfort. In only a few years, anyone who was anyone, from actress Sarah Bernhardt through to the Astors, the Vanderbilts and the Rockefellers, would be clamouring for a few square metres of his magic, paying as much as $10,000 for a single creation. Parisian high fashion at high prices was here to stay.

About the only detractor among European royalty was our own dear Queen Victoria, who declared she'd have nothing to do with such fripperies. The cultural die was cast: for the next hundred years and more, the average French woman would dress like Coco Chanel, and the average English woman like Coco the Clown.

I'd timed my arrival in Paris with the start of its annual fashion week, the defining event in the world of fashion and great-grandchild of Worth's original concept. These days the event is the diamond tiara on the bridal gown of the international fashion calendar, combining themed cocktail parties, congratulatory soirées and endless runway shows from first light till sundown. During these few frenzied days of activity and air-kissing, names as influential as Lagerfeld, Chanel, Christian Dior, Givenchy and Gucci all gather to unleash their latest collections to an adoring press.

My aim was rather more prosaic: merely to pick up some tips and refresh my own image before meeting Julia for our reunion meal. In matters of style I've always tended to take my fashion lead from Harry Worth rather than Charles Worth, preferring labels such as 'Two for One' and 'Easy Ironing' to Paul Smith and Ted Baker. Nowadays the House of Fraser may have replaced the House of Millet in my wardrobe, but I'd come here to France with the express intent of shaking up both outlook and image. Not that I could ever imagine myself dressed in a catwalk creation, but perhaps I could learn about the soul of style in a way that might inform even my own more limited range. In any case, wasn't it the great Coco Chanel herself who stated that 'fashion is made to become unfashionable'? If so, I reckoned I already had a head start.

NORMALLY MY CHANCES of getting a private-messenger invitation to Louis Vuitton or a seat next to the editor of *Vogue* at one of the leading runway shows should have been slimmer than the models themselves, but fortunately I had an 'in'. A journo friend who was covering the event for a leading newspaper had promised to try and siphon off a seat at some of the week's most exclusive presentations.

'But for God's sake, nobody must know,' she'd told me during a hushed message left on my mobile the previous weekend. 'You'll have to turn up at my hotel each morning and ask if I've left you anything. They'll be left at the front desk in a brown envelope with your name on it. Don't hold your breath, and don't acknowledge me if I'm sitting having a coffee with my boss when you walk in.'

I arrived at my own, less salubrious hotel late on Thursday afternoon. Both the rooms and the owner seemed to have had a recent facelift, but in other ways it was typical of small hotels everywhere: the foyer was painted the colour of egg yolks, flaccid pot plants were at the entrance and, as I entered, a cat was dragging its arse across the visitors' book.

By 7.45 the next morning I was already on my way towards my contact's hotel. The weather had changed during the night, and it was now a freezing cold morning with scudding grey clouds and a strafing wind: yet somehow it only added to the excitement. Water carts were hosing down pavements on which bleary-eyed café proprietors unstacked chairs and fumbled with recalcitrant shutters. This is how I'd always imagined myself in the capital of chic: a man in a mac with an upturned collar threading his way through Pigalle towards a secret tryst. Now I was almost there.

At the reception desk of the Hôtel Atlantic, a package bearing my name awaited me. When I ripped it open a number of cardboard invitations fluttered out along with a hurriedly written note:

> *3 invites all I could do no idea if 1st any good but dont miss or ?s about why empty seats land me in ht watr no more likely pls eat this mge x.*

The first show, Lux Aeterna, was starting in fifteen minutes. And it was on the other side of town.

I SUPPOSE IF you want to get your day off to a chic start, being followed by a middle-aged madman blowing raspberries at you every thirty seconds is not the best start. I first encountered him as I hurried down the steps of the metro. When he let rip his first rasper I even wondered if it had been me.

But no: I was waiting for the train when suddenly he jinked in front of me out of nowhere and blew the sort of giant backdoor trumpet I hadn't heard since Harry Secombe on *The Goons*. I ignored it, and the next two on the carriage itself, and another one at the next interchange, but by the time I reached rue Saint-Honoré, site of Charles Worth's original salon and location of the fashion show Lux Aeterna, what feeble thrills it had presented were beginning to wear thin.

I lost him by nipping into a café, but the delay ordering a needless cup of coffee cost five minutes, then a further five when that prompted a comfort stop, and by the time I arrived at the venue, halfway up the rue du Faubourg, I was ten minutes late and sweating like a stuck pig.

I needn't have worried. The doors to the premises were still shut, and a knot of cold, pinched individuals was waiting to be let in. Many were stamping their feet to keep warm, while others huddled in the doorway trying to light cigarettes against the biting wind. The sound of somebody hammering from inside the foyer suggested that preparations might be suffering a hitch. A woman next to me was locked in deep conversation on her mobile, and I passed several minutes trying to imagine what was being said by the person on the other end that could possibly have provoked her twelve consecutive 'OKs' followed by a single '*Mon dieu*'.

Just when I could no longer feel my finger ends, a nervous assistant with a clipboard came out and ushered us inside and up a rococo staircase fringed with oil paintings of elderly generals. At the top was a series of interconnecting panelled rooms, each containing rows of hastily arranged chairs.

Never having attended a fashion show before I'd imagined some spotlit catwalk surrounded by slavering acolytes sitting in the dark. But the room I found myself in this morning wasn't much bigger than my dining room at home, and by the look of it with the same parquet flooring. Apart from a cleaner hurriedly Cifing the dado rail, I was the only occupant.

Lux Aeterna sounded warming if nothing else. 'Christening garments… the white walls of chapels in Greece… black and lace to draw shadows' drooled the small print. I hunched up next to a searing radiator and waited for something to happen.

I don't know what I'd been expecting. Perhaps someone resembling Jenny Éclair in a pair of trendy glasses announcing, 'Ladies and gentlemen, boys and girls, please put your hands together for christening garments, white walls of chapels in Greece and black lace to draw shadows…' Instead, to a sudden splurge of techno-funk, a teenage girl wearing a giant mothball clacked through my room before disappearing out the far end. Her footwear, at least three sizes too large, reminded me of when as a kid I used to lumber around the house in my mum's court shoes.

Nonetheless, both the model and the garment were exquisite. Skin the colour of alabaster, she seemed to have been constructed out of bleached matchwood. Somebody once said that the greatest cause of injury among fashion models was falling through street grates: if so, there could be carnage here this morning, as she was followed twenty seconds later by another, even thinner beauty, this time in a similar mothball combo but with what looked like a vast Terry's chocolate orange stapled to the back. A short delay, then a third lurched through, this time with the hem of her dress ruckled up in the back of her pants.

I was just wondering when I might see some male evening-wear to shed light on my own issues, when without warning the presentation finished. The models, fifteen in total, lined up together briefly in an attitude of collective distaste, before blundering off again and out of sight. From soup to nuts Lux Aeterna had lasted about three minutes. Before I knew it I was back out in the cold. It was nearly six hours until the next show on the carousel beneath the Louvre.

Luckily the rue Saint-Honoré was amply provided with outlets to satisfy the most picky fashionista. As well as being one of Paris's very oldest medieval streets and the site of the Elysée Palace, official residence of President Sarkozy, it's also the top fashion spot in the city, housing Jean Paul Gaultier, Givenchy and Yves Saint Laurent.

I spent some time sheltering from the cold inside their doorways and studying the window displays: but the prices were staggering. Just as I was wondering if any of them did hire purchase, I found myself walking alongside one of the models, the one who'd been wearing the Terry's chocolate orange, who was now in low-slung jeans and a warm windcheater. By her purposeful stride she was on the way to another imminent gig.

The contrast with her professional demeanour was startling: back there she'd scanned the punters as if attending an identity parade of possible rape suspects; now she was gaily chatting into a mobile and skipping artfully over manhole covers like an advert for Special K.

Fashion Lesson Une: Never look as if you're enjoying yourself.

I passed the rest of the morning hopping from hot chocolate

to hot chocolate and taking refuge in the *animaleries*, Paris's famous pet shops, on the section of riverbank opposite the city's oldest bridge, Le Pont Neuf. They may not be on the Christmas card list for the RSPCA, but I know of few greater pleasures in life than entering a shop knowing you can hold a six-week-old Yorkshire terrier for a few minutes.

By the time I'd cuddled some puppies, read the paper, had lunch, walked round the base of the Eiffel Tower and gone back for a second intimate exchange with a long-haired dachshund I'd met a few hours previously, it was time for my next appointment. Alena Akhmadullina was showing her spring 2009 collection in the luxurious Salle Soufflot, part of the mighty underground complex beneath the Louvre. Even the invite was in raised italic lettering on a thick cardboard disc shaped like a circular saw, and so robust it would have done for a game of Frisbee if the weather had been warmer.

The carousel turned out to be a vast subterranean complex of exhibition halls and designer shops linked by sleek escalators. By the time I'd found the venue I was twenty minutes late, but again, I needn't have worried. The queue was yards long. Thirty minutes later we were still waiting.

Fashion Lesson Deux: Never be on time.

Eventually the doors were opened and we were allowed inside. This looked much more like I'd expected. The hall itself was pitch dark apart from a brilliantly spotlit catwalk picked out in tiny acid-yellow runway lights. Camera crews jostled with elegant female interviewers to snatch a few words from VIPs and fashion gurus, none of whom I recognised. At one end, a battery of cameras pointed directly down the catwalk towards a huge wooden flat with the designer's name carved out in black lettering, while above, cocooned in a soundproof booth that looked like the bridge of the SS *Enterprise*, rows of men with headphones sat behind consoles staring at laptops.

I found myself on the back row next to a sixty-year-old man in a red leather trilby and a black one-piece tracksuit decorated like a human skeleton. As soon as I sat down he unfurled a large green Japanese fan with which he began frantically cooling himself, whether as a fashion statement or because of the tell-tale whiff of a dachshund emanating from my sweater I couldn't tell.

According to the programme, Alena, originally from Russia, was theming her catalogue on translucent garments to underline her visible vulnerability. She'd also apparently managed to achieve an ironic play with the Pavloposadskiy headscarf, which was a relief. For the men there was also the promise of some items featuring 'a tailcoat in milk-cotton white with wide open chiffon trousers cut to a pyjama design'.

While I was still trying to envisage the look on Julia's face if I walked into La Coupole in that little lot, the lights went out and we were plunged into darkness. A split second later the air was rent with the sound of John Lennon singing 'Jealous Guy' to the accompaniment of what sounded like someone hitting milk bottles with a pair of pliers.

You could certainly see the traditional Soviet influence at work in the opening model. Bits of knotted rope and bleached wood hung listlessly from her wrists, and what appeared to be woollen handbags swung wildly from her ears. All that, I managed in a single momentary image. The next instant about seven thousand flashbulbs went off, and by the time my eyes had recovered she'd left the stage. In her place the first male member of the contingent was slouching disdainfully down the aisle. I studied his gait carefully. It was a sort of Douglas Bader chic, a stiff-legged lurch with head down, hands deep in pockets, eyes staring disinterestedly up from beneath sulky eyebrows.

There was more than a touch of the dacha about his costume too: open peasant's shirt, designer stubble and large brown leather belt across what were described in the blurb as 'dense seafaring troos with voluminous braided plait inserts'.

It was difficult to see much of this having resonance back in West Hampstead, but I suppose in fashion, as in everything else, one should travel hopefully. A whole sequence followed in which models of both sexes slewed back and forth wearing what appeared to be pairs of suede driving gloves sticking out of the tops of their heads. But, once again, suddenly everyone was applauding and we were being shown the door. Show over. All that cutting, the stitching, the Velcro, the hairspray and corn pads and heel grips. And for what? Five frenzied minutes in front of a load of liggers like me, and men dressed as skeletons.

Nonetheless it was exciting to have a chance to stand on the hallowed catwalk, and in the melee of embracing and email-address-swapping that followed, I found myself ambling up and down trying to perfect the calliper crawl I'd seen so faultlessly displayed by the young man with the seafaring troos. With the hall rapidly clearing, I then stood in front of the giant Alena Akhmadullina logo and had my photograph taken by a blushing design student. I kept my sunglasses on and turned up the roll of my turtleneck till it was nearly covering my chin. Head up, slight profile, and taken from slightly below. The shutter clicked and the young student gave me a thumbs-up. Afterwards she showed it me back in the viewfinder.

'You like?'

The image showed a slim, confident figure of indeterminate age, silhouetted against a fiercely lit background, fluorescent

Cyrillic letters picking out the words *St Petersburg* against a lime-green base tone intersected with raised chocolate-and-cream swirls. No receding hairline, no double chin and no bags under the eyes you could carry your weekly shopping home in. Just sunglasses and black, in a dazzling aurora of refracted light. It could have been anyone from Jean Paul Gaultier to John Prescott and you wouldn't have known the difference. I looked terrific.

Fashion Lesson Trois: Lighting is everything.

My final venue was at the elegant Ecole Nationale Supérieure des Beaux-arts, on Paris's left bank. After five frustrating minutes looking in vain for a taxi, during which it started raining, I spotted a forlorn rickshaw cyclist sitting by himself at the next road junction. I hurried across and climbed in, nearly tipping the entire vehicle over in the process.

As we slewed between lanes of traffic and over tank-buckling cobblestones, I studied the final invite. The exhibition featured Junko Shimada, one of the capital's most famous bespoke designers. Originally from Tokyo, Japan, she had moved here in the mid-1960s. A leading designer of menswear, her boutique on the rue Etienne Marcel was one of the hubs of French fashion.

Again I arrived late and again it didn't matter. A long queue snaked along the pavement and around the corner. I was just sheltering behind a group of photographers each carrying their own stepladders when a woman approached me along the line. She seemed to be looking for someone. Thirty-something, a shock of bleached hair sprouting from above a charcoal-grey Alice band, she wore a huge fluffy white angora sweater deco-rated with strawberry-coloured woollen marshmallows, and was holding an open box file above her as an impromptu rain hat. Either that or it was part of her outfit. I no longer felt confident of anything.

'Michael?'

I looked behind me. It was the first time in ten weeks that anybody had called me by my name.

'My name's Cindy. Thanks so much for coming today, we're very honoured to have you. If you'd like to follow me, we have your seat ready.' She grasped me gently by my arm, and the next moment I was being ushered past the waiting crowd, up some marble stairs and through the barriers.

'We think you'll find today's collection very exciting,' she said breathlessly as we sailed past a couple of beefy security men. 'At least, that's the hope of course. Junko certainly is very energised by it. Did you have a good trip?'

'Not bad, not bad,' I replied carefully. Did she mean the rickshaw, the metro ride or the ferry crossing? Either this was a case of mistaken identity or my newspaper contact had more clout than I'd thought.

This time my destination was a vast white box with white walls, white ceilings and white tiled floor: a photographer's studio for giants. A central walkway bordered by fluorescent lights formed the focal point, dotted every few feet down the middle by giant glass bell jars in which watercress was growing. Inches above the lips of the jars were tiny halogen bulbs, towards which the poor cress was desperately straining, oblivious of its imminent fate in a skip at the back of the Ecole Nationale in probably about ten minutes' time.

'Here we are, I hope you enjoy the show.' Cindy had led me to a bench on which a sign was positioned reading *Reserve VIP*. 'If you'd like to stay behind and have a word with Junko afterwards?' She let the possibilities of such an encounter hang there between us, while I smiled enigmatically back as if considering the request. With a final tender squeeze on my arm she hurried off.

Who on earth did she think I was? And what on earth would I say to Junko if I met her? I turned to the chap next to me, an American of indeterminate age with short back and sides ending in a kiss curl, wearing a herringbone jacket, a pair of jeans rolled up to the kneecaps and black slip-ons with no socks. 'I'm Adam,' he said, offering a flaccid handshake. 'Michael,' I replied moodily. This seemed to delight him and he nodded appreciatively as if acknowledging some unspoken code.

Fashion Lesson Quatre: Less is more.

I knew I was going to enjoy Junko's collection as soon as the first model appeared with a lobster on her head. For a moment I even wondered if it was real. But Junko's versions were mere life-like representations, with the pink shell forming a tiny hat, and front claws curling down round her ears like earrings. The sight of the crustaceans provoked a gasp of delight from the crowd, who burst into applause and chattered excitedly over the sound-track of crunching Japanese hip-hop as the young model loped up and down past the watercress.

My American companion began writing furiously in a note-book. 'Large duck print on silk jersey tunic, crustacean headpiece with attached crabs and plexiglass toes,' he scrawled. He saw me looking over his shoulder and smiled back.

'I wonder if they do chips with that,' I remarked, and immediately regretted it. The fashion world isn't known for its sense of humour, and I certainly wasn't going to ignite it in a bloke with his jeans halfway up his legs and no socks.

Junko's spring 2009 inspiration was fruits of the sea. We had models with crabs, with scallops, with porpoises, blouses deco-rated in seaweed, pink shrimp bathing capes, headpieces in the shape of fish, jellyfish dresses in lilac crumpled organza, and a ballerina bodysuit in duchess satin with accompanying fishnets.

There were high-heel sockettes, organdie camisoles and some startling garments called tonic gym shorts.

But it proved a smash hit. Long before Junko herself bobbed on for the briefest of curtseys, the audience were on their feet and hollering their approbation. Even the American bestowed his benediction by means of a tart smile.

Cindy appeared by my side again. 'Enjoy?' she asked.

I answered with a single diffident nod of the head.

'I'm glad you think so. A lot of work has gone into it this year, I can tell you.' She mimed waving away a hot flush. 'Now then, Junko has to meet the press for some while, but if you wanted to stay behind I'm sure she'd love to...'

Fashion Lesson Cinq: Be impressed by nothing.

'I've got another appointment, Cindy. Perhaps another time?'

'Ah yes, of course, Alexander McQueen, I take it? I hear it's wonderful. Can I get you a taxi?'

'No thanks, the walk will do me good.'

She smiled uncertainly. 'Well, thanks so much again. Can I give you my card?' She pressed one into my hand without waiting for my reply and hovered expectantly. 'And yours?'

'Why not?' I reached instinctively for my wallet, but the idea of her summoning security after discovering I wasn't head of Hugo Boss stopped my hand.

'I seem to have run out, Cindy. Still, I have your email. I'm sure I'll be in touch.'

THE NEXT MORNING I bought myself a designer suit. The deciding factor in my choice wasn't Alena, or Junko's crustacean queen and her plexiglass jellies. It was the security guard I'd swept past with Cindy on my way into the final show at the Ecole Nationale.

I'd noticed his outfit as he'd reached inside his breast pocket for his swipe card to let us through. He was wearing a beautifully tailored, glossy Dormeuil Amadeus number with thin grey and black stripes, high-cut lapels and, briefly glimpsed, an inner lining of crushed purple. He was also black, six foot five and with a shaven head, but he looked absolutely terrific in it. Stay cool, he'd advised. Stay classic, stay black, stay with an eye-catching inner lining, and, above all, if you're over fifty with love handles, stay away from snug fit.

He directed me to a shop called Bruce Field where apparently they were going for a snip. Bruce Field might not sound like the epitome of French designerwear – in fact, it sounded like someone who would open the bowling for Leicestershire – but it turned out to be just the sort of chic, middle-priced outlet I'd hoped for. With my dander now up and my credit card out, I popped a three-quarter wool and cashmere overcoat on my credit card for good measure, and reeled out.

That night in my hotel room I studied myself from the bed in the wardrobe mirror. Even under an overhead bulb it looked good. I felt sure Charles Worth would have approved. If there was mustard on offer at La Coupole the following Sunday, this would cut it.

Chanson d'Amour

WANT TO TELL your partner you love them? Or hate them? That you forgive them, even though they've left you for a younger woman – or man – or both? That though they may be old, ugly or dead, their spirit will forever remain in your heart, even though you're down to your last pair of stockings and are probably going to have to go on the game to satisfy your rapacious landlord? Then French *chanson* is for you.

An art form born in the café concerts and cabarets of the Montmartre district, its concerns are those of the French psyche, and its rhythms those of the French language. Conversational, explosive, opinionated, mercurial, sexy, garrulous and virtually untranslatable, *chanson* mirrors perfectly the national character.

Perversely, given her antipathy to things French, *chanson* is Julia's great musical love, and its greatest exponent, Edith Piaf, Julia's goddess. 'Je ne regrette rien', Edith's paean to a life fully lived rather than rusted away, only has to turn up on the radio or in those infernal ads for Specsavers and Julia turns instantly into a blubbering wreck. When I took her to the recent Oscar-winning biopic at our local multiplex, I had to scrape her off the carpet and carry her home in a bag.

It's Piaf's simplicity that does it, she says. The black dress, the spotlight, the rheumatic hands, the songs reflecting utterly the woman's daily struggles through a life of which, even by the kindest estimates, she made a bit of a Horlicks. Moving, sincere, edgy, tortured, tragic and wonderful is how Julia described her.

I would certainly agree with the edgy, tortured and tragic bit. Piaf has always sounded to me like somebody gargling with wood preservative. I'm sorry that just about everyone she ever touched seemed to be murdered, imprisoned, die in some horrific accident or suffer some other personal catastrophe – but if that were the mark of genius we'd all be listening to Fred West.

Love, loss and forgiveness. These were all potential subject matters for our forthcoming rendezvous at La Coupole. And with Julia already packing her case for the trip over on Eurostar, it was time for me to get up close and personal with some proper French *chanson*.

YOU'D HAVE THOUGHT I'd come to the right city to find it. Piaf's name is synonymous with Paris. She was born here (allegedly under a policeman's coat on the street in Ménilmontant), was discovered here busking on a street corner off the Champs Elysées, and forged her reputation in its clubs, bars and theatres. Yet in reality the musical genre she came to dominate has almost disappeared from contemporary culture. France, and French tastes, has moved on, and although the Little Sparrow's image is everywhere, from tea towels to billboard hoardings, you'd struggle to find any of her songs being sung or even a tribute band anywhere in this teeming city. Imagine going to London to try and find some trace of Al Bowlly and you'll see the problem.

In the end it boiled down to three possibilities. An establishment dedicated to the art of the chanteuses, the Lapin Agile, still existed in an unfashionable arrondissement near my hotel. I might also find some at one of the tourist traps, the Follies, the

Lido or the Moulin Rouge; and the proprietor at my hotel mentioned she'd heard of a caff in Porte de Clignancourt where people still belted out *chanson traditionnelle* each Saturday afternoon. If all else failed…

As it turned out, my options were even fewer. The Follies was currently given over to staging some mainstream musical, while both the other two were booked out for months in advance by tourist groups. I put a call in to a dancer friend of mine back in London who'd once been a famous Bluebell girl at the Lido; but she was on answerphone, and anyway I wasn't even sure she'd remember me. The Lapin Agile seemed the only show in town.

If pedigree counted for anything, I need look no further. Originally called the Cabaret des Assassins, after the initial owner was murdered, the venue was already twenty years old when in 1875 the celebrated Parisian artist André Gill painted the door sign, showing a rabbit jumping out of a saucepan. The name stuck. Its subsequent clientele reads like a *Who's Who* of French populist culture: Modigliani, Degas and Utrillo were all regulars, and Picasso's 1905 oil painting *At the Lapin Agile* cemented its reputation. He even paid for lunch there by painting the proprietor and selling him the result, an item the naive recipient flogged on for $12. Eighty years later at Christie's it fetched $41 million.

The pimps, anarchists and down-and-outers that once frequented this intimate venue may have largely disappeared, but if anywhere was likely to deliver the genuine *chanson* experience, this would surely be it.

I SET OFF for 'an authentic evening of cabaret' just before 8 p.m. on the Friday night. After wandering round the maze of streets in Montmartre, I eventually stumbled upon the venue, a discreet, characterful house on a steeply sloping thoroughfare behind the Sacre Coeur, just as the city is plunging down the other side of the hill towards distant suburbs.

According to the heavy-lidded young man who took my money in the entrance hall, I was in for a treat. The soiree, titled 'Love, Music and Poetry', promised to cover all forms of traditional music – French standards, love ballads, sea shanties and more, as well as a chance to sample the traditional drink of the house. Its pedigree was impeccable. The venue has played host to many of the great names of *chanson*, including at one time Claude Nougaro, one-time lyricist for Edith herself.

I was ushered in through a doorway covered by a curtain to a dark, dimly lit space, about the size of a school classroom. Round the sides, sitting stiffly on dark benches as if stapled to them and lit by dusty table lamps, were the usual collection of bemused tourists you find in any country in the world – portly Americans, sheepish young backpackers from Eastern Europe, as well as the ubiquitous Japanese – while the walls above were decorated with a motley assortment of artefacts designed to provide instant atmosphere. Old clocks and murky oil paintings jostled for space with pencil sketches and nude studies of people who should have known better.

In the centre of the room stood a formidable oak table surrounded by chairs. I stepped round it and took a seat in the corner next to where a wrinkled pianist was bashing out *Liebestraum* on a battered piano. Rumour had it that in its heyday a midget used to perform novelty routines on the lid, but either he'd retired or was having tonight off.

The receptionist had followed me in and now handed me my complimentary drink, a pungent liqueur distilled from tiny cherries, some of which still clustered at the bottom of the glass. It tasted like cough medicine. All very authentic I'm sure, but after the effort to get here I was gagging for a beer. As if reading my thoughts, the pianist began a tinkling rendition of 'Where Do I Begin'.

While I was still searching in vain for a menu, an assortment of individuals ancient and modern trooped in through the curtain, yelling salutations as they did so, and plonked themselves down at the table. Seconds later they launched into a lilting opening chorus in the best *chanson* tradition.

The song was one I recognised at once. In French, the words *'Je n'aurai pas le temps'* teemed with unspoken longing, yet I already knew it by its less poetic English equivalent. 'If I Only Had Time' had been a huge hit in the mid-1960s after it was sung on the ITV talent contest *Opportunity Knocks* by a callow young vocalist called – and God knows where I retrieved this name from – John Rowles. I think I'd even bought the single.

Funny how everything sounds more romantic in French than in English. Unspoken longing hardly encapsulated John Rowles's cheesy version all those years ago, but here, in the original patois, lyrics I recalled as having all the eternal longing of a greetings card seemed impossibly wistful and profound. It would be difficult to imagine anything less calculated to rend your heart strings than, if I remember correctly, something along the lines of 'time like the wind, goes a hurryin' by, and the hours just fly'. Yet now these same sentiments, delivered in the original tongue and thus distilled through a thick soup of rolling r's and strangled consonants, were now pregnant with the message of eternity.

Perhaps, without knowing, I'd already stumbled upon the secret of *chanson*.

The pattern of the evening soon became apparent. Each of the troubadours had their own designated spot, three or four numbers in length, linked together by communal sing-alongs during which all the others would troop back in and slump round the table. The trouble was, there were at least twelve of them in total, and each one possessed a formidable back catalogue of their work. It seemed we might be in for a long night.

Some of the soloists were very good indeed. We had some Jacques Prévert ballads from a smoky-voiced baritone with a guitar, some laments about thwarted love from a young girl in jeans, and a couple of comic numbers about shrewish wives and randy pets from a lugubrious man in his sixties resembling Kenneth Williams, delivered with astonishing facial dexterity and enough shrugs and gurns to satisfy the man himself.

There were songs of love, of loss, of epic journeys and heartfelt goodbyes. The elderly pianist, too, was terrific, and near enough to shoot me a quiet look of wry resignation whenever one of the soloists lingered too long on a top note or was a bit slow on the uptake for the next chorus. But with the clock already showing nearly 10 p.m. I realised I still hadn't been offered a proper drink.

I glanced down at the leaflet, now serving as a beer mat for the forlorn remains of the liqueur. 'The soiree, steeped in traditional Parisian ambience, usually lasts four hours' it read. With half the company yet to perform their solo spot, I was beginning to feel trapped.

Still it continued: French versions of 'Wise Men Say', 'C'est Si Bon', and 'Those Were the Days'. I was desperate to get my lips round something cool and wet, but with one song eliding seamlessly into another it would mean crossing the floor and squeezing past one or other of the performers mid-flow. How would I feel if someone did that while I was performing?

By the time they struck up the old barnstormer 'Alouette', a feeling of claustrophobia was beginning to grip me. I always hated the wretched song at primary school, doing all that *et la tête et le bec et les ailes* stuff: and now, after two and a half hours without refreshment, I was being asked to point to my head and touch my toes when all I wanted was to down a pint and have a pee.

And despite all the glass-clinking and the invitation to clap our hands to the beat and shout *oui* and *non* at appropriate places, the show increasingly felt like a facsimile. It was a valiant effort at giving us the impression of having just stumbled into a domestic living room in time for a jolly sing-song round the piano, but there weren't enough in the audience to get the shindig off the ground. Mind you, if this *had* been someone's front room, we'd have surely been offered something by now, even if it were only some nuts and a face flannel.

I'd had enough. With the clock showing 10.18, the latest chanteuse announced her intention to accompany herself on an accordion, a manoeuvre that required her to halt for a few moments while she strapped on the instrument. In a single bound I was through the curtain and out through the front door. My final image was of the other soloists slumped wearily in a tiny anteroom by the staircase.

I ended my evening outside a pavement café back in Montmartre. What a rum do it had all been. The performers were obviously the real deal, and the photos hanging in the entrance hall suggested this *cabaret artistique* had once teemed with romance and conviviality. Indeed, the yellowing prints on the walls of the foyer clearly depicted the place stuffed to the gills with the bohemian demimonde of low-life Paris, red-faced and happy, all squashed in beneath plumes of curling cigarette smoke. Perhaps I'd just caught it on a bad night.

Or perhaps not. If I knew anything about Edith, she surely wouldn't have approved of being trapped without booze for an entire evening. According to the leaflet, Patricia Schulz, author of *1000 Places to See Before You Die*, had described the Lapin as one of her must-sees – 'An authentic cabaret experience'.

Maybe she's right. It's just that once you'd sat through the full canon of the Family Von Tourist Trappe there wouldn't be much time left for the other 999.

I'D JUST GOT off to sleep when my phone rang. I sat bolt upright in bed and glanced at my alarm clock. No doubt it was Julia, ringing to check the details of our rendezvous. I fumbled clumsily in my trousers and pressed receive.

'Simmo?'

'Yes. Who is this?'

'It's Dawny, darling. Sorry to ring so late. I got your call. I'm in *The Sound of Music* at the Palladium so couldn't do anything till I came offstage.'

'No matter, Dawn, it was only a speculative –'

'Well, it's your lucky night, babe. I've got you a free seat to tonight's show at the Lido. Front row. If you hop in a cab you could still make it, no worries.'

'But it's 11.40!'

'I know, how lucky are you! The show starts at midnight. *Le Bonheur*. It means happiness! Ask for Raymond, the house manager, he's expecting you. *Bon appétit!*'

*

THE LIDO, SITUATED in Paris's pre-eminent thoroughfare the Champs Elysées, is reckoned to be one of the most beautiful cabaret venues in the world. It's also immensely famous: everyone from Laurel and Hardy to Elton John has performed here, as well as it being the home of the legendary Bluebell girls.

With the interior kitted out to resemble the famous Lido in Venice and perfect visibility from all 1,150 seats, it's one of the most ornate and luxurious venues in the capital. In addition to the twenty-five sets and 600 costumes, a team of thirty-five chefs and pastry cooks work tirelessly to cater for the dietary needs of the punters. At any other time than 11.30 on a chilly autumn evening and roused from a deep sleep...

The Champs Elysées was freezing. And packed. When I arrived just after midnight an endless shivering queue was gathered on the pavement still waiting to be admitted. I've never see so many well-dressed people with nowhere to go. The line snaked this way and that, doubling back upon itself many times along the boulevard.

The Lido adheres to the old regime of twice nightly, and it was at once obvious that the previous performance was running behind. When the thousand or so from the 9.30 performance emerged and began mingling with the thousand or so waiting to get in, the scene resembled something out of the January sales. The only person unaffected by the mayhem or the cold was an inebriated street performer who ambled along the queue blowing a version of 'La Mer' across the mouth of an empty vodka bottle.

I finally took my seat just before 12.30. The interior was stupendous, a vast, low-ceilinged auditorium with balconies, booths and galleries, which even at this late hour was full to bursting. Waiters promenaded in and out between the tables, taking orders and dispensing champagne in gleaming buckets. A complimentary beer was plonked on the table in front of me, although some cocaine and a couple of matchsticks would have been more use. No matter – Parisian cabaret on the Champs Elysées, lavish costumes and a line of high-kicking Bluebells – if the legacy of Edith were to be found anywhere, then surely to God…

Just before 12.40 the lights dimmed and a huge, pink furry egg suspended on wires began inching its way through the air just above the heads of the audience. Once it had reached the safety of the stage it was gingerly lowered and a grinning woman in a catsuit climbed out. 'This show cannot be filmed or videoed, it can only be dreamt' drooled a sultry, disembodied voice from the rafters. The way I was feeling that wouldn't be a problem.

I promise I'll never criticise the Lapin Agile for overstaying its welcome again. For the next two hours I sat in a mixture of wonder, bafflement and increasing fatigue as a cast of sixty or seventy chiselled youngsters, many of them topless, twirled, high-kicked and shimmied their way through a series of routines the like of which I hadn't seen since the BBC axed their seaside variety specials and put Peter Gordeno out to grass.

As promised, the routines involved a jaw-dropping array of costumes: feathers, catsuits, sequins, gangster-and-moll combos, and, in one mystifying sequence set in a cattery, a troupe of moggies sitting astride tiled rooftops – in addition to yet more topless dancers, who seemed to be the only constant theme of the evening. Normally I'd have been very happy with such a unifying motif, but the days when I was at my best in that department after midnight had long gone.

The sets, too, were extraordinary: entire Midwest townscapes, Parisian night scenes, a water garden complete with spouting fountains and a colossal Hindu temple that emerged from the bowels of the stage complete with gyrating nautch girls and a full-size wooden elephant on wheels.

These pageants were interspersed with what are called in British variety 'spesh acts'. A teenager with thinning hair and the sort of surprised perma-grin worn only by magicians performed a sizzling routine with fluorescent diabolos, while some time between 1 and 2 a.m., two vast Ukrainian musclemen sprayed entirely gold performed an extraordinary and highly homoerotic strength act. And in one of the oddest combinations, an ice rink came up through the floor and on it a young couple performed dizzying manoeuvres, while behind them a man dressed as Zorro pranced about on a horse.

But for all its razzamatazz, there was an air of pointlessness about the show. Three hours earlier it might have triumphed on chutzpah alone, but fatigue was spreading through the audience like a virus. Heads nodded, applause tailed off, and however many topless catsuits and zappy dance routines were thrown at us, what we most wanted was a chance of some kip. Even Ken Dodd didn't go on this late.

Edith, or at least a projected image of her pinched features, finally made an appearance just before 2.15. I roused myself for a stirring climax, perhaps a rousing medley of her best numbers or a dance drama depicting important incidents from her life. Instead we were subjected to a thumping disco version of 'It's Going To Be A Great Day' to yet more feather-waving, tassel-twirling and breast-joggling. I thought I saw Edith's image wincing upstage, but it might have been the effects of sleep deprivation.

I finally got to bed just before four. The Lido, despite its opulence, had offered no more than the sort of entertainment experience that bedevils tourists in any great European city: an anodyne stew of feathers and shining teeth and spangly costumes which signifies bugger all. Even when they'd summoned the cavalry in the shape of Edith's image, they'd trampled all over her.

My final act was to put a 'Do Not Disturb' sign on the door and switch off my mobile phone. For the next few hours, both Edith and Julia would have to get along without me. My last hope was the transport caff tomorrow lunchtime.

AS SOON AS I saw it I knew I'd found what I was looking for. A tatty lean-to in the bowels of Clignancourt's labyrinthine market, I'd almost given up on finding Chez Louisette after an hour of being misdirected by a series of snotty stallholders down alleyways full of antique postcards and burst sofas. I heard her before I saw her: from somewhere round yet another blind corner, the sound of Edith's famous anthem 'La Vie en Rose' being sung to a wheezing accordion in between someone opening and closing a door. The café itself looked almost derelict, yet there was a queue of people at the door waiting to get in, and inside the place was absolutely heaving.

Five minutes later I was – I nearly said shown to my seat. Rudely shoved in the back towards a single vacant place at a table already groaning with customers would be a better description. The restaurant was in uproar. In every corner flushed diners were tucking into plates of steak and spaghetti and pouring huge glasses of cheap plonk into smeary tumblers. A pall from coffee machines, guttering candles and frying onions hung over the customers like a fog.

The décor, too, was extraordinary: Lawrence Llewellyn-Bowen meets Harold Steptoe. The bar, clad in stained gold Formica and patrolled by a man with a nose like a baked potato, had sets of flashing tracer lights and twinkling Christmas bulbs racing round every surface. The walls were covered in tarnished mirrors, while the entire ceiling was clad in festive wrapping paper from which cracked baubles and paper chains hung down on fraying strings.

But best of all was the live entertainment. On a cramped dais next to the front door, almost shrouded from view behind a supporting pillar decorated with torn photos of Charles Aznavour and Maurice Chevalier, sat a lugubrious pianist with a wall eye pumping away on a Yamaha organ. Next to him a waiter in a stained apron was playing an accordion with one hand and carrying on a conversation at full volume on his mobile phone with the other.

And in front, belting out 'Hymne à l'Amour', was the embodiment of what Edith would have been if she'd lived a lot longer and developed a penchant for cream cakes. A tiny, stout woman in Edith's trademark wool dress, with hair dyed bus-conductress black, was belting out of Edith's greatest hits at full throttle.

If accounts of Piaf's early life are to be believed, she learnt much of her craft in environments exactly like this, working out how to corral and entrance patrons more interested in whether there was mustard with their steaks and ordering another bottle than watching the show. The noise in the café was infernal, but yet this facsimile Edith was giving it her all, pitting both her talents and her life expectancy against insuperable artistic odds. What's more, she was winning.

I found myself rammed against Nitza, an American interior designer here to oversee the refurbishment of some government buildings. Conversation was impossible, but she offered a sympathetic shrug in answer to my desperate attempt to cram myself in my seat, and poured me a glass of red from her own carafe to calm my nerves.

Such was the din that the waitresses were communicating their orders to the kitchens by blowing instructions in Morse code on referees' whistles.

'Oui?' A woman resembling Bernard Manning's twin sister was already demanding my order. A large laminated menu was thrust into my hands. It was greasy to the touch, and so stained with discarded foodstuffs it was difficult to make out the individual dishes.

'OUI?' she yelled again.

Around the edges of the card were apparently testimonials from delighted customers in their own handwriting. I squinted through the grease: Francis Ford Coppola was there ('Thank you for the food and the music'), French actor Alain Delon ('This is the renaissance of the art of the chanson'), a similar testimony from a former PM, Laurent Fabius, and there was even an impromptu cartoon from Serge Gainsbourg himself. Greater minds even than mine had obviously pronounced this the real deal.

A nudge in the spine reminded me that Ms Manning was still waiting. 'I wouldn't worry too much,' bellowed Nitza into the ear not submerged in a large tweed overcoat, 'you'll tend to have to eat what you're given here anyway.'

My first two requests were answered with a savage shake of the head. 'I'd get it in quickly if were you,' screamed Nitza. 'She'll only punish you if you hang about.' At my third attempt, *onglet à l'échalote avec legumes*, the waitress raised her eyes upward in exasperation, but Nitza assured me that the subsequent volley series of peeps was her way of saying she'd see what she could do.

Two minutes later my meal arrived. It was a quarter chicken and chips.

Yet, despite it all, Chez Louisette was fabulous. The food was terrible, the drink was rough as hell, but it was impossible not to be caught up in the *joie de vivre*. Best of all was Manuela herself. She may have been built like a jeep and approaching seventy from the wrong direction, but her love of her idol was obvious in every syllable.

Chanson, the defining musical genre of French life, was forged from the hardships and poverty of Paris's poor and working class. Manuela carried on today, through her backing band taking phone calls, waitresses blowing whistles, customers barging past with fizzing birthday cakes and general uproar from all and sundry, with the sort of indomitable spirit that I can only imagine would have had the real Edith purring with pleasure.

By the time I'd finished the chicken, a bottle of red and a huge slab of half-defrosted apple pie, I was grinning like an idiot, joining in every chorus whether I knew the words or not, and was wondering where I could buy a Piaf CD box set. This is what I'd been searching for. Neither the strained informality of the Lapin Agile, nor the overblown crassness of the Lido, but the real thing: wine, women and song, in a genuine contemporary Parisian atmosphere, finished off with a lavish topping of undisguised insolence. Even the bill was a poem, amounting to a sum that would hardly buy me a cloakroom ticket at La Coupole tomorrow afternoon.

Flushed, hoarse and giggling, I ended my visit by having my photo taken with Manuela. After listening to a final chorus of 'Je Ne Regrette Rien' (for the third, or was it the fourth time?), I staggered out into the market and towards the metro. It had been a revelatory afternoon, and a perfect way to end my trip.

My only sorrow was that Julia hadn't been here to see it.

La Fin

I MET JULIA off the Eurostar on the Sunday afternoon. She looked fabulous. Trendy hairdo, suntan (though God knows how, with the summer they'd had back in Britain) and a new outfit in powder blue. She'd even had her toenails done.

She, too, seemed surprise by my appearance.

'Where did you get that suit?'

'I bought it.'

She fingered the lining and her eyes fell on the label. 'That's a Dormeuil.'

'So I'm assured.'

'How much was it?'

'You like it?'

'Remember, the last time I saw you, you were wearing a panama hat and open-toed sandals. Let's say it's an improvement.'

'Are you pleased to see me?'

She glanced around the station concourse as if looking for a secret listening device. Then she sniffed my cheek.

'What's that smell?'

'Chanel. Pour Homme.'

'Have you got something to tell me?'

'Don't be ridiculous. I've just picked up a few tips, like you wanted. You ready?

'You're determined to go through with this, are you?'

'*Naturellement.*'

'Including the ordering?'

'Leave it to me. You don't have to speak a word the entire day if you don't want. I'm taking care of the whole thing. Food, wine, the whole caboodle.'

Her mouth twitched imperceptibly. 'Well, this I must see.'

FIVE HOURS LATER I asked for the bill. Across from me, Julia looked relaxed and happy. I knew she'd had a great time, as she'd just returned from nipping outside into the doorway for a Gitane bummed off an adjoining diner. Julia rarely allowed herself such hedonistic extravagances apart from first nights or Christmas Day. Now she was sitting with the dregs of a large cognac, enjoying the final few moments of our meal. In ninety minutes more we'd be back on Eurostar, back towards the tunnel, home and half a ton of dirty washing.

'How are you?'

'I'm good. I must say this has been fabulous,' she replied at last. 'Not like the last time. And I haven't even had to speak a word. Well done you.'

Now that the trip was nearly over a feeling of bittersweet relief surged over me. I was looking forward to getting back to England, of course. It would be nice to return to a world and an environment I understood and felt comfortable in, particularly with my feeling refreshed and reinvigorated.

But I left with a heavy heart. In the twelve weeks I'd been here my perspective had changed, both of the country and of myself. Many of the preconceptions with which I'd arrived in Dieppe remained, of course: the French were certainly formal, their bureaucracy could be spirit-sappingly complicated, and for someone who only ever hears our own National Anthem sung on the Last Night of the Proms, their sense of pride and tradition could at times border on the exclusive.

But there were many more things I'd miss. The climate, the food, the space, the ravishing countryside, and the sense of things being done properly rather than being shoved in a metaphorical bap, smothered in tomato ketchup and gobbled down on the move while you're thinking of something else.

Above all, I'd miss their appreciation of what is important in life: their attitude to money as a means of purchasing time with loved ones rather than the next modish gizmo. I'd also miss a rail network that had delivered me everywhere I'd needed to get to without so much as a leaf on the line.

There were people I'd miss too. Not only Dandrine and her circus folk, but Emile the hospital courier, Isobel at the casino, Anne-Sophie and her collection of lighthouses, Paulina and her dreams of ripping white denim, Jean-Paul and his obsession with all things Scottish, Eddie George and his tape measure, and Leo the hotelier who had turned things around for me in Vichy. Plus all the other receptionists, ticket inspectors, hotel porters, waiters, fellow travellers, oddballs and raspberry-blowers whose paths I'd briefly crossed. I'd even miss that strange little man with his transistor I'd glimpsed on the beach at St Marc sur Mer, the one who had first thrown up such a sharp reflection of what I'd come here to escape.

And then there were all the things I'd seen: the *fest-nozzers* of Brittany, the water jousters of Agde, the bull racers, the naturists, the stoic, smiling pilgrims of Lourdes: it seemed now, in the warm afterglow of a couple of bottles of red, that my trip had consisted of one long endless summer's day, in which it was I who had remained still, and France that had been spinning past me on a continuous loop, offering up wonder upon wonder.

Most of all, I'd miss the stranger who had been myself. We'd not met before, but this summer, left alone with him for the first time, he'd proved a worthy if at times unpredictable companion. Would he return with me to London, to chip in the odd thought or comment of his own in the years that followed? Or would I find, when I unpacked my suitcase back home, that I'd left him at the entrance to the tunnel? I hoped not.

Jacques Tati's own daughter, Sophie, hadn't appeared in the film *Monsieur Hulot's Holiday*, as she'd been too shy to pass in front of the camera. She admitted years later that after the unveiling of the bronze statue to her father, she walked across the spaces she couldn't bear to bring herself to cross as a child: 'purging her old fears, achieving a sort of closure'.

I knew how she felt.

MY REVERIE WAS blown apart by a ferocious blast on a referee's whistle. It was nearly five. The taxi would already be waiting out in the street. I looked across at Julia. 'You haven't finished your dessert.'

'I can't eat it. It's still frozen. Anyway, ssshhhh, I want to hear this last number.' Even as she spoke the electric organ launched into the intro, and for the umpteenth time this afternoon her eyes moistened. Across the room, semi-hidden behind a pillar and a poster of Jean Sablon, Manuela was powering into Edith Piaf's iconic anthem to a life lived without guilt or remorse.

It had been my decision to change venues at the last moment. I had no desire for the stuffy, frigid French formality as offered by La Coupole, with its snobbery, its overbearing opulence, its waiters who had perfected the art of xenophobia with a simple,

'Certainly, madam: sparkling or still?' That France was easily discoverable if you wanted it. But I had no need.

Instead I'd discovered another country, and it was typified here, within the fug of Chez Louisette. Warm, welcoming; 'a cacophony of song and friendship' is how Laurent Fabius had described it on the menu, and he should know, he'd been PM. And as for the French's infamous rudeness, at least you knew where you were with the girls here. Better a referee's whistle in your lughole than the frosty raising of a left eyebrow.

At the end, Manuela came round with the hat. We popped in a few final coins, and she leaned across and gave us both a departing hug. The waitress was already fumbling for our overcoats on the hat stand. Time to go.

'What an extraordinary place,' said Julia huskily as she blew her nose. 'Right then, let's go. Looking forward to coming home?'

'What do you think?'

'And what about your trip? Has it been worth it? God knows you bored us all rigid planning the thing. Glad you came? Any misgivings?'

I leaned back in my chair. Somewhere in my pocket I had a final Café Crème. I might just enjoy a crafty one back at the station before boarding.

My reply was easy: 'Je ne regrette rien,' I said.

Michael Simkins is a familiar face on the west end stage and TV screens, usually playing experts, policemen or unsuspecting husbands. Most recently he's played Billy Flynn in Chicago and the Pierce Brosnan role in Mamma Mia (or as he'd rather think of it, the Michael Simkins role which Pierce Brosnan subsequently played in the film). Countless TV and film appearances include *Foyle's War*, *Minder*, *Lewis*, and *Doctors* - as well as turns on the silver screen in such films as Mike Leigh's *Topsy-Turvy* and *V for Vendetta*. He is a frequent contributor to Radio 4 and writes for the *Daily Telegraph*, the *Guardian* and *The Times*.

His first book *What's My Motivation?* was Radio 4 Book of the Week and his second, the critically acclaimed *Fatty Batter*, was shortlisted for the 2008 Costa Biography Award.

Michael lives with his actress wife Julia in London.

Follow Michael's journey online at:
www.detourdefrance.co.uk

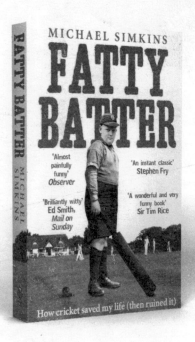

An instant classic – *Stephen Fry*

The childhood recollections, suffused with warmth and
spangled with pain and humour, are the book's unique selling
point. Lovely stuff – *Daily Telegraph*

Simmo may be a shockingly average amateur cricketer, but when it
comes to self- deprecating wit and telling a good anecdote, he's as
sprightly as Garry Sobers in his prime ... anecdotes and quirky
characters hurtle down at us like yorkers bowled by a fast bowler
that I'm not quite knowledgeable enough to name ... an
entertaining read indeed – *Sunday Times*

At last the work of genius that will finally bring the long-suffering
cricket addict a measure of understanding in the world.
A wonderful and very funny book – *Sir Tim Rice*

Extremely funny - whether or not you know your bails from
your balls – *Daily Mail*

One of the funniest sporting memoirs ever – *Sunday Telegraph*